Celebrating Single
and
Getting Love Right

Art by Ann Feild

LJAllen

At least if I join a convent,
I'll get a wedding band and a job with benefits.

CELEBRATING
SINGLE
and
Getting Love Right

ⓑ   ⓑ   ⓑ

From Stalemate to Soulmate

L. Joan Allen, M.A.
with
Marc Kusinitz, Ph.D.

CAPITAL
BOOKS, INC.
Sterling, Virginia

Capital Books, Inc.
P.O. Box 605
Herndon, Virginia 20172-0605

ISBN 1-892123-30-4 (alk.paper)

Library of Congress Cataloging-in-Publication Data

Allen, L, Joan.
    Celebrating single and getting love right : from stalemate to
soulmate/ L. Joan Allen with Marc Kusinitz.
        p. cm.
    ISBN 1-892123-30-4
        1. Single people—United States—Psychology. 2. Baby boom
generation—United States.
    3. Man-woman relationships—United States. 4. Dating (Social cus-
toms)—United States.
    5. Self-realization—United States. I. Kusinitz, Marc. II. Title.
    HQ800.4.U6 A59 2001
    305.9′0652—dc21   2001025631

Printed in Canada

First Edition
10 9 8 7 6 5 4 3 2 1

In loving memory of my parents,
Jeannette W. Allen and William Allen,
and my dear friend,
Judith Johnson Foshee.
—JOAN

To my sons,
David and Ken Kusinitz.
—MARC

Acknowledgments

My Experts

Thank you for your generosity of spirit and for sharing your expertise, time, and ideas with me. Marc and I believe your contributions will help thousands of single men and women around the country get love right.

ⓥ   ⓥ   ⓥ

Carolyn M. Ball, M.A.

Martin Blinder, M.D.

Jalaja Bonheim, Ph.D.

Sylvia Boorstein

Fr. Joe Breighner

Eve Bruce, M.D.

Judith Burch, M.S.N.

Patrick Carnes, Ph.D.

Patty F. Cummings, L.C.S.W-C

Mark R. Ginsberg, Ph.D.

Sol Gordon, Ph.D.

Angela Grayboys

Gloria Gregg, Ph.D.

Rebecca Hartman, L.C.S.W-C

Charney Herst, Ph.D.

Barbara Harris Whitfield

Sara Kittrie, L.C.S.W.

Mark Komrad, M.D.

Doree Lynn, Ph.D.

James McGee, Ph.D.

Pia Mellody, R.N.

Marilyn Mendoza, Ph.D.

John Millbrook, Ph.D.

Mark Crispin Miller, Ph.D.

Suze Orman

Rhoda Posner Pruce, L.C.S.W-C

Susan Rabin, M.A.

Carl Robbins, M.S., L.C.P.C

John Sanford

Everett Siegel, M.D.

Anne M. Stoline, M.D.

Charles Whitfield, M.D.

Karen J. Wilson, Ed.D.

My Support System

Special thanks to: My editor, Kathleen Hughes, and her assistant, Noemi Taylor. Anne Roadman for leading me to Capital Books. Shana Bender for steering me to my authentic self and helping me change the direction of the book. Jane Hughes for her support and writing contributions and for making me laugh through the process. Sandy, Phil, and Merrill Bender for believing. Ira and Liz Allen for their lovely accommodations, finding me singles to interview in Seattle, schlepping me to the interviews, and their special editing services. Diane, Steve, and Lisa Bienstock for the use of their five-star quarters and car and for their help in finding singles to interview in Phoenix. Lisa Bullwinkel for her list of contacts in Berkeley. Bob Friedman of Hampton Roads Publishing Company for his contacts, support, and encouragement. Patsy Schneider for her list of adoption resources. Linda Janzik, Janet Weber, Elaine and Eric Aiken, LeOuita Nicholas, and Sharon Goldner for their love, support, and friendship. Carol Sorgen and Les Bradley for their editing skills. Yvonne Rose for her marketing expertise. Peggy Cullen and Andy Matlow, Buffy Murphy, and Karen Panasevich for their inspiring stories and for letting me use their real names. Elin Gursky for the subtitle. Sylvia Gordon, Geri and Ralph Deitz, Aunt Margaret and Uncle Sol Weisberger, my special family. Elizabeth Whitmore, Andrea London, and Anne Stoline, the doctors who changed my life. Marc Kusinitz for his friendship and devotion to this project.

Contents

Introduction

*"The great lie is that in order to be happy you have to
find someone else. The truth is unless you're happy
yourself, you're unlikely to be happy in a
relationship."*

—PACY MARKMAN

This book is dedicated to single baby boomers—the 22,118,000
divorced, widowed, and never-married men and women born in the
United States between 1946 and 1964. Joan and I, single baby boomers
ourselves, wrote it to console and inspire our peers who are looking for
a healthy relationship and to help them create a fulfilling life with or
without a partner.

With divorce rates skyrocketing, longer workdays, and families
scattered around the country, many single baby boomers feel lost and
alone, without a forum to share their concerns. *Celebrating Single* was
written to offer singles a sense of community, a feeling of comfort that
comes from knowing there are others who share the desire to make
peace with their lives and relationships. It also offers hope and inspiration to those who've given up on their dreams.

Throughout these pages you will hear from us jointly and individ-
ually. Sometimes we will argue, sometimes we will agree. We are
friends, after all. We've invited other friends, as well as people around

the country whom Joan met while researching this book, to offer their stories and advice. Joan also interviewed experts to provide you with the best information and advice on relationships available. Through our commentaries, "he said/she said" dialogues, and Joan's poems, we've added our own experiences about love and loss.

In the first part of this book, "The Journey," we discuss why common reasons relationships fail and identify stumbling blocks to forming healthy relationships. And we tell you how to get help. In the second part, "Celebrating Life," you will meet people who've created and maintained a healthy relationship. You'll read true stories about people who seemed fated to meet each other, and the (often unlikely) ways in which they actually met. We will also introduce you to women and men who found purpose in their lives instead of waiting for love to complete them.

When you've finished reading our book, you'll be prepared to answer these questions for yourself:

How can I be happy whether I'm in a relationship or not?
What should I know about a person before getting involved?
What are the red flags that warn, "don't get involved?"
What is a healthy relationship?
How can I stop making the same mistakes in relationships?
How have others learned to find joy in being single?

Finding joy in being single, whether you are in a relationship or not, is the theme of this book. But, you may ask, if you want to be in a satisfying relationship, what's there to celebrate if you're single? Yourself and your life. The single life doesn't have to be merely a dreary netherworld where you mark time until, if you're lucky, your romantic ship comes in. That's a lot of wasted time. So celebrate being single. Grow intellectually, professionally, spiritually, artistically—in whatever ways make you a happier and more fulfilled person—whether it's finding a mate or thriving on time spent alone.

As part of your growth you may have to resolve some unhealthy behaviors. Many people tend to replay past hurts, angers, and frustrations. That may be part of the healing process, but after a while, doesn't it just take up valuable time and energy?

Celebrating Single faces these behaviors with an unblinking stare by delving into the personal lives of real single people. Many of these stories may remind you of your own; many may startle, anger, or upset you. Yet these anecdotes are full of hope. These baby boomers, male and female, speak from their hearts. They are healing and learning. They have gained wisdom that comes from putting hindsight to good use. Many have grown, become happier, and learned how to celebrate being single. And some have even found healthy relationships that enrich their lives.

The "destiny stories" in this book? Yes, they're wonderful and full of hope. What they represent, however, are not dreams or wild strokes of luck. They show what can happen when a person is ready for a truly fulfilling relationship with another emotionally healthy person. They represent what can happen when you have a prepared heart and a clear mind when that ship comes over the horizon.

Celebrating single means feeling fulfilled in many ways and being happy and eager to face the day with a clean slate, whether or not someone wakes up next to you. And it's about being wise enough to avoid jumping into a relationship just to have one.

You've got a life to live. Every day is a potential first day of a new relationship with yourself and/or another person, if you want it and you're ready for it.

Get out there and start celebrating.

—JOAN AND MARC

To help you and other singles connect and share your concerns, we have set up a Web site: www.celebratingsingle.com. We look forward to your comments and questions.

Part I

The Journey

1

Looking Back

"The journey itself is home."

BUDDHIST SAYING

The female psyche is a lush green garden
where happy endings hang from the vine
like Sonoma grapes,
ripe for harvest.

These seeds of hopes and expectations
are planted in our wombs and souls
by the unfulfilled dreams of our mothers
and theirs before them.

The fantasy is the same.
"This will be the one."
Only the characters
and clothing change.

Are you my leading man?
Do you share my goals and dreams?
Perhaps I just project mine
upon your empty screen.

EXCERPT FROM "THE KNIGHT IN SHINING
ARMOR"—JOAN

Joan's Story

The theme of *Celebrating Single* is captured by Oscar Wilde's words, "To love oneself is the beginning of a lifelong romance." It took me four decades to appreciate the meaning of that remark.

Growing up with an overprotective, opinionated Jewish mother, I never considered being single as an option. To my mother, "single" evoked images of a childless, hunchbacked spinster like my Aunt Yetta. To her, single was an unacceptable choice. Sadly, up until a few years ago, I shared her vision.

When I was a girl my mother encouraged me to learn bridge so I would meet "refined, bright, single men." (I've never met an interesting single male bridge player.) Anyway, the only card game I excelled in as a child was Old Maid.

At age 39, with the mantra of my family ("You will marry and have children") haunting me, I took a serious look at my love life. I had been in four relationships in seven years. With this much practice in breaking up, it struck me that I was getting better at mourning failed relationships than I was at finding a healthy one.

But I wasn't alone. My friends in "perfect" marriages were divorcing. My colleagues' long- and short-term relationships were crumbling around me. We shared a lot in common: similar experiences, disappointments, and relationship scars. I kept asking myself: Why have our relationships and marriages failed? Why do our relationships just end instead of ending happily ever after?

I decided to take a year off from my work as a documentary film producer and write a book about singles, a lifelong dream. By sharing real baby boomers' stories I believed I could help other singles understand their own relationship patterns and make better choices about whom they get involved with—or whether they get involved at all. I traveled around the country and talked to more than 100 single baby boomers and dozens of relationship experts, authors, and spiritual leaders.

During that time, I was also collecting "destiny stories" for *Celebrating Single*. These are true stories of couples who met despite life's obstacles and against the odds. And when I interviewed Barbara Harris about how she met her husband, fellow author Dr. Charles Whitfield, a simple theme for this book emerged, a message of hope for my wounded generation. Barbara said, "No one can love us the way we want to be loved until we first learn to love ourselves in a healthy way."

Initially, my motivation in writing this book was to find out why my generation's relationships weren't working. Through example, the advice of experts, and my own experiences, I wanted to show single baby boomers how to love and heal themselves, find a passion besides romance, and celebrate their single status, not mourn it—in spite of societal and family pressures. To include the single male perspective, I joined forces with fellow baby boomer, dear friend, and colleague Marc Kusinitz, a published author, media guru, and divorced father of two teenage sons. We have sprinkled our personal stories and commentaries throughout each chapter.

As I researched further and after some serious reflection, I realized my motives were more personal. I wanted to know why my relationships hadn't worked and how I had contributed to their failure.

I had long resisted looking at my past and what I termed psychobabble. But I learned Robert Anthony's message the hard way: "Whatever you resist, persists." Eventually I examined, with a therapist, my childhood experiences, my relationship with my parents, and their expectations of me. I was able to see my mother's powerful influence on me—and on the romantic choices I made. I also uncovered mysterious unconscious patterns in dating based on my relationship (or lack of relationship) with my father.

I looked at my baggage, forgave my past and myself, and moved on. Then I was able to ask myself "What do I want?" As author Natalie Goldberg says to writers, "Your first job is to get your own story straight." The same is true in love and life.

Here's how my journey began.

Joan: Don't Cut Your Toes to Fit Your Shoes

"You're still single? A pretty and intelligent woman like you?" my blind dates ask this question frequently. Eventually they get over their surprise, but my mother never recovered. My never-married status was the bane of her existence.

My mother, who thought "America's Most Wanted" was a show for singles, threatened to send my name, telephone number, and photo to the producer so I would get national exposure and receive numerous marriage proposals. I already get collect calls on my message machine from a young man in prison. (Duane, if you're reading this, you've got the wrong number. Please stop calling.)

When I discussed the joys of being single on "To The Contrary," a television program that aired on 200 PBS stations around the country, my mother blamed me for her skyrocketing blood pressure. The topic was "Why Marry?" She feared that if available single, heterosexual men who watched that program met me, they might not ask me out.

Trying to be the Dutiful Daughter, I always went on blind dates that she and her cronies set up. They included the transvestite ballroom dancer who borrowed my rhinestone earrings at a black-tie event, the 350-pound inventor, and the unemployed candy salesman. My theory is, I'm being punished for bad karma from another life.

I adored my mother, but sometimes her pit-bull tenacity incited my sarcasm, especially when the conversation went like this:

MOTHER: "You've been dating Gary for six months, shall I call the caterer?"

ME: "By the time I get married, I'll have to wheel you down the aisle."

That line usually succeeded in fending her off for a few weeks, but my mother never quit. Every year on my birthday, from the time I was 19, she took out a spiral notebook and edited my wedding list in front of me. On the eve of my 41st birthday, and after a year of therapy, I finally had the nerve to say, "Mother, I'm not playing this game anymore."

The irony was, I brought home a constant stream of men whom she did *not* want me to marry. There was, for example, the cheap fiancé who was secretly romancing two other women while he was courting me. One Thanksgiving, a day after we arrived at my parent's house in New Jersey, he refused to go sightseeing until I offered to fill his car with gas. Mother overheard this conversation and whispered to me, "He'll only get worse after you marry him."

My mother complained that another fiancé wasn't smart enough. "Don't worry that all your friends are getting married. You're the one who has to talk to him over breakfast every morning," she said.

So despite my mother's growing dread that I might never marry, she insisted I break off my last engagement. She thought I might be "settling." Her advice still rings true: "Joanie, don't cut your toes to fit your shoes." The first time she said that I thought she wanted me to marry a podiatrist.

A few years later, Mother passed away. I think about her wit and wisdom every day. I understand now that she didn't mean to torment me. She, like many women of her generation, felt I needed a man to bring me happiness, to take care of me. If only she could see that I did that for myself; I'm living my dream. I just needed time to fall in love with myself. I believe the man I attract now will enhance my life, not complete it.

Deep in my soul, I know that when my mother hears about this special man, she will find her way back—to help me edit the wedding list.

> I don't want a cookie-cutter wedding:
> a parade of cotton candy dresses,
> and rows of Mother's friends
> standing stiffly like stuffed corsets.
>
> Surrounded by my sea of friends,
> I will wear Mother's trousseau gown,
> and float down the aisle
> with my life mate,
> like a Chagall painting.
>
> EXCERPT FROM "THE WEDDING LIST"—
> JOAN

Joan: Find Your Self First

Learning how to find happiness within as a never-married woman is like climbing the Himalayas without a companion. You have your family at the bottom begging you not to take that journey: "You'll be alone. You won't have anyone to protect you. . . . " Yet your inner voice says, "You need to do this. You won't be up there alone forever."

Barbara Harris Whitfield, author of *Spiritual Awakenings*, describes this dilemma:

> If we're not finding Mr. Right, the universe is being kind to us, because we're not ready. Whoever we'd catch up with at that time would match our own emptiness, our own places that we need to heal. What we need to do is learn to love ourselves. We can heal through psychotherapy, other personal growth experiences, anything that's going to teach us more about who we are. And once we do that kind of healing, once we find that the love we're looking for

is inside ourselves . . . once we find out who we are, then we'll more likely find someone. But we may not find it before that.

How Do We Fall in Love with Ourselves?

Many women have more than they know in common with Dorothy from *The Wizard of Oz*. Like Dorothy, they've had relationships with men who lacked a heart, courage, and a brain. But Dorothy also teaches that the answers are inside us all along. If we listen to our Self, we can go home.

Tapping into that power of listening to our Self is like discovering precious gems. Once we heal old relationship wounds, erase outdated tapes that replay past hurts, forgive the past, strip away ineffectual patterns in relationships, and begin loving our True Self, our fears dissolve like the soggy Wicked Witch of the West.

But how do we unearth the answers inside? How do we learn to fall in love with ourselves? How do we become whole and join with another complete person in a relationship? First, we have to heal.

Janet F. Quinn, author of *I Am a Woman Finding My Voice* writes, "No one grows up without wounds—emotional wounds; spiritual wounds; psychological wounds. I may want to forget how I have been hurt; bury it and just move on, but sometimes my wounds keep me from becoming all I want to be, and so I need to pay attention to them."

Although an exploration of our psychic cobwebs can be painful, bringing these wounds to the conscious mind can help us heal ourselves and our relationships. Quinn describes her personal healing journey: "Healing is discovering all the secret places inside of me, especially the ones I feel ashamed of or frightened by, and befriending them. Healing is the process I am engaged in and not a specific outcome."

Marc's Story

After years of doomed relationships on the singles' scene, Joan and I realized that we were failing to learn from our experiences. Rather, we tended to react to them. Bitterness and cynicism were becoming our Saturday night companions. Then Joan decided to tackle this challenge with insight and understanding instead of anger and frustration.

She started out on a journey of self-discovery and took me, her co-author and friend, with her.

We older baby boomers went from the innocence of high school dances and girls sporting crinoline skirts to the summer of free love in San Francisco. No one was prepared for that. Not our parents. Not us. Baby boomers began by breaking the rules and ended up buying books about how women should date by certain rules.

Along the way, self-help books and seminars, weekend encounter sessions and spiritual journeys of discovery began to replace a frenetic do-your-own-thing lifestyle. We wanted to know why so many of us felt unfulfilled in our selves and our relationships. It took me many years to reach that point. I went through my marriage with all good intentions, and as clueless as a Keystone Kop. For years afterward I struggled with myself and my relationships, shifting from feelings of inadequacy to anger over transgressions I felt I suffered at the hands of the opposite sex. I chafed at the condescending attitude of women who said "Men don't get it," while legions of them seemed to willingly throw themselves into self-destructive relationships with men.

It seemed like the world of single baby boomers had gone mad. And I was eager to defend my gender. I needed an outlet for my anger in response to women's criticism of men and relationships. I had a bone to pick with women.

It was only after I started to learn more about my own lack of understanding of what healthy relationships are all about and how to avoid slipping into unhealthy ones, that I finally made peace with myself and the opposite sex. Nothing changed overnight, and I'm still on a learning curve. But dating is not so much a gamble anymore as a night out, a friendly encounter that may or may not evolve into something else.

Along the way I met Joan Allen at a brunch arranged by mutual friends specifically to bring the two of us together. We dated for a month or so, but we drifted apart. When we reconnected during a professional collaboration, we began a very long, spirited friendship, the likes of which I could not have foretold and would never have guessed. I say "spirited" because we've had our differences over issues of dating, sex, and relationships. We've also helped each other through a number of tumultuous relationships. Through it all we have remained great friends.

I'm proud to report that after several years of introspection and personal growth, Joan and I are now both happily single and ready to share our insights and personal experiences with you. *Celebrating Single* is a wake-up call to single baby boomers who have outgrown the "me generation" and are searching for more meaning in their lives and relationships.

Writing this book with Joan has helped me to see both men's and women's views of dating issues clearer and to realize neither side is completely wrong. *Celebrating Single* is a tribute to our ongoing friendship and to what we've learned along the way from experts, from our peers, and from each other.

2

The Truth about Dating

THE LAST BLIND DATE IN BALTIMORE

Is there someone worth the wait,
the endless stream of chatter with a new stranger
at the same espresso bar?
Mistaken identities.
One-hour dates.
"Who pays?"
Furtive glances at my watch.
Slanted crow's feet filling pregnant pauses.
"How 'bout them O's?" ★

—JOAN

Blind dates are like bungee jumping. To some, they evoke the thrill of anticipation. To others, the dread that the date, like the bungee cord, might be too long.

—JOAN AND MARC

Marc: **Will I See Her Again?**

And I wonder: Will I see her again? She seems at ease and ready to laugh and have a good time. Maybe it's been a while since she's been out with a guy. Or maybe she likes the way I act, talk, dress, look?

★ Baltimore Orioles

She's ready, eager to get into small talk. Friendly chatter about her day as we drive to the restaurant. The weather. Work. Traffic. The city. A funny incident at the office. A wacky co-worker. A cranky boss.

I talk to her as if we've known each other for months. I smile as I drive and make a joke. She laughs. I quickly turn my head from the road to catch her glance. She's smiling. Her eyes almost sparkle, but maybe it's just because she doesn't know me that well. I'm a tiny bit disappointed. I wanted to see her eyes sparkle. I love seeing a woman's eyes sparkle. Even if we don't kiss goodnight on a first date, that's okay. But I want to make her eyes sparkle.

Somehow, I find it reassuring to see a woman's eyes sparkle. She's not just killing time with me. She's really having fun. I'm not wasting my time. I'm not wasting my emotional energy. I'm not wasting my best jokes.

I wonder: Will I ever see her again?

The evening passes at the restaurant she chose. I wanted her to feel comfortable so I suggested having our first date in her neighborhood. Her territory. Make it easy on her. Help her relax. Make her smile. Be warm. Tell a joke. Make her eyes sparkle.

We walk into the restaurant—a cross between a family diner and a wannabe swank eatery. Nothing too pretentious for a first date. More small talk as we sit across from each other in the restaurant. We start talking about ourselves. The waiter breaks into our private world and drops off menus, asks if we'd like something to drink, and mentions the specials. He leaves.

We get deep into conversation, each of us grateful to have some-one of the opposite sex with "potential" to talk to tonight. The waiter returns several minutes later and we tell him, somewhat sheepishly, that we haven't even looked at the menu. He smiles and forgives us. And disappears.

We pick up the menus and change the subject from past lives to present hunger. I wonder if I'll ever see her again.

It's been a half-hour since I picked her up at her house, which has photos of her children and her ex-husband with her children—and her brothers and sister and parents and cousins and friends—on the refriger-ator, the living room walls, bookshelves, the hallway. A previous life of togetherness is artificially patched together with images on Kodak pa-per, carefully placed around the house so she'll never be without her family and friends. Even though they're scattered across five cities and three states, and she never sees more than three of them at a time—

when she can get away. Not like the old days, when her family and friends could gather in one backyard for a summer evening party, like the one captured forever in that photo on the living room bookshelf. And now she uses her museum of photos as a buffer against the gnawing realization that her life is an emotional diaspora.

She looks at the menu hungrily. She's happy to share a meal with me. And I with her. She's talking about her children now. My two sons, who've spent a decade with a live-away father, pass through my mind. I keep listening to her as I drop my glance to the menu and wonder if there's anything here that my finicky son Ken would like. I like taking my sons Ken and David to sports restaurants. It's guy bonding time, fun time. They grew up knowing me as a regular weekend visitor—no matter where I lived.

I pop my head back up and look at her. In my mind's eye I see all the photos of her family and friends again and compare them to the scarcity of images in my apartment, where some few precious images of my sons at different ages are displayed.

They grew up with a live-away dad.

She stops talking about her children, suddenly conscious that I might be hungry and want to order. She asks me what I'm going to order. I look up again from the menu and smile, acting like I've been deep in concentration over the appetizer, salad, and entrée options splayed out across the piece of cardboard I'm holding.

I tell her I can't decide and ask if she can suggest anything—especially if it's a fish dish. She's not familiar with the fish dishes here. She prefers chicken. She's from the Midwest. She's never been on a sailboat or gone fishing.

I find a nice fish entrée and urge her to continue talking about her life. I'm tired of going through my life over and over again on each first date. She continues to tell me about her children. That's a good sign, I think. She wouldn't talk about her children with so much warmth and pride if she didn't like me, didn't want to see me again.

Or is she just trying to draw a line in the sand, to tell me that her joint custody of the children means that they will be in her life day-to-day—and the life of any man she gets deeply involved with—for several more years at least?

I wonder if I'll ever see her again.

Dinner ends and it's only 9 P.M. I had left open what we'd do afterwards because the neighborhood is fun and funky; it'll be easy to kill an hour or two just wandering in and out of stores and bars. And it gives us time to talk. We find things to talk about as we duck in and out of antiques stores: The stodgy antique wicker chair. The grouchy-looking old rolltop desk. The preposterous old ball gowns that look like they were the toast of some long-ago Mardi Gras.

A final drink at a pub, then I take her home. She invites me in for coffee. I accept and ask for decaf. There's more small talk, like we're each waiting for the other to make the first move. I figure, "In for a dime, in for a dollar." I ask her out for the following week. She accepts. More small talk and then I stand up from my chair and stretch. I thank her for a wonderful evening and walk to the door.

She steps ahead of me and opens the door. Then she smiles, thanks me again for a wonderful evening, and offers her hand. I embrace it.

Her eyes sparkle.

Victory.

She wouldn't have accepted a second date with a sparkle if she didn't think I had long-term potential. I start thinking of movies and museums and plays I want to see with her. A trip out of town I want to take with her. I'm planning out how I'll make her happy. Show her how special she is to me. Make her laugh. Make her eyes sparkle.

This was just the first date.

And then I think to myself, "What will it be like when *this* relationship ends?"

BLIND DATE

Anticipating my blind date,
I gathered, lathered and slathered.
He never bathed, shaved or slaved.

—JOAN

Paige's Impersonal Personal Ad

Paige is an energetic chef and a fun-loving divorcée with an optimistic attitude. Here she serves up her advice on answering personal ads and her favorite blind-date story.

I enjoyed the personal ads because they kept me out and about so I wouldn't feel isolated. I didn't realize how many men were into going out with a 42-year-old woman. There were tons. There were more men than there was time. It kept reassuring me how many single people are out there. Not everyone was normal, but there were some real nice guys. My barometer of "normal": common courtesy, manners—if we meet for just coffee, they offer to pay. Some men did request $2 for coffee. Many offered to pay. After a first meeting, I expect to pay my way, but I know the man's a gentleman if he pays for my coffee.

I was truly looking for a friend, not the date of a lifetime, so if someone asked me out, I usually said yes. I made two male friends by placing an ad in *Pennysaver*. I met both of them and we stayed friends. It's nice to hang out with just guys sometimes.

Another advantage of dating through the personals was after almost every date I learned about new places to go—restaurants, cafes, cultural events, hangouts for singles where I'd feel comfortable. By dating so much, it gave me a chance to know what I really wanted and how to ask for it. Also, placing a personal ad in *Pennysaver* was free and they ran my ad for four weeks.

When I wrote my ad, I didn't make any sexual references whatsoever; I didn't mention my height, weight, figure or color of my hair or eyes. Many men said they noticed there was nothing about my personal appearance and they liked that. That's how you weed out shallow men from the others.

A red flag for me in a personal ad was a hint of anything sexual. I avoided meeting that person. Please, do not under any circumstances talk about where you live or work with people who respond to your ad. Be very general until you get to know someone. Pay attention to something as simple as whether they do what they say they're going to do. Are they reliable? You can see in just a few dates if a person is reliable or responsible. And always let someone know where you are going, with whom, his phone number, and about when you're expecting to be back home. For your comfort.

I met one potentially dangerous guy who wouldn't go to a state flower show because they didn't have organic flowers. He screamed at me on the phone and hung up on me. Big red flag signal: Do not go anywhere with this man. Ever!

Know what you will and won't accept. Do you really want a smoker? A person with children? I knew I didn't want children. It's very important to know before answering ads.

I found that through this process of dating, if you do it carefully and don't jump into anything, you learn what your real values are and aren't. Is that acceptable to me or not? Do I want to go out with a man who's just recently separated? Do I feel comfortable going out with a younger man? Someone of a different religion? It challenges your own beliefs about yourself. It's ultimately your life. You are looking for a person who meets your needs, not the other way around.

The best lesson I learned while dating through the personals, after doing it for a year, is if you take it very slowly in meeting another person, you will find they are not the person you thought they were on the first and second date. Give yourself the time to see who the person really is, not the fantasy in your mind. Men you thought were nerdy, you may see such beauty in; you can't go by physical features to help you decide who a person is.

Gary contacted Paige within the first few weeks her ad ran. When she met him, she stopped dating other men.

My ad said I am fun and funny, artistic, creative, gentle and warm; that I love the countryside and historic towns. It said I was in search of a man who is humorous, warm and down-to-earth. Gary and I share these attributes exactly. He lives in the countryside in Pennsylvania. He's a fabulous artist and inventor; he's fun and funny, down-to-earth, warm. When me met the first time, I wasn't familiar with his kind of looks. Being from the city, I was used to a more sophisticated, tailored, stylish, every-hair-in-place guy. Gary is 5′9″ and has a beard, mustache, beautiful blue eyes, thinning hair. He's rugged, a "man's man" admired by other men.

On our first date, we met at Chi Chi's for appetizers. It turned out to be more than appetizers. That was the first and last time I let him pay for me. He met me at a time I was financially comfortable. I didn't want a man to be my rescuer financially or in any other way.

Many women look for a man to take care of them. Gary and I are equal people. He really is my best friend. I've never had such a good friend who's been my partner.

During the first five months we only went out once a month. That was him. He wanted to be friends; he didn't want to rush. We both wanted time to be cautious and to figure out who the other person was.

After dating six months, this was all a coincidence, we ended up making separate plans to be in the same town at the same time. Before I even spoke with him about my trip, I had made reservations for a bed and breakfast on a farm, by myself, for two nights.

When I spoke with Gary I asked him if he had ever heard of the town where I was staying. He said, "I'm going there next weekend and I'm staying there for several days. I have a trailer there I'm fixing up to sell. I hope I won't be infringing on you but would you consider extending your stay a few more days so we can spend some time together?"

It was perfect. I stayed in the B&B and Gary stayed at his trailer. There was nothing sexual.

I enjoyed spending time alone exploring the historic sights and visiting crafts galleries and Gary worked on preparing his trailer to sell. Sometimes we connected with his friends, sometimes we met for dinner. On that trip we found we had many of the same interests—especially anything to do with art. And we both love funny movies. Most important, though, was the way we spaced our time together and our time apart. It's the exact pattern of our marriage today. We each have a need for our own space.

On our first date, we talked for four hours. We were shocked when the restaurant was closing around us. After three years of marriage, we continue to have conversations that last three and four hours. We are friends like we were at the beginning of our relationship. Our friendship has remained the core of our marriage.

Joan: Dating.com

First and second dates serve a purpose. As Paige says, "You are looking for a person who meets *your* needs. It gives you a chance to know what you really want and who you really are."

Or, as in the following case, what you really *don't* want.

ⓦ   ⓦ   ⓦ

"You really should try it, Joan," my friend Carol persuaded.

"Internet dating? I don't think so. People could present themselves in any way they want. They could be married. They could be serial killers—or worse, serial daters."

"I've met some decent guys. Just fill in your profile and send your photo to this address. Do it once and I'll never ask you again. You spend too much time alone writing that book."

It had been a few months since I'd been on a date. A line from an old Ann Landers column reverberated in my mind: "The best match that ever came out of Baltimore was Wallis Simpson's."

"Oh, OK."

A few weeks later a man responded to my Internet profile. He lived in Baltimore; he sounded warm, confident, and intelligent on the phone. After several conversations, we agreed to meet at Starbucks for about an hour. That seemed safe enough.

When we met for coffee, his in-person demeanor was 180 degrees different from his phone personality. He sat slumped in his seat with his hands covering his face while he talked. It was strange body language. I thought maybe he was just shy.

He asked me out for New Year's Eve, a few weeks away. A black-tie event at his country club. My first instinct was "no." Something didn't seem right—The wrong chemistry? His shyness? I studied his face. His blue eyes implored me. He looked so boyish and vulnerable.

"OK," I said. "I'll meet you there."

His smile stretched from ear to ear; I thought his face would burst. And I felt touched.

About a week later, I came down with a killer flu that kept me in bed with bronchitis for two weeks. I called him and declined, saying I'd love to get together again when I felt better.

He called after New Year's and we made plans to meet that night for dinner in my neighborhood. I still wouldn't drive in the same car or give him my address. My instinct was get to know this guy better.

We sat in an Irish pub and made small talk. He ordered a merlot for me. Strange, I thought, has his demeanor changed again? He seemed more confident, more like his phone persona. Is this his twin brother?

After swilling two gigantic kamikazes, he ordered another wine for me. I said, "I'm afraid I'm a cheap date. This one will last me forever."

He said, "That's OK, I'll drink yours."

"Tell me about your New Year's," I inquired. "That's great you went alone."

"It was incredible. My golf buddy and I sat together. He brought his girlfriend. She's a drop-dead gorgeous masseuse."

"A certified masseuse or a masseuse-masseuse?" I teased.

"Well, she says what goes on behind closed doors is her business."

"Oh," I gaped. I've always been a terrible actress.

"My friend, his girlfriend, and I stayed up drinking and dancing until 6 A.M. After the party we went out to breakfast. Then she gave me a pill."

He ordered a third cocktail.

"Aspirin? It must have been a brutal hangover."

"Hangover? No. It was Ecstasy."

"Ecstasy? I thought people die from that. Heart attacks."

"Anyone can have a heart attack. It's safe enough."

Trying to maintain the conversation until we finished dinner and I could escape, I said, "I'm not sure I could have made it till 6 A.M. I'm an early-night person."

He replied abruptly, "I don't see how we could be any more different. I stay up till 4 A.M. every day."

"How do you entertain yourself that late?"

"I watch movies on HBO and then gamble online."

"Are you winning?" I tried to be cool.

"So far."

"I thought gambling online was illegal in the U.S."

"This is out of Costa Rica."

"Oh."

"I've got to be honest with you," he said. "You're just too prim and proper for me."

"I think you're right."

"Dating is so hard," he said. He looked at the bill. "And so expensive."

"Can I help with the bill?"

"No, that's OK."

He walked me to my car and said, "See ya."

The events of the evening flashed by like a van Gogh painting: sad, dark, and swirling. Driving home, I cracked the window and inhaled the icy air to clear my thoughts. "OK, so that one didn't work out. Look how far you've come on your journey, how much you've grown—now you know who you are and what *you* want." I felt so empowered that I couldn't restrain my triumphant smile as I turned the key to my apartment and entered my cozy, warm oasis.

Women and Their Cats

Sometimes pets create that cozy, cuddly atmosphere single men and women crave. But what happens when the pet and the hostess forget their manners and you feel like an unwelcome guest in their home? Marc shares his thoughts on this scenario.

If it weren't for single women, cats would probably be an endangered species.

Thousands of abandoned and orphaned felines would have their last meals at cash-strapped animal shelters staffed by overworked caregivers struggling to feed their furry charges and filter their hairy remains out of the air.

The majority of women I've dated have had cats. My friend Joan wants one more than she wants a baby, but she's allergic—to cats, not babies. She loves babies, too.

There's something very nurturing and reassuring about a woman who can love a furry being that haughtily ignores her all day and then hisses and spits at her when she (the woman, not the cat) comes home after spending the night away with her boyfriend.

I once went out with a woman whose cat had the run of her home. It was a first date—with the woman, not the cat. At the end of the evening, she invited me back to her place for a late-night cup of coffee. I sat on a stool in her kitchen, resting my arms comfortably on her small kitchen table.

She placed a small cup of sugar and a small pitcher in the middle of the table. Then she busied herself, with her back toward me, preparing coffee for both of us.

In the meantime, her cat, rightfully feeling more at home than I, hopped up onto the kitchen table. I watched, riveted, as ole Tabby strolled across the table, stopped in front of the pitcher, dipped her head into it, and casually began lapping the milk.

Ole Tabby's owner turned around in time to espy the violation of my coffee additive, pushed the cat gently away, and turned back to tend the coffee.

I sat, stone-faced and quiet, awaiting her response to this filthy turn of feline events.

When my date turned around again and placed a cup of fresh hot coffee in front of me, I sat still, awaiting her response to the cat's public health transgression.

She pushed the pitcher of milk toward me.

I told her, politely and calmly, that I'd prefer not to use the milk because the cat had used it first. She did not offer me a new serving of uncontaminated milk.

I drank the coffee black.

The most incredible part of this entire scenario was the fact that I asked her out again. The woman that is—not the cat. That was still early in my post-marriage "happy bachelor" days, when I was running on automatic.

But that was the old me. No longer would I tolerate a member of a species further down the evolutionary ladder partaking of my coffee additive. Nosiree. Either the cat shows manners or the woman gives me fresh milk.

I will say, however, that I've reached a détente with cats owned by single women. In fact, I've actually managed to make friends with some of those cats, a circumstance that was not lost on some very impressed women.

Now I wonder whether those cats or their owners remember me. I sure remember them.

The moral of the story: Love your cat, but don't let your feelings for your pet disrupt a potential relationship with a man. There's room for them both at your kitchen table.

Joan: If He's Too Good to Be True, Run

Speaking of kitchen tables, my mother's best advice to me was, "It doesn't matter what anyone thinks about your fiancé but you. You're the one who'll face him every morning over breakfast."

What happens when the person staring at you across the kitchen table is your legal mate and you realize, a bit too late, that you made a big mistake? Sometimes even the best advice from family and friends can't prevent us from learning our soul's lesson. That was the case with Beth.

You've talked on the phone for two hours. You agree you have a lot in common and the anticipation of meeting is delicious. Your heart races. Your hope returns. You feel the rush of excitement, the thrill of the unknown. If you're a woman, you probably buy a new outfit, at least a new shade of lipstick. And you can't wait to talk to your girl-friends.

We sat around the table at a local tavern three years ago. It was my birthday and five attractive, professional, savvy women from 25 to 40, took me to lunch.

Our dear friend, Beth, a television news anchor who resembles a young Grace Kelly, sat shell-shocked from a recent breakup with her boyfriend. To take her mind off the past, we offered Beth advice about her first date the next day with a dashing new man.

Their romance started like a fairy tale.

Bill cared for disabled adults so he could earn money for graduate school. When his group requested a visit to meet their favorite television news personality, Bill called Beth. Beth, in her generous, gracious way, offered to make his group lunch and give them a tour of the studio.

She spoke frequently by phone with Bill to make the arrangements; she was impressed by his kindness and eagerly anticipated their first meeting at the studio. Sparks flew. The day they met, Bill asked Beth to go on a boating picnic.

The conversation at my birthday luncheon about Beth's first date with Bill quickly hit a frenetic pitch. I felt like I was back in high school, surrounded by friends at a slumber party, trying to figure out the opposite sex. Well, some things don't change.

Our discussion energized the sunny little room. Even waiters wanted to join our stimulating sorority. The discussion whirled into a life of its own—a free-for-all, no-topics-barred brawl. The conversation went something like this:

BETH: I have my first date with Bill tomorrow.

GIRLS: Ooooooooooh!

(The waiter takes drink orders.)

JENNIE: Hot date! Don't hold back on us, girlfriend. Where are you going?

TINA: How could you wait so long to tell us?

BETH: We're going boating and on a picnic.

LAURA: Mrs. Beth Bradford. I like it.

CHRIS: She hasn't even gone out with him yet and you're marrying them off?

LAURA: Yeah. So?

TINA: Well, what are you going to wear?

BETH: Shorts.

TINA: Oh no. Promise me you'll change outfits. You need backup clothes to bring with you. Come over to my house after lunch and check out my closet. I have a really cute little black knit dress if you need to change for later. It'll roll up in a ball in your carry-on bag.

JENNIE: You should wear a bikini and show some skin. Every guy loves a girl in a bikini, so go for it. Show plenty of skin.

BETH (laughing): More is definitely more in this case. I'll stick to a one piece.

TINA: What's so funny?

BETH: This whole thing is hilarious. Can you imagine Bill sitting around with his buddies, seeing if his name sounds good with mine? Or deciding what he should wear: boxers or briefs?

CHRIS: Question. Off the topic. When, after how many dates, do you sleep with a guy?

JENNIE: I want to know right away if the guy is worthy. If we're really attracted, I don't want to waste time, so I let him know.

JOAN: How?

JENNIE: By seducing him.

LAURA (stunned): I can't believe this. I'm not going to sleep with anyone anymore that I'm not going to marry. I found my boyfriend in bed with another woman, and I'm not going to be that vulnerable ever again.

JOAN: From learning the hard way, I think it's really important to be friends with the guy first. If you sleep with someone you don't know well, it clouds your decisions about him. Do you like him as a person? Do you have the same values and goals? Keep talking, ladies. This is great material for my book. I'm going home to get my tape recorder. Be right back.

(I start to leave, then call over my shoulder.)

JOAN: Oh, and what about AIDS?

JENNIE: I use condoms.

BETH: Happy birthday, Joanie.

JOAN: I'm coming back.

As I left the table I noticed our shy waiter considering when he should take our order. Laughter filled the preppy forest-green room and people from surrounding tables tilted their ears toward us to eavesdrop on our lively conversation.

LAURA: Let's do this next week. I have a date.

(Glasses clink.)

Two years later, I spoke with Beth about her memories of that famous birthday luncheon.

The funniest thing was, there was no consensus. No two opinions matched. I also remember still feeling shaky from the breakup with Larry. I hadn't healed yet. Just a few weeks earlier I had confided to Marc at your party that I hadn't done enough to make the relationship with Larry work. I felt I had made a huge mistake. I thought I wouldn't meet anyone again, and a week later I met Bill. Sitting at your birthday luncheon two years ago, I hadn't moved past my pain with Larry. I was still healing. I still really needed to talk about it.

Beth fell in love with Bill, and after their two-year courtship, they married on a New England beach. I felt grateful to be among the handful of family and friends who were invited. Gentle waves and soft harpsichord music filled the silence as Beth walked through a rose path on the sand. The sun, so large and red, reminded me of a child's drawing as it dissolved behind the kissing couple.

I observed what I thought was the perfect wedding; but the marriage ended one year later. Beth admits she jumped into a relationship with Bill too quickly, and she ignored the red flag signals during their courtship.

Bill kept putting off the wedding date, even after I had the dress and had made the wedding arrangements. We put off the wedding four months from the original date we had picked. Then, a week before the wedding, we flew to the resort to set up the clambake for the out-of-town guests, and Bill was still unsure about getting married. He spoke with the minister, trying to get clarity, the morning of the day we were married—which I didn't know until a week later, on our honeymoon. If I'd known this the day of our wedding, I think I would have had it and called off the whole thing. But by the day of the wedding things were better.

The scary thing was, when we first met, he pretended to be everything I wanted him to be—charming, and gracious to my friends and parents. After we married, I realized he was extremely self-centered. Everything was about him—from his special diet, to his two-hour-a-day workouts—whatever *he* wanted to do. He had none of my best interests in mind. He put me through an emotional roller coaster. If I hadn't been so tired and worn out, I would have seen that I needed to get away to get clarity. My judgment was clouded. I wanted to believe he was the person I thought he was when we first met. The person I met didn't exist. He was trying to be the perfect guy. He was too good to be true.

When Beth told me calmly over tea that she had filed for divorce, she said she had no tears left. With the support of her therapist and loving family, Beth is now ready to move on with her life.

I see this as a learning experience. Next time I'll trust my instincts. Right now, I'm working on making myself happy and spending time alone. I'm going skiing by myself for two weeks and then I'm going to cooking school in Europe and doing some traveling. I finally feel happy and free.

Advice from an Expert

Sol Gordon, Ph.D., author of *Why Love Is Not Enough,* says many marriages don't work because people don't know what love is. "They think if you can't eat or sleep it's love, but that's not what love is all about." He shared his expertise in an interview.

Q: *What is love about?*
A: If you think about it, if you feel yourself to be in love, you are. And it's foolish to even attempt to say that's not love. It's love. Unfortunately there are two kinds, mature and immature. Mature love is energizing; mature love is creative. You want to be nice to the other person, you want to please the other person. When you are in an im-

mature relationship, you're exhausted all of the time. The process of having an immature relationship means you're going to be mean to people; you have what we call a "hostile dependent relationship"— you can't stand to be with the person you're in love with and you can't stand to be without them.

People need to think a little more seriously about marriage. It's surprising how many people that I've spoken to say things like, "Oh there's Joe, he's wonderful, he's so pleasant and so nice to me, but he doesn't turn me on; but there's Jim, who's a psychopath, an alcoholic, a gambler, a liar, but wow, he really turns me on."

So many people marry the person who turns him on. You can be madly in love with someone and after a few months of marriage, you're just plain mad. Love itself is not a criteria, it's another matter of mature and immature relationships.

And by the way, you can't tell the difference between mature and immature relationships in the first few months. Things appear to be the same at first, and then some clear patterns emerge. Meanness emerges in immature relationships. Kindness, caring, intimacy, sharing, having fun together, playfulness are traits of mature relationships.

Q: *What is your advice for single people over 35?*

A: Marry a good friend. It's not enough to establish a relationship on love or sex. Sex is not a good indication of whether or not you're compatible. There are a lot of people who have perfectly good sex with people they don't even like or care about, and there are some people who don't understand that those first experiences of sex are not very comfortable. Sex is something you're supposed to learn. The best sex comes in time, when people are able to share intimacies, when people can communicate with each other. It's possible to have inadequate sex with somebody you really care about. There is no connection between love and sex. None. You can have a wonderful sex life with somebody you love and with somebody you don't like. And you can have a not-so-great sex life with somebody who's wonderful, who you really care about, who you are fully in love with, and hopefully with time and patience and communication, you'll be able to figure things out.

Q: *Where do you suggest single people meet?*

A: I think single people try to meet others in the wrong places. I don't think singles bars are appropriate, or even singles dances (although I'm not totally opposed to them). I don't think that's the right place to meet people. You need to meet people in the context of meaningful experience. In Hebrew, there's a word "mitzvah." In traditional usage it means following commandments, but in modern usage it means to do good work. The best place to meet people is in the context of doing good work, doing mitzvahs. Help the disadvantaged, work with people with AIDS, teach a kid how to read, conserve nature. Here are places where you meet like-minded, interesting people. Another good place to meet people is in a learning place.

Q: *What's on your Top 10 List for couples trying to evaluate their relationship?*

A: Number one is intimacy: Caring about each other, being able to talk freely and openly with one another, being available in times of hardship. That's the number one aspect of a relationship. It's also the number one aspect of a really good friendship.

Number two is a sense of humor and a kind of playfulness. Without a sense of humor, relationships don't work. Without a kind of playfulness, the relationship doesn't work.

Number three is communication.

Trust or being able to count on the other person is fourth.

Tolerance for problems or dealing with the not-so-perfect aspects of the relationship is fifth.

Six is sharing common interests.

Seven is respecting the other's differences.

The eighth is excitement in making plans together.

By the way, number nine is sex.

And number 10 is sharing household tasks together. So you get a sense of how I put these things in context.

Q: *How can you tell if a person you're dating is seriously pursuing you?*

A: In a very brief period of time, you'll discover a very important aspect of the person, which is reliability: Can you trust that person? Do they lie a lot? Do they seem in some way distracted by other issues? There are people who are deceivers; they pretend they're not married and they are, for example. They're not really serious. You can judge it by the level of attention someone gives you. People who are not serious have lapses of attention, they lie quite a bit, and they don't remember your birthday or anniversaries.

Q: *Why is it so hard to let go of a relationship that is not working?*

A: It's hard because the person feels insecure and has low self-esteem. They feel they won't be able to find another relationship; they feel doomed. They feel this is their last chance—somehow or other there is some notion this is all they can get and they deserve this situation. It's based on low self-esteem. People who have high levels of self-esteem don't stay in bad relationships.

Why, for example, do people stay in abusive relationships? It's incredible, we hear of so many couples where one is battering the other and they still maintain the relationship. It's based on the assumption that they don't deserve more or they have this weird notion that if it's real love, they need to be patient and the relationship will work.

If there's a single incident of some physical violence, just a single incident, and the person is sorry and says, "I'll never do it again," you might say, "Look, I'll forgive you this one time, but if you ever hit me again, our relationship is finished." I'm not talking about abuse, I'm talking about a single incident; it could be episodic, it could be based on lack of control for a moment, loss of temper for a moment.

I once met with a young woman who had a black eye. I said, "What happened, honey?"

"My boyfriend beat me up."

I said, "Has he ever done this before?"

"Oh yes, several times."

"He beat you up several times. Why do you stay with him?"

"I love him."

"You love him? I have news for you, if someone hits you it means they don't like you."

It seems like a simple matter, but it's dramatic. We have to convey to people in this country that if someone hits you, they don't like you.

Q: *What kind of person would you advise our readers* not *to marry?*

A: A person who's addicted in any way. It's important not to marry someone who is an addict, whether it's an alcoholic, a drug addict, workaholic, sex addict, or gambler. Addicts characteristically make false promises. "Don't worry honey, when we get married, I'll stop fooling around with other women (or men)" or "I won't gamble anymore."

Don't count on such promises. An addict has to get treated first. Don't marry someone who hasn't been sober for at least two years if they have an alcohol problem. A bad situation always gets worse in marriage. Walk away when there's violence, of course, or when there's a tremendous amount of ambivalence: "Should I, shouldn't

I?" It could take years before they're willing to make a commitment. They're not usually good bets for marriage.

Q: *How long should you give someone who's commitment phobic?*

A: Maximum is a year, especially if you're over 25.

Q: *What do you do until you've found the right person?*

A: The worst thing to do is to get desperate. If you're desperate you give off negative vibrations. People don't like to be with desperate people. They'll be wallowing in self-abuse and self-pity. "Nobody cares about me, nobody loves me." The best things to do while you're waiting to meet somebody are learn something new, enjoy every day of your life, dress well, pay attention to your health. This is a good time to be attentive to your own needs—clean up your room, buy a new apartment, go abroad, do something exciting and interesting. Don't wallow. Wallowing gives rise to desperation, and desperation gives off negative vibrations.

Q: *What role should romance play?*

A: I'm all for romance. I think romance is the greatest joy of all things, but it should not be a substitute for intimacy. You can have a romantic evening based on a line, and you can have a romantic evening as part of an intimate, caring relationship. You can have a romantic evening that's just one deception after another, with all this lovey-dovey stuff. And you can have a romantic evening with a lot of integrity. So romance has to be sort of evaluated for its true meaning; it has to be tested. It's OK to have a romantic evening or month or two—it doesn't matter, it still has to be tested in the relationship, in the intimacy. You still have to find out whether or not the person is really selfish or has intimate feelings for you.

Avoiding Red Hot Topics

And what happens when your date tries to get intimate too fast? Marc offers advice on the art of verbal intimacy.

Giving advice to women about men and romance is like trying to speed up a barbecue by squirting lighter fluid onto red hot charcoal briquettes. I've learned that if you want to jump-start such a fire—or debate—it's best to step back once the fluid hits the coals. But I'm so eager to inflame a discussion on how women should *not* treat men that I'm going to take advantage of this chance to speed up the barbecue and have my say.

This is my advice to women, offered in the spirit of support and cooperation: Be nice to guys. Don't harass or criticize them in public just to show off to your female friends how in control of men you think you are.

I know that many women have had lousy experiences with fathers, boyfriends, and ex-husbands. But that's all the more reason for those women to deal with their issues before plunging into the singles scene and alienating potential partners.

Another hint: When you're talking to a man during that intro cup of coffee or cocktail, don't start prying shamelessly into his private life three minutes after you sit down. Don't interrogate him as if he's a criminal until proven otherwise. And if you just chuckled to yourself while reading that statement and said, "Well, he is a criminal until proven otherwise," then maybe you need to take a vacation from dating.

I've been on first dates during which the woman, however coyly, appears to be interrogating me rather than engaging me in conversation. The questions start out innocently—about family, school, jobs, birthplace. Then they take a subtle turn, "Do you see your mother often? Are you in touch regularly?"

Now, I'm not denying that the answer to that question is pregnant with ramifications about the man's ability to form lasting bonds. And I'm well aware that advice columnists cajole women into asking such questions early on. But the question is so patronizing and obvious that it makes it seem as though you're carrying on the conversation with a clipboard. That level of efficiency can be off-putting. Any guy with a brain can play that game and tell you what you want to hear.

While some first-date questions, such as how often I call my mommy, are simply tiresome, others are disconcerting. Years ago on a first date I was taken aback when the woman heaved a heavy sigh and said, "Now the big question. Are you still in love with your ex-wife?"

That was our only date.

Years later, another woman asked me an even more personal question on a second date. First she shared some heavy baggage with me about her strict religious upbringing and lack of experience dating. She said this inexperience had led her into a variety of relationships with cads and beasts.

Then the zinger: "Did adultery play a part in your divorce?"

"No," I told her, "adultery didn't kill my marriage; it was lack of communication."

Here's another point about rushing verbal intimacy with a man. Many men find it confusing and misleading. Bells go off in their minds: If you're so eager to be so personal on a first date, then shucks, by the third or fourth date you should be ready for sex, right? You want guys to "Take it easy so we can get to know each other first?" I'm all for that. But if you don't want the guy to rush things sexually, then hold back on verbal intimacy for a few dates.

Also, what if you or he or both of you decide after the first or second date that the relationship isn't worth pursuing? I don't know about you, but I get tired of disclosing intimate details about myself to women who listen for no other reason than to be entertained. Or who turn out to be killing time until their imaginary knight in shining armor appears. Or who just aren't emotionally ready to establish a healthy relationship with a man and substitute intimate secrets for real intimacy. Just remember, even though you have a right to know intimate details of a man's life before you get into a relationship with him, he comes to the table with his own issues about how he's been treated by women.

So skip the inquisition. Be patient. Men worth becoming involved with have their own reasons for saying, "Let's take it easy so we can get to know each other first."

3

Patterns and Fears

I stand alone
in a crowded mahogany room,
filled with silver awards and hors d'oeuvres.
Glances and glasses twinkling,
toasting new business.
My psyche feels him trace her outline with his stare.
But I do not want to see.
A thick black widow's web
veils the signals from my soul.
In his trance
he longs for the tip of Lara's classic nose,
the curve of her white swan neck.

They had been lovers—
shadows dancing on the wall,
while pet cats poked at moving blankets
and licked salty, sticky skin.
She lusted for his brilliance,
but did not love him.
He is now a shell, a man obsessed.
I hold him to my ear,
but do not hear the ocean's music.
He will not let me in.
We are together and I am alone.

"Do you still love Lara?" I ask.
"How can I love an unfaithful woman?"
He turns pages in an upside-down thriller.
My black lace teddy does not lure him.
Sleep comes slowly and the dreaded dream recurs.
He and I are holding hands,
drinking beer in a desert resort.
He seeks a low-cut woman at the bar.
Their eyes flirt and he is gone.
"You are on your own," he calls over his shoulder.

My soul screams the truth each night.
The same dream, a different setting.
But I stay.
I stay still.
What is my prize?
Is there a Cracker Jack box with
a Zircon diamond?
A 14K Purple Heart?
A chocolate chip for my shoulder?
Or a sterling badge of courage?
Am I afraid of the loneliness monster,
who lurks beneath my single bed?
Of getting old alone?

EXCERPT FROM "ON MY OWN"—JOAN

JOAN: I think our unconscious thoughts have lead us in and out of some pretty disastrous relationships.

MARC: I never did understand why you were in a relationship with that guy in the poem.

JOAN: I was drawn to brilliant, unavailable men. When I met Chris, he seemed passionate about his life and work, and I was searching for that passion in my life. Instead of putting that energy into my own purpose, I channeled it into a dead-end romance with him. He was in love with another woman and I allowed myself to get sucked into his bizarre romantic dramas. It was one of my patterns. I know better, now.

And speaking of patterns, I interviewed a really great guy named Will, who said he played the role of the savior, the white knight, in his relationships with women. These women were attracted to his strength and ability to care for them. He, in return, enjoyed the role. Does this sound familiar?

MARC: Oh yeah—the savior thing.

JOAN: Well, if the shoe fits. . . .

MARC: I'll admit in some of my relationships I fulfilled a temporary need of a woman in emotional distress. The usual plot line was that I'd meet a woman going through a divorce. All her familiar support systems were degenerating or had disappeared. And she saw me as her rescuer. I provided companionship, sex, and whatever self-esteem she needed, because I showered her with attention. I got companionship, sex, and the satisfaction that I was able to save someone. In saving each woman I thought I was building strong bridges for a relationship, but instead I was throwing a life preserver that the woman tossed aside when she was safely on shore.

JOAN: What did you learn from all this?

MARC: I've learned that in a relationship, especially with needy women, I can be my own worst enemy if I don't recognize I'm being "used," so to speak. Not viciously, but used as an emotional and ego crutch. And crutches have limited use for people once they heal. So I've made peace with myself. I won't invest a lot of emotional energy in a relationship just for the sake of the possibility of sex and companionship.

JOAN: How did you change your pattern?

MARC: There were three things that helped me. My therapist, discussions with you, and a lot of honest introspection. It didn't come easy and it wasn't always comfortable learning about myself.

JOAN: How long did it take?

MARC: This process took five or six years. Mostly because I didn't work hard on it at first and spent a lot of time in denial. Now if I get into a similar situation, I know what's going on. I'm not flying blind anymore.

JOAN: For me, the biggest challenge was: How do you confront your demons—unhealthy relationship patterns—when they are buried in the unconscious? Once my therapist showed me how to identify them, I was able to change my behavior and choose available men. But that took several years.

I believe this chapter will help people understand why they repeat unconscious patterns and go from relationship to relationship.

MARC: I think writing this chapter has helped us both.

The Jung and the Restless

Some people change lovers as often as dance partners. Many people who leave the relationship blame the other person ("You've changed") or the nature of the relationship itself ("The magic's gone"). The Swiss psychiatrist Carl Jung suggested an explanation for this romantic behavior. He believed that men typically project their feminine side (which is unconscious to them) onto women, and women project their unconscious masculine side onto men.

When we meet someone we think is a potential partner and start projecting our anima or animus onto them, it sticks. Soon that projection is a vital part of the other person's image, at least in our own eyes. And that other person is blissfully unaware that he/she is carrying around his/her partner's projection. Even more problematic is that, in our view, that projection becomes a responsibility for our partner. It's an image we expect that person to live up to. If he or she doesn't, we feel betrayed, frustrated, or disappointed. And we never even asked that person if he or she wanted that responsibility. We simply dumped it on our unsuspecting partner.

For example, Jungian analyst John Sanford explains in his book *The Invisible Partners*: "If the woman projects onto a man her positive animus image . . . of the savior, hero and spiritual guide, she overvalues that man. . . . She feels completed only through him, as though it were through him that she found her soul."

This was the case for both Marc and Will, a 44-year-old mason in California, who found himself in the role of savior and hero in his romantic relationships. It was a pattern he grew tired of and changed with the help of a hypnotherapist.

Sir Will

I really didn't know it at the time, but I feel that one of my lessons in life was to discover self love. That was a big change in itself. I loved being the savior. It's a lot of fun being the white knight, but it's a lot of work, especially if you don't love yourself. The part of me that wanted to be the savior was always seeing the problems in other people, trying to change them, to help them find some happiness in life.

I felt I was happy. I found out later I could be a whole lot happier. That happiness came from that discovery of the pain that I didn't know was there, the pain I had denied completely and fully in the conscious mind. I discovered the only person I could change was myself. When I was the white knight, I was drawn to women who were really screwed up and who were drawn to me. They were desperate to be in a relationship. Something was lacking in their lives, and they thought they could fill that gap with me.

I found out a woman I was seeing had had a very traumatic experience with her ex-husband. He shot guns around her feet. I wondered, how could someone so beautiful and loving have these horrible things happen to her? He had broken out of jail and kidnapped her. She had become so afraid of men that if something I did bothered her, she'd just shut me off and say, "You're out of here." Anything that happened—arguments, treating her the way she didn't want to be treated—she couldn't discuss it, she'd just get upset. I would try to discuss things, and she'd say, "You're treading on thin ice."

Then there was the girl from hell. She was a drug addict. She was escaping reality because she didn't want to deal with her pain. It's not easy to be with yourself. My therapist suggested I find someone on a similar spiritual path and stay away from basket cases. I thought it was great advice. Finding someone of a like mind with similar interests, spiritual beliefs, values and views on life—like how you want to save the world—and what you want out of relationships.

I know now I want total bliss. I want someone who is open-minded, communicative, emotionally expressive, willing to share any and all that comes up in life. Good, bad, or indifferent. Someone with a willingness to deal with life head-on. When problems come up, we'll see where we can find a resolution.

Now I find out why a person really wants to be in the relationship, what they want to get out of the relationship—co-dependence, filling a gap or need, or to have the best time possible in life. I think that last reason is really what love is all about.

Unknowingly, the women in Will's life projected their animus traits onto him. And Will gladly assumed the white knight role. But what happens when a man projects his anima energies onto a woman? In *The Invisible Partners*, Sanford explains that this woman becomes the "source of happiness and bliss. A woman who carries this projection for a man readily becomes the object of his . . . sexual longings, and it seems . . . if he could only be with her and make love to her he would be fulfilled."

This, says Sanford, is the definition of "falling in love."

Falling Out of Love

Mark Komrad, M.D., a psychiatrist at Sheppard Pratt Health System, a psychiatric facility in Baltimore, explains:

> Jung said these energies [anima and animus] become part of our unconscious life, the part that peeks out between the lines, or comes out in our dreams. . . . These things stirring in our unconscious want to have a voice and come out, and sometimes manifest themselves through projection.
>
> Projection means simply, rather than seeing something in yourself, seeing it in someone else. Maybe seeing it in an exaggerated way in the other person. . . . In relationships, we're very prone to seeing the unconscious part of ourselves in the other person.
>
> And ultimately . . . relationships call forth the projections. . . . And that comes up at first and it's really good because it kick-starts a relationship. Then you start to see in the other person things that you overvalued, frequently you don't see in yourself. So relationship starts to occur. And the task of every mature relationship is to eventually start that way. . . . But [the task is also] to eventually weather the storm that's coming. Because it's always coming. And that is not unique to any one individual. Disillusionment comes and the projections begin to wear off. . . .You see anima and animus have positive and negative qualities.
>
> The negative quality of animus is violence and aggression; the negative quality of the anima is being a harpy or bitch. Eventually you start seeing some of your negative aspects of the anima and animus in the other partner. And every relationship goes through that. It's not to be taken personally, it's part of the psychology of romantic love. You then reach a crossroads and you need to ask yourself: are you going to start seeing the other person for who he or she really is and yourself as you truly are? Are you going to own [take responsibility for] your own stuff, your own negative anima or animus qualities?
>
> Are you going to account for those and your positive qualities such as your own strength or your own capacity for tenderness and nurturing rather than having to rely on the other person to do it for you? Or are

you going to be angry or disappointed when the other person doesn't come through for you?

That's the place where the rubber meets the road. That's where you are capable of breaking through into a higher level of consciousness about yourself, owning your own stuff. Typically the accusation is they've changed. To some extent that's true. Some people are on their best behavior when they first start a relationship. But it's not just that they've changed. It's just that your blind spots have started to fade. Projections are very mercurial and ephemeral things—the positive can flip to the negative very easily. So somebody you overvalued can become devalued just as easily.

When projections flip, falling in love can turn into falling out of love and into the arms of someone new. That new someone, according to spiritual counselor Jalaja Bonheim, Ph.D., is a person who you believe will complete you.

Whenever we get into a relationship there is a conscious or unconscious desire to complete ourselves, to become whole. Quite naturally we look for qualities in the other person which we lack or that complement us. A shy woman might look for a very outgoing man. Sometimes we find in the relationship that it is our task to own the qualities the other has. The timid woman may begin to own her own strength. That man may find his growth may be owning the introverted, receptive qualities traditionally defined as feminine: nurturing or gentleness, receptivity.

I think it's useful to look at how my partner is manifesting qualities on my behalf that I need to own for myself. When I'm fighting with my partner, [I look at] those aspects that drive me crazy. Where do I find them in myself? We are mirrors of each other.

When a person has stopped functioning as a mirror that inspires consciousness and growth, then this relationship may no longer serve its purpose. It is interesting to look at how my partner challenges me to reclaim aspects of my wholeness that are denied or underdeveloped.

Dr. Bonheim, author of *Aphrodite's Daughter,* recalls the turmoil in one of her female patients who was married to an outgoing man. At first, she was attracted to this attribute in her husband that she thought she lacked. Eventually it became a source of conflict in their relation-ship.

> I think of this marriage in which the man was very outgoing and con-fident and the woman was extremely insecure and shy. His outgoingness was the cause of many fights in the relationship. It would make her feel jealous; she would feel threatened by it. As we worked together, her challenge was to develop some of that in her-self. As she did so, she was not so threatened by his extroversion.

Joan: From Fear to Love

I agree strongly with Dr. Bonheim that often we are attracted to what we lack in a potential mate. In my early twenties, I lacked self-esteem and was drawn to men who appeared confident and strong. I sought men who I thought could save me from taking responsibility for my life. When we withdrew our fantasies, the relationships ended. In my mid-thirties, I let fear run my life: fear of the social stigma of being single, fear of being a spinster, fear of dwindling savings and a lack of an IRA, fear of living alone in my old age, fear of pursuing my goals, fear of attending another black-tie event alone.

With that list of fears, the Hunchback of Notre Dame may have looked like a suitable mate. After all, he was kind and gentle—and he was a movie star. Unfortunately, back then I was not attracted to kind and gentle. I thought those qualities were a sign of weakness.

Domineering, arrogant, brilliant, critical, workaholic, financially successful men turned my head. If there was one man like that in a room of 50, we would meet and develop a doomed romantic relation-ship.

I played the role of the shut-down victim, denying my needs and dreams, because I wasn't sure what they were. I craved their goals and passions.

I wrote a song in memory of the woman I outgrew like old bell-bottom jeans.

> I'm hungry for your touch.
> I'm hungry for your soul.
> I'm hungry for the strength in you
> that I cannot control.

I'll be what you want me to be.
I'll do what you want me to do.
Can't you see, I've lost myself in you.

EXCERPT FROM A SONG CALLED "THE LOVE
ADDICT"—JOAN

I would fall in love with what I wanted a man to be, whether he possessed those qualities or not. My animus projection worked overtime to convince me that this man was my hero and savior. If only I had read this line from John Sanford's book *The Invisible Partners*: "When we fall in love with someone instantly we can be sure a projection is involved, for how could we love someone whom we do not yet know?"

Falling in love through projection of anima or animus is often a one-way journey to failed relationships if one or both partners can't get past this stage. Sanford explained this dark side of falling in love in an interview with *Celebrating Single*:

> The difficulty with that projection is it's a hopeful thing in one way because it initiates a relationship. But if it keeps on, it keeps the man from seeing who the woman really is, in and of herself. . . . And of course she's a red-blooded woman in her own right, so she can't be someone's anima image. She has to be herself, and that often causes a great disturbance in the relationship. . . . [If the man cannot] transcend that projection, he never learns to love the real woman. . . . The woman who can be loved for who she is, is the real woman; and that's the woman who we see when we withdraw the projections.

Joan: Falling in Love For All the Wrong Reasons

I grew up believing that "in love" and "love" were the same. Over time I learned that love is a conscious decision, not just romance or a sexual attraction, and the key to laying the foundation for a long-lasting relationship is to bring the unconscious "Invisible Partners" into my conscious awareness. As Sanford explains in his book, "Real love begins only when one person comes to know another for who he or she really is as a human being and begins to like and care for that human being."

This knowledge would have helped me immensely nine years ago, when I was the "imagined woman" in a three-month relationship. By the time David saw the real woman, he had already moved on to his next goddess. The red flags emerged early on. David told me at dinner on our first date, "You are everything I want in a woman. I'm very attracted to beautiful, accomplished redheads like you." That evening, David called the woman who introduced us and confessed that he had fallen in love with me. I was so ill that night from a reaction to a rubella shot that I didn't have time to process his empty compliments. I left my food untouched and disappeared into the night like Cinderella.

The next day he sent an exquisite flower arrangement to my office with a "hope you're feeling better" note. I felt very flattered. On our next date, we met for a romantic brunch at a country inn and he brought me a beautifully wrapped book about the Victorian era, one of my passions. He was doing all the right things.

I thought David was nice, but I didn't have that instant, "Oh my God, I have to marry this man" reaction. I found him attractive, worldly, intelligent, but I wasn't choosing my bridal party yet. Over the next few months, as we spent more and more time together, I started to fall in love for all the wrong reasons. We became intimate within six weeks, after he pressured me with accusations that I was cold. I wasn't comfortable with this decision because I felt I didn't know him well enough. My instinct told me something was wrong, but like many women in this situation I thought I'd lose David if I didn't sleep with him.

A few months into the relationship, I invited David to Baltimore for a Sunday afternoon picnic and to opening-day festivities at Camden Yard the next day. He became moody and sullen and didn't speak to me—even during the Orioles game. When I inquired what was wrong, David admitted he had wanted to play coed softball in Washington instead of coming in for the picnic. What was going on? I felt very confused. John Sanford could have told me why:

> Anima is the quality inside of the man—his own feminine side. He's usually not aware of it because he's so identified with being a man. The anima characteristic carries some of the aspects of what we call soulfulness, feeling, sensitivity, perceiving things through the unconscious. . . . The anima is the soul of the man he's not aware of. When he's not in touch with this, it can bring out his dark side. It usually comes out in moodiness. The way to transcend it is to recognize the

source of his moods may be this moody feminine side of himself. And when men are into a mood, women can get very frustrated because they can't find the man. He's lost in a fog somewhere. So men who fall into a mood are not very relatable. So if he has an awareness of it, he can say to the woman, "I need to be alone now, or, [I] need to think something through." And most women can accept that, and they know what that's all about. If a man is caught in a persistent kind of moodiness, he's not available for a relationship. He often gets very negative and critical.

Bingo. He's caught in a persistent kind of moodiness. He often gets negative and critical. He's not really ready for a relationship. David became very abusive and critical of me—from putting my opinions down in front of salesclerks and friends to blaming me for his dwindling sex drive. I was emotionally invested by this time and chose to continue the relationship.

The next weekend we went to an art exhibit at the Smithsonian. As we took an escalator down to the first floor, David, standing behind me, whispered into my neck, "You're not a natural redhead. I see dark roots." Thinking he was joking, I turned around and smiled at him. His face froze in an ugly mask, like Sardonicus. He sulked the rest of the day.

If I had understood the world of unconscious projections, I might not have felt so wounded or taken it all so personally. In spite of the red flag signals, I was trying to make the relationship work—cutting my toes to fit my shoes. After all, I was 39. I was supposed to be married by now. And hadn't David said we would have beautiful children and he loved me?

Our relationship ended on Mother's Day weekend. I invited him to meet my family at a luncheon at my house. He declined by saying he was working with a freelance writer on a project during the day and would come to Baltimore for dinner instead.

The writer had invited David to a party at her house that evening. He called me and said he needed space and we'd talk. "Oh no," I thought, "the old 'I need more space' phone breakup."

I found out through a mutual friend that David was "seeing" the writer, while I thought we had an exclusive relationship. I broke it off.

A year later David called me from a business trip out West. He said, "I heard you were engaged and I'd really like to be in his shoes."

I said, "Thank you."

He said, "No, you don't understand, I'd like to be married to you."

I said, "You're a bit late." I suggested he see a therapist.

He answered, "Oh no, I don't need therapy. I've changed a lot since you and I dated. I've read some self-help books."

Perhaps David did grow by reading self-help books. Or perhaps he, like so many of us who think we can do it by ourselves, chose not to do the healing work necessary to have a lasting relationship, to go on a guided tour of the unconscious with a therapist.

John Sanford explains why people resist self-knowledge.

> I think it has to do with egocentricity. Self-knowledge usually begins with looking at the dark side of ourselves and the traits of ourselves that we would prefer to deny. So the beginning of self-knowledge is usually the destruction of the ideas of ourselves that we carefully cherished all our life. . . . You have to be ready to get a new estimate of who you are and what you are really like. And this may include having to own up to . . . some negative things about ourselves. Although as we hold them as our own, they don't seem to be as negative. You might say it's like a psychological conversion.

So, can someone read a few books, go to a weekend conference on spirituality, and be healed? Not according to Sanford: "Growth is a matter of growing in small increments at a time; and becoming conscious is a matter of adding small increments of consciousness, one bit at a time. . . . That's why the building up of a new consciousness requires a considerable amount of time."

Gradually, in therapy, I learned to become more aware of these unconscious thoughts and to focus on my own abilities, goals, and dreams. I wanted to find my inner voice and sing out loud—no matter who listened. When I focused on "What do I want?" I found the courage to create a satisfying, purposeful life. I could take care of myself, no matter what. Whatever I lacked and sought in a mate, I tried to develop in myself.

Marc: Looking My Anima in the Eye

I think the concept of anima/animus is a useful model for keeping track of your responses to partners and potential partners. When you've been without a relationship for a long time, there is an emotional part of you that's so empty that when a potential partner enters your life you mistake thankfulness for love. You're looking for an end to the pain of aloneness.

I think people need to be mindful of the potential confusion that occurs when members of the opposite sex project their anima or animus onto one another. Sure, the projection gets the relationship into gear. But projections change from magnets getting lovers together to heavy weights that must be borne.

I once dated a woman going through a divorce (hey, that's a switch). Her husband left her for a younger woman (hey, there's a new wrinkle). Jan, the woman, got angry at me once after I took a call on my car phone from my ex-wife. My ex and I had a mild disagreement, and somehow I compromised on whatever was bothering her. After the call, Jan got snitty at me, saying she had thought I "had it together" better than that and should have been able to lay down the law to my ex. I was mortified.

Now, mightn't this incident be related to the fact that her soon-to-be ex-husband was an aggressive salesman who wanted bigger and better possessions, including a house too big to be practical? Or the fact that her husband took charge and dumped her? Or that she fantasized in general about guys takin' charge? Apparently, she projected onto me her image of what a strong man would do in that situation.

So projections—yours and your partner's—are good instruments for making that beautiful music at the start of the relationship. But the music grows stale if you don't get beyond those same old first bars of the love song. You gotta grow past the projections. And you gotta be alert to what might be the other person's projections onto you. Forewarned is forearmed. Get straight on what's happening in your own mind and try to fathom what's happening in your partner's mind. If you can't guess what's happening in your partner's mind, then ask. (I know from experience this is not an easy thing to do.) The extent to which he or she can, or cares to, explain honestly what's going on in his or her mind is a helpful marker of how healthy your relationship is to begin with. Then, of course, you're stuck with facing up to the task of honestly assessing whether the relationship is worth your time and effort to make it grow and flourish.

At that point you can look at the relationship as if you're playing the stock market. Are you interested in slow growth, dependable stocks that will repay you for your patience with steady earnings over time?

Or do you want to take a chance on hopping a rocket to Wall Street heaven on a hot dot.com stock that promises the world but might just as likely tank in the next quarter? If you don't mind gambling on love, then by all means hop onto the rocket. But just remember: You pays your money and you takes your chances.

Introspection: Questions for You to Consider

What qualities in a prospective mate do you wish to have yourself? How can you go about making those changes or building those qualities within yourself?

4

Love Junkies

THE LOVE JUNKIE

Driving through the countryside,
we applaud Nature's fall fireworks.
He holds my hand.
We speak with smiles.

Then winter's fury finds me pacing.
Suddenly, a phone call.
We share a crackling fire,
wrapped in warm silence.

We sip hot chocolate
in a cozy cafe.
He reads personal ads.
I swallow sobs he never hears.

He fills my emptiness
and leaves silently at dawn
to another's satin sheets
and melted candles.

Silence.

—JOAN

JOAN: Pacing. Emptiness. Silence. Those words describe a love addict's life. Staying by the phone, waiting for a call. Waiting for life to happen. Accepting inappropriate behavior from the object of love. Surreal—as if this must be someone else's life.

I know this world of surreal images that swirl around the mind like a draft on burning leaves. I know because I am the woman in the poem. I am the woman who looked for the knight to rescue me so I wouldn't have to find my own way in the world. I am the woman who lost myself and went on a spiritual journey to reclaim my own purpose—to find my inner voice.

In this chapter, you will meet people I talked to while on this journey: Pam, a recovering love addict; her therapist, Judy Burch, M.S.N., a family counselor in Baltimore, Maryland; and Pia Mellody, R.N., the nationally known author of *Facing Love Addiction*. You will also meet a dear friend and counselor, Jane Hughes, who, while editing this chapter, discovered a mysterious truth about her past.

MARC: You are not alone, Joan. Many baby boomers grew up clinging to the fairy tale of meeting a prince or princess, getting married, and living happily ever after. Time passed—as did several relationships and maybe a marriage or two. Yet some of us relationship-ravaged boomers still clung to that fairy tale, as did Pam, an attractive and successful entrepreneur.

Pam's Fantasy Men

I was in a series of relationships where I went for very wealthy guys to take care of me, like a knight in shining armor. I went for the fantasy. It was always the same. We'd meet. It would be intensely romantic. Sex would happen immediately, and it would be over in three months. The relationships always failed. I was attracted to men who were addicted to sex or were professional daters. In four years I went through nine relationships like that. Finally, I was in so much pain I went to a therapist. I said, "I don't want to be here in six years telling you I've been in thirty-four relationships." I had reached rock bottom.

Pam's relationships were more than simple infatuations. She valued these men above herself, investing too much of herself in them. Experts in the field of psychology call this type of obsessive relationship "love addiction."

Author, lecturer, and counselor Pia Mellody, R.N., a nationally recognized authority on °codependence, and a consultant at The Meadows Institute, a treatment center for addictions in Wickenburg, Arizona, says,

> With love addiction . . . the person is obsessed with the other person he or she is trying to have a partnership with. The love addict thinks about him or her all the time. She has a fantasy about the person being her knight in shining armor and doesn't see him as the person he is. A male relationship addict may see his partner as a goddess. The second fantasy is, "He can heal my wounding, do what my parents never did for me."
>
> Love addicts, in a funny way, look to the other person to take care of them, like a child to a parent. Actually, they see their partners as better than they are, they are in a one-down position. They empower the other person and make them a god or goddess who is responsible for them.

In her book *Facing Love Addiction*, Mellody explains, "Making another person our Higher Power is, I believe, the heart of love addiction, an addictive process of its own."

A Love Addict's Story

Pam, a classic example of a love addict, empowered her partners and lost her self-esteem.

> I was in one relationship that absolutely devastated me. We were engaged. He kept changing his mind. I was blinded by the fantasy. He was wealthy. What happened was at the end of six years, he had finally cheated on me. He had cheated on his wife for 17 years. I thought I had come along to change him and save him. He was indecisive about marrying me. I had moved in and out of his house. It was a roller-coaster relationship.
>
> Only later, in recovery, I found out that intensity in relationships— the yes, no, back, forth—was my drug of choice.
>
> Then I went to a therapist. I remember through the whole session I was sobbing. I felt better. She explained things to me. I thought I

could brush myself off and go back into the world of romance. . . . Then I met a totally different kind of man, a compassionate man, 14 years older. We were spiritually connected and had a lot in common. He was in recovery and was willing to go to my therapist. I did therapy my way—every eight months. I wasn't working a (12-Step) Program. He did group therapy with my therapist, and six months later he broke up with me. I was devastated. I went back to see my therapist. She begged me to go into group therapy. I said I didn't have the time or money.

Finally I went into group. I couldn't fool these people. Everyone could feel the controlling part of me. They saw my shame, how I live in my present: "He'll take care of me and my daughter." I learned devastating facts about myself.

My therapist told me not to get together with any male friends. "You will get the strength you need from women." I thought she was nuts. But I was in so much pain, I did whatever she told me. I thought my life was over. I got into a 12-Step Program for sex and love addiction. When I went to recovery meetings I heard other women share what I was thinking and feeling. God, this is me. I realized the men I had been dating were sex addicts. They were mean and sarcastic and always kept in touch with ex-lovers. I felt the shame from my past. I didn't feel good enough to be loved. My insecurities came out in my need to control. When I'm controlling I can't experience intimacy in a relationship.

Old boyfriends would call. I'd say, "I'm sorry I can't talk to you. We're in different places right now. Good-bye."

My group of 12 women became my family. Every weekend we would go to meetings, movies, dinner together. I had a great social life with just my women. I wasn't longing for men. For the first time I felt really loved and connected—like I belonged. They would do anything for me and I for them. We laughed and played, had slumber parties, went to the ocean. We celebrated birthdays together, cried together.

After 16 months, I announced in group I was ready to go on a date just to practice. I went out with a divorced guy I met at an engagement party. I could feel the excitement of that drug again. We went to dinner, we talked, and he was nice. We went out two weeks later and I knew not to rush anything. I was ready to practice my new rules. On the second date I smelled liquor on his breath. My friends in recovery said he had been drinking before he saw me. The red flags went up. I just observed them. On our third date he said he'd like to make me dinner at his place. In recovery you wait six months before you even hold hands. I said, "No, I'm not happy with that."

He said, "We'll just watch football."

I said, "No, I'm just unhappy."

"Fine, we'll go out to dinner."

I had people to ask for feedback. The men in my group said, "Do you want to go out with this man?"

For the first time in 47 years, I called up and canceled a date. I would have never recognized the signs. I would have still been in my fantasy.

Then I got a call from Mark, a man I had known for 19 years. He had been my insurance agent. He ran into our mutual friend at a funeral and called me to say his wife had died and he had nursed her through her illness. He asked if he could call again. He called later that night. We had so much in common. We set up a date to have coffee. I looked at him for a long time and thought he was nerdy. Then I thought, "Beauty inside, a place I never looked before." I had dated money and bank accounts. I never dated who they were.

I fell in love with who Mark was inside. I still love who he is. He's a very special man. In group therapy, he found out he still needed to do recovery work following the death of his wife. He said if we were ever going to have a healthy relationship he would need to go off and do his work. I knew he was in love with me, but it was hard to let him go. I loved him and wanted to be with him, but I knew this was important for him.

For five months we didn't see each other. This time I wasn't devastated. I knew I had women to go back to and I needed more recovery time. I did date and found out the man I was seeing wasn't Mark inside. I called the other man and canceled him out of my life.

Mark and I don't fight about small things like cooking or cleaning. When you have the same values and goals it makes it a lot easier. We share a spiritual life together, we go to therapy together and read the same books on spiritual topics. We make sure my daughter is taken care of. We're both entrepreneurs, in our own businesses. We both respect and understand the other's business. We both network together. Meeting and connecting people is a value we share, and learning is another important value in our lives. We both exercise together.

When you have your own strength, you don't need anybody for anything. I don't need him for anything other than for his companionship, intimacy, and love. We're good friends.

I absolutely will never give up my women friends. I'm having a birthday party with all my recovery women. I just want women. Women need to get away from men and get their strength all the time. You lose it if you don't go back to get that strength. Like a car needs fuel.

Pam and Mark were married in June 2000.

Recognizing Love Addiction

Pam's therapist, Judy Burch, M.S.N., treats relationship addiction in her Baltimore practice. Burch defines addiction: "When you continue doing the same behavior even though there are adverse consequences."

I am particularly interested in relationship addiction because it goes undiagnosed so often. The pain is excruciating. . . . I used to teach a course on loneliness in the late '70s, early '80s. The definition of loneliness is the lack of being "meaningfully related" to another person. When I taught that course I began to realize that "meaningfully related" becomes translated into addictive relationships instead of meaningful ones.

People get into addictive relationships thinking they are meaningful. When a relationship begins, for example, it's like a drug. There is an actual change in the levels of endorphins. The person (or couple) is obsessed. They are constantly thinking, "How will we get together?" "When will we see each other?"

We can choose alcohol, money, men, women, food—whatever thing we pick—to keep us from feeling shame and pain. I believe that money, food, and sex are the monitoring addictions. We need those as part of our life to survive, as opposed to drugs and alcohol. We have to monitor sex and money and food, which makes the addiction more difficult to detect.

Relationship addiction may be the most difficult one to deal with. The adverse consequences don't seem to come as quickly and they're more socially acceptable. People forget there is a withdrawal from relationship addiction. I believe there is a psychological withdrawal that strongly affects our physiology. There's a physiological change.

Whatever change does occur, there is certainly an emotional surge that contributes to the addiction. And what feels better—a broken heart or the surging excitement of a new relationship? The instinct for many of us is to pursue that "in love" high. So going cold turkey while experiencing such an emotionally addictive feeling isn't something that you can expect to do easily—or the first time you try. One of Judy Burch's patients faced this challenge as he went through a divorce. Losing one partner and looking for another, he jumped at the chance not to be alone.

Paul, a man in his forties, came to me initially for help going through his divorce. When he had been separated four months, he met a separated woman casually through a friend. She was in her late thirties. They had coffee and kept seeing each other. On the second date they had dinner. By the third date they were in bed. They spent the next 21 days together.

In Paul's situation, neither he nor his lover thought about the adverse consequences of their actions, particularly for my client. In the beginning of a relationship you naturally want to be together. They just stayed with each other for three weeks. They didn't go to work.

I always ask people not to get involved sexually with people while going through a divorce, for a number of reasons. The new relationship blocks the pain of the divorce. Sooner or later you will go through the pain. It's just a matter of time. Another reason is, you can't end a relationship and begin one simultaneously. People tend to make the same mistake again, as reflected in the divorce rate.

For first marriages there's a 51 percent divorce rate and in second marriages it's two-thirds and climbing. The average length of a second marriage is five to six years. People find they're attracted to the same person they married the first time. "I'm so much in love this time, she's so different. She's professional, has dark hair. My first wife was blonde." But the dynamic hasn't changed.

My patient (Paul) says he can't stop with this separated lady. He says it's not about the sex, it's about the way she makes him feel. In relationship addiction there is an intensity, an excitement. Everything they do is intense. I asked him what will have to happen for him to stop being in this relationship. "Will you get charged with adultery? Will her husband, who is rageful, who doesn't want the divorce, hurt someone?" He hadn't even asked her about that. Her ex might be violent. In today's world this happens much more frequently than we care to look at.

Intensity really characterizes relationship addiction. High intensity and low ability to put anything (emotional) into it. When intensity wears off, there's not much there.

High Intensity, Low Self-esteem: The Treatment

Therapist Judy Burch has some practical advice for people with relationship addictions:

I ask my relationship-addicted patients not to be in a relationship, not to date for six months. When they're out of the dating scene, it feels like six years. What they miss is the intensity.

You start to feel like, "I'll die if he doesn't call and ask me out. What if I have nothing to do on Saturday night? My whole life revolves around this other person. Whatever I'm doing depends on whatever he's going to do or not going to do." So then the question becomes, what do we call this? We have a thousand names for any way one wants to look at something. People would rather use any other name than "addict."

Love addicts are frequently attracted to love avoidants. There are men (and women) who are empty, dead inside, with nothing to give. They can only get through stage one of a relationship, the excitement—the intensity.

Love avoidants can't reach stage two in a relationship. Stage two is where you begin to deal with issues and differences. You begin growing in a very different way—to more intimate kinds of things. Dealing with issues leads to intimacy.

What I learned about single women and men is that when people have that high intensity out here, they are empty and have little substance and confidence inside. When they come in my office I can see them become another person in the chair. My patient Pam brought a couple of guys in (not simultaneously) because this was the relationship she was in at that time.

She didn't consider what she wanted or needed. On the surface she wanted the good dresser, broad shoulders, dashing conversationalist. He wore designer clothes and drove an expensive car. But after the glitz and the intensity faded, the other person left her and moved on to the next relationship. He only had a little bit of a repertoire, so he needed to start all over with a new person.

The relationship addict, the person in Pam's position, can't understand. She said, "I gave him everything, whatever he wanted to do." She always waited till he called. I intentionally have people not date so they can be more sensitive to their own feelings. "What is going on with me? What am I feeling?" People can't do that until they get some separateness.

Women tell me, "Gee I can relate to men so much better than women." We can manipulate men more easily and use our seductive powers, and of course we're going to get along for a while. The truth is, women get their strength from other women. Pam did not believe me until she joined a 12-Step Program for relationship and sex-addicted women.

Women give up who they are for a man because they don't know who they are. I don't believe women have ever gotten a chance to get in touch with who we are. We're so busy trying to see who we can get, because of pressures of society.

Most people would tend to deny the symptoms of relationship addiction. That's why it's difficult to treat. I look at the person's track record and their past history. Women who are more immature . . . are more needy. That neediness will draw the guy who is empty and needs to take care of a woman. . . . He is attracted to powerlessness in a woman. It can go either way, not necessarily one gender. When this guy leaves a woman, she crumbles.

Avoidance Addiction

Love addiction is the opposite side of a dysfunctional coin that also carries the face of avoidance addiction. These direct opposites, says Pia Mellody, R.N., author of *Facing Love Addiction*, are also drawn toward one another:

Love avoidance is an over-sensitivity to feeling engulfed in a relationship. The two problems are caused by the opposite kind of relationship trauma, emanating out of the family of origin or caregivers.

Abandonment or neglect by major caregivers can cause love addiction. The parents don't provide the resources their child needs.

The opposite is true for avoidance addicts. In this case, the parent enmeshes with the child; the parent attaches to the child to get taken care of by the child. When the parent bonds (rather than enmeshes), the parent attaches to affirm, nurture, and sets limits for the child. This takes enormous energy. In enmeshment, the parent drains or uses his or her child by getting him to care for the parent. Love addicts believe that if they don't get close enough to their partner, they will die. Avoidance addicts believe that if they let a partner get close, they will die.

This double-sided coin metaphor reflects the emotional tribulations of our next baby boomer, Steve.

Steve's Story of Avoidance Addiction

Steve, 45, a never-married counselor, speaks freely about his life-long problem committing to a woman. Poking fun at himself, he says that his biggest fear is finally getting married and then meeting the woman of his dreams in the buffet line at his wedding reception.

I'm from an upper-middle-class family, the youngest of three. My father was a doctor. A chronic low level of depression, largely from my mother, filtered into the family. My mother was rigid, compulsive. When I was a kid, my father brought home a calendar for me. My mom made him keep it in the trunk of his car because it would clutter the house.

Pretty nutty stuff went on between me and my mother. She was at times very intrusive, overbearing. At the same time she would withdraw emotionally for days at a time. She would get angry and completely withdraw. There was a pattern in her relationship of being too close and other times being too far away. The positive was that all of my material needs were met, and there was opportunity for a diverse set of experiences—enriching activities such as travel. I was very athletic. Both of my parents were very supportive of that.

My relationship with my mother gave me a feeling of being claustrophobic in committed relationships. I confused commitment with confinement. I had an ambivalent combination of anxiety about being consumed or overwhelmed by it, and at the same time being afraid of abandonment. Once my claustrophobia takes over, I start hoping for abandonment and that the person I'm dating will find someone else and leave me alone.

The women I dated in my thirties were a lot like my mother. I only realized that in my forties. They were concrete and judgmental and angry, chronically depressed. There was safety in being with a depressed woman in that she's not too demanding in a way—demanding of me in terms of my time and attention. There's a passivity that keeps her from being too obtrusive, like my mom when she was withdrawn.

I have forgiven my mother. Personally and professionally, I'm not into intentional forgiveness. It's something that evolves over time. Some therapists say you have to forgive that person. In my experience, expressing forgiveness too early can interrupt that process.

Now my relationship with my mother is better than it's ever been. I've grown up a lot. I have no expectations of her. We have a cordial and a mutually loyal relationship. Like a nephew might have with an aunt. I call her by her first name. It helps—it's a reminder not to bring mother stuff into it. If I need nurturing or comforting, I'll go elsewhere.

My singleness is not without ambivalence. This whole business about finding the right woman—I'm finally going to settle down with the right flawed woman. Then I'll finally meet the right woman at my wedding reception by the shrimp cocktail. Then it's too late.

I have fewer and fewer fantasies, no fantasy that there is the ideal woman. I've dated enough fine women to know it's me. Of the women I've been seriously involved with, there's probably only one I might have been able to marry. We broke up and got back together. And at my initiation, we got into couple's counseling to see if I could get past my fears of commitment, and I couldn't. She clearly wanted to be in a long-term, committed relationship. She wanted to be married and later got married. I have a bit of regret about this one. I really tried hard and it didn't work. I tried to make myself commit a couple of times. There's something deep in my soul that rebels.

Steve's story is poignant. He recognizes his anxiety about commitment and its source. Yet he has chosen to use his free time creatively and productively, to build his therapy practice and make a difference by helping others.

The way I manage my own anxiety is to constantly remind myself that this is my path, to be single and have the life I've led. It's not for everyone. It's consistent with the way my life works best. I'm in a pretty supportive position for my friends and clients and have a lot of time and emotional energy to be available. I can work every night until 9:30; I can channel all my financial resources into buying equipment for my practice. A lot of energy and resources that might have gone into marriage and kids can be channeled into my friendships and my practice. Maybe my soul knew it wasn't right for me to get married. Maybe there is wisdom in my anxiety.

I think my purpose is to teach some of the people I come into contact with about dealing with fear and about courage. I see myself as somewhat of a shaman. In my early twenties I went through a personal hell, dealing with fear and panic. That became my life-defining wound. I have finally found a place in my own life where I can be helpful to other people.

A Q&A on Love and Avoidance Addiction

Pia Mellody explores further the issues of love addiction and love avoidance.

Q: *Why do love addicts seem to repeatedly fall into relationships with people afraid of commitment?*
A: The love addict and avoidance addict are attracted to each other because they are attracted to what is familiar. The love addict is familiar with looking at her father's back. She's attracted to someone who's trying to get away from her (or who wasn't there for her emotionally, physically, etc., when she was a child). This feels comfortable. What's familiar is someone walking away, fearing a level of commitment. The avoidant [person afraid of commitment] is used to

taking care of needy women. He [or she] doesn't want to get too close. But he feels guilty if he's not taking care of the person. He uses walls to create spiritual abandonment. He walls in, so he's there but not there. While the partner feels abandoned, it's confusing because the avoidance addict looks like he's there. When the avoidance addict uses a wall in a relationship, it looks like he's intimate, but his partner feels unloved. There's no truth in the relationship, the person builds walls instead of creating boundaries.

Being spiritual is about truth and love. Behind this invisible wall, there can't be truth and love. If you love a fantasy or illusion, are you loving a real person? No, you are loving a fantasy. It's only real love when people are being real. The avoidance addict feels if he is real, he will be killed or suffocate. The love addict feels abandoned.

Q: *How can someone know if he or she is a love addict or an avoidance addict?*

A: If it strikes them as a possibility, they need to do some reading and have someone evaluate them. Everyone will have a hint of these traits to one extent or another. Focus on the question: "Am I having harmful consequences as a result of my choices in relationships, ignoring them and doing them anyway?" If the answer is yes, then you may have a problem. Frequently there is cycling in love avoidance or love addiction, going from one to another extreme. If you identify cycling, this is another signal to seek help. A love addict enters in fantasy, then when his/her partner avoids him/her, the love addict will deny it. When reality strikes, he or she becomes panicked, enraged, or homicidal, may drink, smoke, try to get the love avoidant back, and reenter fantasy. Or she may go to the next person.

The love avoidant may return out of guilt, make the person feel special (although he/she doesn't really care), escape the relationship, or leave and create intensity and then reenter out of guilt. He/she's really not taking care of his/her partner, the love addict. If this cycling is identified and progressive, you may have an issue that needs exploration.

Q: *What should a single person know or inquire about a person he or she is dating before getting seriously involved?*

A: Be aware of a person who wants to get sexually involved in order to create a relationship. Being sexual should come out of relationship, not create it. If a person is wanting to start off being sexual, suspect that it isn't going to work. This person probably doesn't know how to be intimate in other ways. Becoming too deep too fast trivializes the relationship. Love addicts use sex in a compulsive way to trap a person; a love avoidant uses sex to create intensity and often treats sex like going to the bathroom.

In heterosexual relationships ask (not on the first date), what kind of relationship has he had with his mom? If he was enmeshed or abandoned, stay away. That's the first question I'd ask. The second question I'd ask is what kind of relationship did his parents have? If the answer is "perfect," then beware, he is deluded. If the person has a history of violence, or is unable to commit, stop dating. The person needs lots of work to have a healthy relationship. [This also applies to men asking women these questions.]

Joan: It's All a Choice

In this compelling commentary, counselor Jane Hughes explains that although she experienced the symptoms of love addiction in her past relationships and marriages, she had no name for the emotional pain, intensity, and drama until she read this chapter.

In late February 2000, my good friends Joan and Marc asked me to read the draft of this chapter for *Celebrating Single*. They felt that I could offer some insights and suggestions because of my counseling background. I agreed.

This was truly an example of helping yourself when you reach out to help others. I also happen to believe that there are no coincidences in the Universe. I finally had a name, a description, an explanation, a recognition of what interfered with my ability to maintain a healthy romantic relationship all my life—up until now.

Yes, I've done a wealth of work in becoming aware of my own magnificence and creating an ongoing relationship with my Higher Self, Higher Power, the God within me—whatever you want to call it. I became conscious of and very interested in nourishing my spiritual path about 10 years ago. But up until that time I kept making the same unhealthy choices in relationships. As I read this section, I could really relate to the issues discussed and remember how I felt in relationships. *Celebrating Single* has helped me recognize my problem and give it a name. "Hi, I'm Jane. And I'm a recovering love addict."

I remember a relationship in which I thought I was madly in love. "Mad" was an appropriate description. I was madly out of my mind.

My thinking became very unclear and was clouded by the intensity and drama of the relationship. Sex was the best, or so I thought. It was my way of convincing myself that all of the pain I had to endure from his lying and deceitfulness was worth it. Whenever we had sex, I felt so close to him.

But now I realize it wasn't really me that was close to him; it was someone I was becoming, and that was someone with very low self-esteem. His self-esteem issues started filtering into my being, creating a real toxic reaction on my part.

My system became so confused by his excuses and defenses that not only did I suffer from severe depression, but my body started to break down, as one's does during any long-term addiction. I remember saying to him, "All I want to know is who you really are." This was a question that, sadly, he could not answer. So I tried to fill in the blanks according to my own fantasy about who he was. The whole relationship was built on untruths. I became intoxicated with my own fantasy about who he was and the outcome of our relationship.

I began to question my own self-worth and discernments about things that seemed so clear before. There was a place in me, however, that always told the truth. It was my intuitive self that knew the truth and what I needed to do to experience a healthier, more loving, joyful life. But I would not listen. I shut out that voice until it cried so loud I couldn't ignore it any more. It was my Spirit saying, "Please save me. You are suffocating me." It was the same voice that encouraged me to get out of a dying marriage.

It was the same voice that told my lover, "I'm not going to participate in this charade anymore." When I ended the relationship, I was terrified. What would I do? How could I survive this heart-wrenching loneliness? I literally went through a withdrawal from my "drug" of choice.

Ironically, I had spent 18 years counseling at-risk kids and their families in their homes. Part of my job was studying models of dysfunctional families and attending workshops held at Sheppard Pratt, a nationally renowned psychiatric hospital in Baltimore. I wouldn't have been able to heal myself if I hadn't had that job. I had learned from my work how to uncover the reality of my own family of origin. My issues evolved around an alcoholic father whose behavior towards me was sexually inappropriate. I also felt he abandoned me at the age of five, when he and my mother divorced.

In therapy I learned not to blame my father, to take responsibility for my own choices. I also discovered that my patterns with men mirrored my relationship with my father. My father was not emotionally available; that was the thread that ran through all of my relationships. For example, the man I was involved with was emotionally unavailable and suffered severe abuse in his childhood; his father was an alcoholic. So what chance did we have of creating a healthy relationship?

I recognized my problem on a visceral level: I was always looking after someone else's needs and not knowing what mine were, I fell in love with the intensity of the relationship more than the person. If you don't have a knowledge of yourself in a relationship and the other person leaves, either physically and/or emotionally, then what you have left is zero, the empty, bottomless pit of abandonment.

Well, what you *perceive* you have left is zero. But I can tell you starting with zero is a great place to be. You can create whatever you want on that empty plate and that's what I did.

Judy Burch's advice about staying out of a relationship for a period of six months is extremely effective. You see, we love addicts need to discover who we really are. This cannot happen when you are distracted by an unhealthy relationship. What happens is when we don't do the healing work, and we don't accept responsibility for our own happiness, we keep repeating the same unsuccessful dramas. It's always contingent on an outside experience.

You have all you need within you to be happy and to be at peace. Don't anesthetize yourself from the pain of being alone. It only lasts for a little while. Soon you truly begin to see your own magnificence and strength.

After four years of staying out of an involved relationship, I can say that the next one is going to look and feel very different from any of my past relationships. I will ask, "Does this relationship have *my* best interest at heart?" "Do I feel good about myself when I'm in the presence of this person and do I feel whole when we are apart?" If the answers to these questions are "yes," then I will participate and be my playful self. If the answers to these questions are "no," I will walk away with a knowing smile.

JOAN: I shared Jane's epiphany. Indeed this condition has a name. And once you hold it up and look at it, it's easier to let it go. Hearing the stories of single baby boomers interviewed for *Celebrating Single* propelled me to face my own love addiction, that agonizing, powerful desire to be in a relationship, no matter how unhealthy. It also inspired me to write poetry about my experiences.

You know how your mother told you she was always right? (Or maybe just my mother said that.) Anyway, I realize now she was 99.9 percent right on target with the advice she gave me, especially about my choice of men. Unfortunately it took me two decades to grasp the meaning of her advice.

> Like Dorothy,
> I chose frightened,
> hollow men and
> dreamed of happy endings.
> With help and time,
> I learned my truth.
> My voice lived inside me all along;
> I clicked my heels and freed it.
>
> Now late at night when I am still,
> I conjure up my mother's voice.
> "If you don't cut your toes to fit
> your shoes," she says, "the man
> will be your choice."

EXCERPT FROM "DON'T CUT YOUR TOES TO FIT YOUR SHOES"—JOAN

MARC: I don't think I've ever been a love addict. Sometimes I pursued women who, it became clear to me upon later reflection, were not going to give me anything more than the opportunity to take them to dinner and have a nice chat. Good people usually, but not interested in a relationship. One woman—a divorcée—told me she was interested only in "casual dating." I ignored her clear message and continued to pursue her. Eventually, I got tired and got the message. I don't consider such behavior on my part love addiction. I consider it stupidity and my inability to respond intelligently to red flags.

I finally recognized I had to change. I spent many very valuable hours with a therapist, who helped me confront myself. This took time and work. I don't care how you describe my past behavior in relation-ships. The goal was getting past it. And I did.

Introspection: Questions for You to Consider

Does your life revolve around the person you are dating? Do you feel you need to be with him or her all of the time?

Do you find yourself needing to be in a relationship with this person even though he or she is abusive or doesn't return your feelings? Why?

What was your relationship like with your father? Your mother? Do you see a correlation between your family of origin and your patterns in dating?

5

Red Flags

Like an ancient Greek soothsayer,
a man will share his inner truth
when you first meet him.
Many women seldom hear it.
They tune out red flag signals
when warnings slap them in the face,
forgetting raw wounds from the past.
Women store flags in their psyche
until they crawl through splintered glass.

EXCERPT FROM "REVELATION"—JOAN

JOAN: I overlooked some glaring red flags. Sometimes because I wanted to give the man the benefit of the doubt. Other times I discounted the signals so friends and family would stop criticizing me about being too picky.

MARC: What signals?

JOAN: Signals like the man who had photos of half a dozen past lovers on his refrigerator, and said he could easily go back to any number of them. I wonder if my picture is still up. Oh yes, and he was an alcoholic, just beginning treatment. And although he denied it, my instinct said he was in love with another woman. He was also the one who read personal ads in front of me, after an evening of intimacy, while we were having breakfast at a cozy cafe.

Your turn.

MARC: Give me a minute. There are just so many, I'm still plowing through them. One thing that hits me is the woman who said her husband just left her, and I still got involved. In those days I saw it as an opportunity, now I see it as a red flag.

JOAN: Why do you see that as a red flag?

MARC: She's in a free-fall mode and she's ready to grab at anything that even superficially looks like love to validate her worth as a desirable woman. When I pursued a woman who was just getting divorced, I usually wasn't looking for a relationship; I was looking for sex and companionship. When I was looking for a relationship and pursued a recent divorcée, I was like the fish in the joke, "What did the fish say when he hit a stone wall?"

JOAN: I'll bite.

MARC: "Dam."

JOAN: Do I really have to keep that joke in the book?

MARC: Yes.

JOAN: Damn!

Ginger's Story

The fragrance of freshly ground Kenya coffee wafted by my nose as I sat across from Ginger, a shapely, petite blonde. I smiled and thanked her for meeting me, but my instinct told me not to set up my laptop for this interview. Ginger, 38 and never married, had that distant, doe-eyed expression of a broken-hearted woman. We had met recently through a mutual friend at a girls' night out party. Ginger said she had been dating Ted, a very successful businessman in his late fifties, for just over a year. She told me she had given a dinner party at Ted's house that would have pleased Martha Stewart.

JOAN: How did the dinner party go?

GINGER: The dinner was a success. Not that Ted helped me. His only job was to take drink orders. And he only asked the guests what they wanted to drink one time. I'll admit, I was a little embarrassed. But that's not the half of it. After the guests left I was exhausted. It took me several days to shop and prepare the food, and my back hurt from standing so much. So I asked Ted for a back rub and soon after I took a sleeping pill and fell asleep. I've always had insomnia.

A couple hours later, he was leaning over my face, screaming, "I want you out of here and out of my life." He was angry because I had gotten a lot of praise from his friends for making a wonderful meal, and they didn't make a fuss over him.

"What's wrong? What did I do?" I said.

He dashed out of the bedroom with his pillow and slept in the den. I got up for an hour and started packing some of my things and went back to sleep. The next morning, I noticed his pillow was back on the bed, next to my face.

"I almost suffocated you with the pillow last night while you were sleeping, but I didn't want to end up like O. J."

A couple of hours later he acted like nothing ever happened and asked me to go shopping with him.

Tears spilled from Ginger's soft brown eyes and I handed her a tissue.

JOAN: Has he ever threatened you or hurt you before?

GINGER: Only emotionally, not physically.

JOAN: What do you mean?

GINGER: He criticizes me constantly, he doesn't appreciate me, he's very self-centered, he never listens to me, he's emotionally closed, and he told me he's thought about going back to his ex-wife because they have more in common. He's been separated for over a year.

Ginger's bizarre tale flooded me with memories of my past relationships with emotionally abusive men. I had stayed too long in these dead-end soap operas in which, at first, I was the leading lady. Then I gladly took the role of best supporting actress. I knew what low self-esteem looked like inside and out. The question was not "how do you mend a broken heart?" but "how do you mend low self-esteem?" "How do you learn to listen and respond in a healthy way to red flag signals?"

JOAN: What are you afraid of, Ginger?

GINGER: I'm afraid of being alone, that I might not meet anyone else. And I'm at a crossroads with my career. I want to do something else, but I'm not sure what. I feel like I have this hole somewhere in me and I don't know how to fill it.

JOAN: I've felt that way, too. I'm writing this book to help women and men learn to make better choices in relationships, strengthen their self-esteem, listen to their instincts, and find their passion in life.

GINGER: I guess this relationship has taught me a lot. I don't know why I keep repeating the same patterns with men. I'm just so angry at myself. I gave him so much. I helped him through his mother's illness and her death. I want revenge. I want him to know he lost the best thing he ever had. I'm so tired of learning through pain.

I want to learn from joy, not pain, had become my mantra. I screamed those words to the sky just seven years ago when, after the breakup of yet another dead-end relationship, I started my personal spiritual journey. More pain followed in my relationships, more therapy followed the pain. More reading and meditation, and then a change in perception, finally brought me inner peace. I'm still learning every day.

JOAN: Can I make a suggestion?

GINGER: Please. Yes.

JOAN: Try to use that energy to work on yourself, to find your purpose, what you really want to do. If you need help setting goals or working on patterns, I can refer you to some excellent therapists in the area. You just recited a list of red flag signals in your relationship with Ted, but it seems your fears prevent you from leaving him.

GINGER: You have good insights. Thanks, Joan.

I am happy to report that after three years of enduring Ted's criticism, public humiliation, and lies, Ginger broke up with him. She went to a therapist and worked on her self-esteem issues and became aware of her pattern of dating abusive/commitment-phobic men. Ginger took six months off from dating and created joy in her life: she took her mother on a cruise, started pampering herself with facials and manicures, and began writing a screenplay, something she had always wanted to do.

Then she ran into Bill, a colleague in the advertising industry, who shares her values and passion for travel. She called me and said she and Bill are moving south to start a life together. I heard the joy in her voice. It was the voice of a woman who had fallen in love with herself and with a vibrant, warm man who could love her back.

Reading the Flag's Stripes

Your new love interest blames her ex-husband for all her problems.

You wonder why your new boyfriend is not available on weekends.

Your lover constantly criticizes the way you look and dress.

Call them danger signals. Call them red flags. Or just call them fair warnings. You may spot them quickly in the love lives of your friends, yet ignore them when stars are in your own eyes. And when it ends, you ask yourself the age-old questions: "Why didn't I see it?" "Why did I put up with it?" "What was I thinking?"

Susan, 41, a vivacious California girl, has a zest for life, and a strong desire to be a mother. When an exotic lover stepped into her life, pursued her, told her he wanted to have a baby with her, and absolutely wowed her friends and family, she thought she'd found her prince. Up went her spirits and down went her guard. With hindsight, Susan now sees the red flags and confides, "My prince was really a toad—a toad with a bad habit."

> I keep trying to make lemonade out of lemons. I'll find a guy that's not up to par and think "I can bring him up to par," or "If I nurture him, he will be a better person." It's the benefit-of-the-doubt thing: there's someone way inside there that's good. I'll keep digging until I find him.

> I met this tall, dark foreign man. I was gaga over this guy. When I got into a relationship with him, everyone loved him, including my family. But when we got to my place, it was like I was invisible. He would pick up the newspaper, and I was fluttering around on the periphery. We were spending a lot of time together. He was calling me all the time, pursuing me regularly. But I found out his socialness was because he had a major alcohol- and drug-addiction problem. I was stupid enough to still move in with him.

I look back on that time and think to myself, "You were a psycho. Were you so desperate that you were willing to overlook all these major things?" He sucked away any self-esteem I ever had. He was the kind of man who said, "You really ought to try wearing more makeup." Once he told me while we were making love that maybe I needed to think about exercising. He was trying to turn me into something I could never be. I met him when I was 35 and I really wanted to have a baby. That's what he said he wanted to do. He was divorced twice, with no kids. He lied to me and totally misrepresented what his goals were in life.

Red Flags: Ignore Them at Your Peril

Jay, a freelance writer in his forties, disregarded a searing reality: The woman he wanted to build a relationship with was sleeping with another man. So Jay put time, effort, and substantial money into a dead-end relationship. Like Susan, his self-esteem diminished because he stayed in a relationship built on self-delusion:

> I was attracted to a 42-year-old divorced woman. She was dating a guy with several young kids. The children were causing tension in their relationship, and she was planning to break up with him. Normally if I met a woman like this, I would have given her my card and said, "Call me when it ends." But I went out with her and my self-esteem went out the window in two months.
>
> I was taking it slow. We would go out to dinner and for long walks. We went out once or twice on weeknights and she was with her boyfriend on weekends. I was totally stupid. We were not being physical, no sex, and I was dropping major dollars—many $150 dinners. Here I am getting more involved, and then 24 hours later she would be lying in bed with this guy.
>
> We were talking about traveling together to Italy. She was selling me a bill of goods. When we started discussing traveling, she said it would be no problem to take time off from work. But when I called her to confirm our plans, she said she would need approval from her boss.
>
> She said she couldn't just go from one relationship to another.
>
> A lot of this was my fault. I was too giving. She felt that it was too hard to go from ending one relationship to starting a new one without a break to gather her thoughts. Sometimes, when you are physi-

cally drawn to someone, you lose perspective. When it ended, I felt very unappreciated.

No More Ms. Nice Guy

Donna, a 37-year-old quality assurance manager for a food manufacturer, ignored a red flag telling her she was being taken for granted:

> A big danger signal I found in relationships was lack of commitment. I've come to believe that if they can't keep a simple commitment like a date, then this is indicative of problems in other areas. If someone can't follow through on their small promises, what makes you think they're going to follow through on the big promises?

> What it boils down to is, when I dated guys I was always giving, giving. Now the guys are going to have to step up to the plate and show me they're interested and get things going. I would cook dinner and breakfast for them, arrange camping trips, get plans lined up. He just had to come along. I would get the ball-game tickets through the company, get invited to parties, weddings, social events. I was more well-connected. My last boyfriend ended up riding that wave. I wouldn't have cared if he just had cooked hamburgers on the grill, but he never reciprocated. I even baked chocolate-chip cookies for him while he sat and watched a football game on my TV. Instead of putting my foot down, and seeing this behavior for what it was, I ignored it. At the time I felt, "It's better than being alone."

You Can't Change Them

Some people delude themselves that they can change their partner in order to make a relationship work. Susan was forever optimistic. Jay put his money where his fantasies were. But Dean, a 40-year-old jazz musician and song writer, seeks women with sizzle, women who challenge him. He finds "nice" women boring. Red flags seem to attract rather than warn him.

> I tend to go for the rocket, the woman who blasts me into orbit and then tears me up. She's high maintenance.

> I had met Alexis when she was in a relationship with another guy. We were just friends for years and I knew what she was like. She was en-

gaged, and I could see what was going on. I said to her, "I know what your gig is." Her boyfriend told me after they broke up, "She's really good. She says all the things you want to hear. She's like 'Love Potion Number Nine.' Like the serpent on the tree that says, 'Bite the apple.'"

She's evil. It's like your arm is getting cut off, and she's making you feel like it's good. And I dated her anyway. She was so good at pushing my buttons. I don't know why I liked her.

Take and take and take—like a vampire, she sucked my pocket and emotions.

Once she ordered a lobster. The dinner was $150. The cost didn't bother me. But she took five bites, said she was full, and took it home to her dog. I wouldn't have cared if she had just eaten the dinner. She had a really good job, but she never once bought or made me dinner in six months. I must have had a welcome mat lit up in neon on my chest. It was as though she said, "Let me find the most expensive thing on the menu."

She also lied a lot. She would tell me one thing one time, and change her story later.

There was too much inconsistency. One night I brought her a pumpkin for Halloween. When I went to her door to drop it off, she had company. She was seeing someone I didn't even know about while we were dating seriously. "I just see him once or twice a week so I can figure out my feelings for you," she said. I broke up with her. A week later she wanted to get back together with me. By that time, I wasn't interested. Soon after we broke up, she was already engaged. Her engagement ended at Christmas.

You can tell if someone is using you. All those little signals were there. Was she trustworthy? No. Compassionate? No. Honest? No. Did she have integrity? No.

She's taught me the red flags, and I put song titles on them. This relationship really hurt, so I used my pain to write my music. I need turmoil to write good songs.

Two Wives, Too Close

Beth, a 46-year-old never-married teacher, has learned a hard lesson: Stay clear of men who are momma's boys. After a three-year relationship with a man and his mother, she says it was "too close for comfort."

Mothers are great red flags. I met a wonderful guy from a personal ad. When he looked at me, his eyes lit up. We had a great dinner in a cozy, romantic restaurant. We shared a bottle of wine. We were talking about his family, and he said he had recently lost his dad. His mother lived with him. My last boyfriend, Tom, who I was with for three years, also lived with his mother, so I saw the flags. My date and his mother were building their dream house together. He was designing the kitchen. He said he came home to a cooked meal every night. It was so disappointing to me. It was the first good date I had since Tom and I broke up. I only went out with him once. He was 51, a good-looking doctor, never married. Now I like orphans or men with mothers who live in other states.

I always tell my dates about why I broke up with Tom: "He left me for another woman, his mother." Tom and I had talked about getting married. The way he proposed to me was, "Do you think you could live with my mother and me?" His other idea was to have two households and go one night to his mother's house and stay with me every other night. He came up with this plan because his mother didn't want to be alone. He just couldn't break away from her.

When I first met Tom, his mom lived across the country. During the first six months of our relationship, he lived temporarily at home to take care of his parents when his dad was dying. After his dad died, he moved in with his mom. He seemed like such an independent guy. I didn't pick up on this thing of his being a momma's boy. It was a sick relationship.

A Happy Ending

In her thirties, with a successful track record in personal goal setting, Beth achieved a career as a professional singer, bought a house, and traveled the world. By her late forties, she avoided dating momma's boys and focused on meeting a wonderful man and getting married. Thanks to a positive attitude, a satisfying life, and a joie de vivre, she accomplished that goal, too. Here's the ad that brought her Marty:

"Beautiful and Jewish. Bright single professional female ISO [in search of] single, divorced, white professional male. Seeking well-educated, financially secure man who's a great conversationalist."

This simple ad may not find the man of every woman's dreams, but it worked for Beth, then never-married and approaching 50. After receiving nine responses in a week, she chose Marty.

MARTY: The only reason Beth returned my call was my voice. I left her a message saying that I was an executive for a large company, an attorney, and I belonged to a country club. Then I added at the end, "And if I pass your audition my telephone number is . . . "

BETH: His voice is unbelievable. He could have been a radio announcer. He has a pretty Delaware accent. We met for the first time in a bookstore.

MARTY: I walk in this bookstore and don't know what Beth looks like. I see this woman approaching me, smiling. She knew it was me because I was wearing a suit.

BETH: I go crazy over men in suits.

MARTY: We got to talking over coffee. At first I didn't think it would work out. It was difficult to find a time when Beth was available to meet me. I thought, "This girl is beautiful and has loads of responses to her ad; she's probably meeting three or four guys before me."

BETH: That wasn't it at all. The weekend he wanted to meet me fell on my sister's birthday, my birthday, and my parent's anniversary. We're a close family and we always celebrate that week with one big party.

I thought he was really nice-looking. I thought he looked wonderful in his gray pin-striped suit. That lovely voice. I just thought you were cute. We had coffee and talked.

MARTY: I invited her to dinner that night.

BETH: I had a fever. I was sick as a dog. So I went out to dinner, even though I had no appetite.

MARTY: She was such a good actress. Well, she was a professional singer. Ate everything on her plate. It's part of her personality. That's good.

BETH: I'm very dramatic. After I met Marty, that first week I placed the ad, there were about nine or ten responses. I listened to them all and selected Marty. Once you find someone really wonderful, why continue meeting other people? I had put an ad in *The Sun* once before. I changed my ad a little, and whatever I did, it just drew. I placed it just after New Year's. I think people were ready to meet people in January.

MARTY: She had a verbal telephone message in addition to the print ad. It's recorded in your voice. The fact you spoke well appealed to me.

BETH: I talked on the voice message about things I think men my age would be interested in. I said I play golf, like to travel, like to sing, and enjoy classical music. Marty also loves the fact I can have an intelligent discussion on football or baseball. I like talking about sports.

MARTY: I found in answering ads, the best philosophy is to be honest. For me, I was interested not only in meeting someone, but in having it turn into something. If you're deceitful, there's little chance that the person you meet is going to be compatible with you or trust you. Being honest creates a foundation for having a good relationship. Beth and I were very compatible. We each recognized the ingredients of compatibility based on our phone conversations. You don't want to waste your time because of lies or exaggerations in ads.

I separated in June 1998 and had gone on three dates through personal ads between then and the time I met Beth. One was a lady I met for coffee. There was no interest, attraction, or compatibility. After coffee we said good-bye. Another woman was never married, in her late forties. We had dinner. There was no interest on my part. She seemed to be angry, self-centered, argumentative, aloof, and just an unhappy person. She thought she was beautiful. She was set in her ways and only wanted to talk about herself, not about me.

I went out on about a half dozen dates through the personals. I also had gotten fixed up on a blind date with a woman from Delaware through my sister-in-law. Her friend had recently divorced and had gone to a palm reader. The palm reader told her that she was going to meet an executive in Baltimore and it would lead to a long-term relationship. My sister-in-law fixed us up. If it was fated I meet her, how could I turn my back on fate? It turned out that I knew her, we were both from Newark, and I knew her ex-husband well. She was attractive, smart. I invited her to Baltimore, and we went out several times. But I wasn't divorced yet and didn't feel I was in love with her. I felt I didn't want to start a relationship where I had to spend so much time out of state.

BETH: Dating through the newspaper worked for me because I was totally honest. It's easy when you're honest and sincere about what you're saying. That comes through in the voice mail. I was at ease because what I said was the absolute truth. I didn't lie about my age or interests.

MARTY: In my opinion, the voice mail is the important ingredient. You find out whether they're nervous, if they planned what they said. That says more than they could write in a small ad. The voice mail was the main attraction when I called Beth.

BETH: My voice training for singing helped a lot.

MARTY: Some voice ads turned me off. They hemmed and hawed, their grammar wasn't good. That was an important requirement for me—to have someone well-educated, who could speak well.

BETH: I said I was seeking someone well-educated and financially secure. I have those attributes and I'm looking for my equal. I didn't ask for someone rich, I asked for someone well-educated and a great conversationalist.

I made notes about what I would say on the voice mail. Marty and I are very much alike. I wrote what I wanted to say, so I was ready. It was scripted. That's what Marty did.

MARTY: I didn't read it aloud, but I knew the contents beforehand.

BETH: My focus was finding someone to share my life with. I told every guy that up front on our first date, and I scared some of them. I separated the men from the boys that way.

MARTY: One of the things that attracted me to Beth was that she had a good time being single; she did all of the things she wanted to do in her single life. Some women are very bitter about being single; that self-centered woman I went out with had been unhappily single. Beth was not disappointed about her life. She just had reached a point where she wanted to experience married life, doing things with a husband. I found it very refreshing to know I was dating a woman who was happy and enjoyed herself—even though she said she wanted to get married from the beginning. People want to be with those who are healthy and happy. If you come off bitter and frustrated, I think you're going to end up alone.

BETH: I never sat and waited for life to start. I never waited for prince charming. I bought a house and traveled to Europe alone. I was so used to being the extra person at a party or wedding. You have to enjoy life, make your own memories, not worry about what's going to come. And then something wonderful came.

MARTY: Beth almost turned me off in the beginning, because she said she's been single 47 years and it was time she got married. She had

had a couple of serious relationships, and now she wanted to date men not just for fun but to get married.

BETH: I was looking for my life's partner. I'd never been married and I wanted to try it once in my life. In my thirties I didn't want to get married. I never thought about it. That's when I was singing.

MARTY: Beth seemed afraid I might want to date a lot of women. I had dated a bit already. When I met Beth, I liked what I saw and stopped dating other women; I didn't want this one to get away.

BETH: We like the same things. We look at the world the same way. One thing Marty likes about me is I'm sensible; I have a lot of common sense. Marty really appreciates that. He's easygoing, and I appreciate that in him. He'll talk things through. We don't really have fights.

MARTY: The reason is we're compatible; we enjoy each other's company, and physically, there's a lot of mutual attraction. It's hard to think about life without Beth. I think I would be missing a lot if I wasn't sharing it with someone I loved. I felt happy doing things married couples do. Being married to Beth is a wonderful experience, and it has made me a better person. It gives me a lot of satisfaction seeing Beth happy. Of course, she was also happy before she met me.

BETH: I've always set goals for my life, and I recommend other single women do that. Just before I met Marty, I had thought about buying a larger home and may have gone ahead and bought that home without a spouse. If you want to travel around the world, go. If you are thinking of changing your career, go on and do it. Don't make excuses that keep you from enjoying life.

My advice to other single people is, don't live for the future or you're going to wonder where your life went. I have single girlfriends who still seem to be waiting for someone. They're afraid to buy a house or travel. They want to wait till they meet the man of their dreams. Someone should enhance your life, not make it.

Beth married for the first time at 48. She and Marty have been married for more than a year and a half.

Trying Too Hard to Please

April, a 44-year-old woman with a doctorate in health policy and management, stewed over making a gourmet dinner to please her man.

The experience made her realize she was wallowing in anxiety instead of floating on love:

> I knew something was wrong when I started trying too hard and becoming someone else for the sake of that person. I spoke and dressed a certain way to please him. I realized something was wrong when all of a sudden I wasn't being true to myself. What I was doing was for the approval of that person. I was going out with a physician. By virtue of the fact he was a doctor, I felt I needed to be smarter, to be on my best behavior, to mask my imperfections for this person. I remember inviting him for dinner. I took off a whole day from work. I had to prepare the perfect meal. Three-quarters of the way through cooking the meal, I realized something hadn't turned out right. I got in a panic. Do I replace it? If it had been a friend, the thought of replacing it wouldn't have entered my mind. I would tell the friend, "It didn't turn out, but I'll do it right next time." I wouldn't take a whole day off if I was cooking a friend dinner. That's a very simple example. You know in your gut or heart when something is off. If we would pay more attention to those senses or feelings, rather than ignoring them, we'd probably be in better shape.

Control Freaks

Victoria, 35, a West Coast gynecologist, saw red flags the first night she met Frank. They didn't stop her. She lived with him for three years.

> I should have known the night I met Frank. He told me within a few seconds of meeting me that I was the woman he was going to marry. That's a red flag in itself. That's controlling. He was hosting a dinner party with my friend Carol. Carol and I were reminiscing about our travels to France, having fun. During our conversation, which everyone else was enjoying, Frank said, "Can't we change the subject? This is getting boring."

> There were so many signs. During our first Christmas together, we went to a party. I was aware there was a very handsome man staring at me, who seemed to want to talk. I was conscious of looking out for Frank. He was very jealous. He was hiding and watching me.

When I finally spoke to this man, Frank came out from nowhere and called me a bitch and a c———. No one had ever called me that before, and I allowed it.

I come from a conservative background, and because we were living together, I was committed to make this relationship work. We had so many differences. He was a multimillionaire, but he was so cheap. He wouldn't spend any money. He kept written records of everything he spent and I spent. I'm a much more generous person. I don't keep track. If it was my evening to make dinner, I couldn't just get carry-out—he took it as a sign I didn't love him.

The second I would come home from work, he wanted my attention. I had no downtime.

Gradually, he became resentful. He resented my friends, especially the history Carol and I had, because she knew me better than he did.

One night I found him home drunk. I had been out with a girlfriend. He was out with a friend. I came home five minutes later than he did and asked him to move his car. I turned on the lights. He started grabbing me and threw me. I drove to the hospital and stayed there overnight. I realized I wasn't going to live with a man who's drunk and enraged and who owns a gun. I took his gun to a friend's house.

When we met, we were both physically active. But together we only watched football and drank. After three years, I had put on 25 pounds. It was a very destructive relationship.

Six Degrees of Separation

Elizabeth, 51, and Larry, 54, met through an online matchmaking service. Originally Elizabeth had some misgivings about Larry—he's a clergyman, and she isn't religious. But by the end of their first rendez-vous, she thought he was a man she could fall in love with.

They went to an art museum, had lunch, walked through the museum's sculpture garden, and three hours later, he took her hand and gently kissed her lips. Ah, romance!

If only she had paid attention to the warning signs.

Within a couple of days of his first e-mail to me, before we'd even met, he started addressing my messages with *"Bonjourno Princepessa!"* We hadn't had a date yet. My immediate thought was that this was a line. I'm not big on lines, so I had my guard up. Another warning sign I tucked away: before we met Larry said, "If you count each one of these e-mails as a date, then by the time we meet we will have already started on a full-fledged romance."

As our first date progressed, Larry indicated he would like to stay over my place, which I thought was too quick. I even said, "I'm not going to do that on the first date because I'm not looking for a fling." The next time we got together, I went to his apartment for dinner. When I got there, before dinner, he said, "Let's go into the bedroom." I thought that was a little pushy. I said, "Let's eat instead."

Then everything was fine. He had to go to New York for a week for a conference. He e-mailed me the first day from his meeting. He wrote that he looked forward to seeing me and told me about the conference. Then I didn't hear from him for the rest of the week. I was getting upset. I thought things had been going well. I thought, "There are always two minutes to make a phone call. If you really want to be in touch with someone, you find a way." Over the next few weeks I discovered an advancing and retreating pattern. He'd e-mail, call, and then he'd vanish. This happened several times.

I kept saying to my friends, "Maybe he's fooling around, because he's only a few months out of a recent marriage." And everyone said, "He wouldn't do that; he's in the clergy." I also pooh-poohed it and ignored my instincts, because I thought a clergyman would not act that way. I hold clergy to a different standard; they're supposed to be ethical and family-oriented. I assumed he would be that way, that he would put himself in someone else's shoes. He had been married twice and said his second divorce was very painful. I believed he had enough experience to know how his actions would affect somebody else.

We talked about getting together in our last e-mail. He said he was back in town, and he'd call. He initiated all e-mails. Another warning sign was that he didn't phone much. He said he wasn't good on the phone and e-mail was better. To me that indicated he wasn't a good communicator, and he was using e-mail as a distancing thing so he wouldn't have to get intimate. Either that, or he was cheap. He lived out of town, a little over an hour away.

I'm a member of several Internet dating services, and that's how I met him. He got in touch with me. One night two months after he and I had first met, a woman e-mailed me just to say she had seen I was on-line, she was new to the matchmaking thing, and she wanted to know how the experience had been for me. I wrote back saying it had been fine; I hadn't had any bad experiences. Most people had seemed nice, I said, but I cautioned her to take things with a grain of salt because a lot of guys come on strong and then retreat—like a guy I had been seeing recently.

She e-mailed back to say, "I hope he wasn't the chaplain that I was seeing."

I said, "Uh oh, I think it might be." How many chaplains could there be?

She wrote back with his name, and it *was* the same man. She said, "We need to talk." I gave her my number and we spent an hour and a half on the phone the first night. It turned out they had met and started dating about the same time we had met. When he was calling me from New York, she was in New York with him. I also learned he addressed his e-mails to her the same way and even made us both the same seduction dinner.

Then she came to find out he was seeing a third woman simultaneously, who was also getting the same e-mails, calls, dinners, and sleep-over invitations. (They slept over; I didn't.) He even took them to his place of worship.

I just couldn't believe he was seeing three of us (that we knew of) at the same time. They got suspicious when he slept with them and then started disappearing. Then his e-mails to them started becoming scarce. So they each laid a little trap for him. (They didn't know about each other then.) They observed his on-line habits and saw he was on-line all the time.

This was while he was involved with them, and he was telling them there was nobody else, and at same time telling them he should force himself to date other people so he wouldn't rush into anything. He was also telling them that he wasn't sleeping with other women, when apparently he was.

There's a way to know if someone's using the on-line matchmaking service. If you see a little lightbulb next to the person's screen name, you know that person is on-line at the moment. It also says when the last time you checked in was. For example, "last log-in 8:45 P.M."

I had never checked to see how often he was on the service because I think it's an invasion of privacy. I thought it would just make me feel bad to know he was on-line so often and obviously looking when he was saying he felt he wanted to see me, couldn't believe he'd met somebody like me, and wanted to spend all of his time with me.

This was while he was involved with them, and he was telling them there was nobody else, and at the same time telling them he should force himself to date other people so he wouldn't rush into anything. He was also telling them that he wasn't sleeping with other women, when apparently he was.

One woman had her girlfriend call him and pretend to be a wrong number. The friend became very suggestive on the phone with him and pretended to be a 20-year-old girl. He fell for it and tried to meet her.

The other woman created another account on this Internet dating site with a different e-mail address and forwarded sexually suggestive e-mails to the chaplain. He was telling both women—this made-up e-mail person and the made-up phone person—that he wasn't seeing anyone, and that all his dates hadn't been any fun, that he was kiss-deprived.

A fourth woman surfaced after the first woman sent an e-mail to age-appropriate women on this service saying, "If you've gone out with this guy, get in touch." This other woman had a week of e-mails from the chaplain, and they had gone out to dinner. He also began his e-mails to her, *Bonjourno Principessa*.

We all agreed he was "not my type" physically, and that we all just didn't pay attention because he had that clergy thing going for him. We thought a clergyman was someone you could trust, someone who was honorable. The fourth woman sent a letter to the administrator of the Internet site asking if there was anything that could be done to prevent him from hurting other women, and they kicked him off the site. One of the women had arranged to place an article in a magazine featuring him as a prominent member of the clergy. She called the editor and he pulled the story.

One of the women, out of revenge, subscribed him to an alternative lifestyle matchmaking service. When he complained to find out what was going on, they traced it back to her. He sent her an e-mail saying shame on you and never contact me again. Interestingly enough, he never asked why she did it.

Later I found out through the woman from New York that he lied to her about his age and said that he didn't have children. He has one child. To me, lying about not having kids is dishonorable. I can understand lying about your age.

Dating this man has taught me to listen to my instincts even when everyone is telling me there's nothing to back my instincts up, to be very wary of people who come on strongly, not to be so hard on myself, and not to think, "What did I do wrong?"

I learned there are sociopathic people who can fool you and many others. You had one guy with four women who all thought that this relationship could be something. These are four very intelligent, attractive women. He fooled us all into thinking that we were each special to him. Another lesson to be learned from this is no matter how vigilant you are, and no matter how carefully you try to read the warning signs, there are people who can fool you. It doesn't have anything to do with being naive, but with how good they are at fooling you. You have to keep your guard up, while at the same time to stay open enough to trust in other people.

In spite of her experience with this insincere Lothario, Elizabeth will continue to use the Internet as a means to meet new men.

I just consider Internet dating another avenue. I'm as careful with it as I am with any other way I'd meet people. By and large, most of the people have been nice, and who they say they are. I'll also continue to meet men in my usual ways: bookstores, traveling, through work, and introductions by friends.

The Psychic Background Check

Susan Rabin, M.A., a relationship therapist in New York City and author of *101 Ways to Flirt, How to Attract Anyone, Anytime, Anyplace,* and *Cyberflirt,* suggests running a face-to-face background check on your next potential mate, with your red flag detector on full alert:

Find out the nature of their relationships, how they ended, why they ended. Do they throw the blame on everyone else? Has he or she grown? What is his/her communication style? Does he withdraw or argue? It's very important to respect each other's style, especially if yours is different. Pay attention to what has happened in his past relationships. Older single people have a lot of history and baggage.

And if you're already in a relationship, Rabin suggests calling it quits if your radar picks up these ugly warning signals:

Does the person lie, cheat, disappoint you constantly, say one thing and do another? When the pain becomes greater than the pleasure, get out. Unfortunately, a lot of us can tolerate a lot of pain, and many people don't have a lot of self-esteem. They don't know they've been put down or what they should tolerate. In a good relationship, there's mutual respect. It nurtures and makes you feel good, enhanced. It's not about constant anxiety and tension.

Therapist Charney Herst, Ph.D., author of *Mothers of Difficult Daughters: How to Enrich and Repair the Bond in Adulthood,* advises singles to observe the yellow signals before they become red—and before you're already walking down the aisle with your beloved. Dr. Herst suggests asking the following questions before you get involved with someone:

What are your and his main values? Does the person steal, drink, make up stories, sustain friendships, see his family? It's a clue when two people are getting married and there's no one from his or her family at the wedding. The person says, "I don't have anything to do with my parents or siblings." People don't stop and pay attention at a yellow signal. If this is historic, there's a problem. Then the person says, "If I had only known."

I often ask my clients, "How long did you wait to get married?" "How long did you go together?" "Why does this have to be instant marriage?" The answer to the last question might be to have a baby, please parents, be considered acceptable by his or her family, enter the mainstream, do the right thing for the wrong reasons.

Dr. Herst also recommends observing your romantic partner's basic values and how they react in a crisis:

How do they handle money? Are they kind? How do they handle obstacles like a flat tire? How do they act at family events, Seder, Christmas, Easter, get-togethers? How do they hold up under an illness or death in the family?

Many couples today don't interact with other people. When I ask them, "Who are your friends?" They say, "We don't have any friends."

"Where or with what groups are you affiliated?"

"We just rent a movie, order pizza."

I say, "You have excluded the homeless, poverty, seeing what's happening around you. You have excluded reality." They are not equipped for tolerating crisis. That's when their relationship falls apart—their first car accident, first serious illness, first miscarriage.

I know of a couple who had been married five years and got a divorce following the wife's miscarriage. Her husband realized the only reason he stayed with her was for the child. After the miscarriage, they couldn't sustain the relationship.

Dr. Herst believes that the most important red flags concern how the significant other relates to other people.

That's the best indicator of how you will relate to life. How does he or she adjust and rehabilitate after stresses? Does the ex-husband choose not to see his kids? Does the new man in your life avoid closeness, responsibility, intimacy, and financial responsibility? If he can let his kids go, he can let his wife go—without guilt.

A person needs to sustain a wide range of emotions, including feeling guilt when he or she does something wrong, or remorse when he or she caused something bad to happen. It's important to feel joy as much as sadness. You have to hang around with someone until you see the rest of it. You may become a victim of this person's one-sidedness. You need to see someone angry and observe that he or she is not destructive or violent, that he or she can handle anger. If it's not shown, don't think it's missing. Perhaps the person is afraid of feeling anger. He or she has to get past that and learn to handle it. Professionally speaking, I think people need to get therapy before marriage—to be prepared. Life is not a sitcom, it doesn't all get worked out in 30 or 60 minutes.

Feelings You Shouldn't Ignore

Martin Blinder, M.D., a psychiatrist practicing in the San Francisco Bay area for more than 20 years and author of *Choosing Lovers*, says red flags are sometimes just gut reactions, feelings you shouldn't ignore.

When your head tells you everything is going fine and your gut says there's something not right, when the inner picture doesn't match with the outer picture, you're picking up stuff your eyes and ears aren't ready to pay attention to. A patient may say, "When we talk, we don't really talk" or "When we make love, she's not really there."

Other red flags may be: lots of drinking and smoking goes on, sex goes away, someone is clinically depressed or angry all of the time. Someone is cheating. But if anybody gets physically hurt, that's not just a red sign; that's *maroon.*

What danger signs in the beginning of courtship indicate a person might become violent? Sara Kittrie, a clinical social worker who works with domestic violence clients on behalf of the Washington, D.C. Superior Court, suggests that women (and men) be wary of excessive jealousy.

In the beginning, sometimes the abuser expresses his jealousy as a proof of his love. Jealousy has nothing to do with love. It is a way of possessing and controlling and not having trust in the partner. One signal is when a man always wants to know who his girlfriend has been talking to. He may even become jealous if she spends time with her children or her friends. Jealousy can become even more acute; it can become a real problem when a man is too possessive.

Kittrie offers advice to those wondering just how long abusive behavior takes to surface:

Everybody is on their good behavior in the beginning. But you cannot keep that up for very long. That phase can last one day or two years, that phase of the relationship that we call the honeymoon, where "I am for you and you are for me." The couple does everything together. You have to be able to identify signals. It doesn't really matter when, just be aware of them. Quite often, the men and women get involved emotionally and sexually very rapidly, before a friendship develops. It's a kind of impulsive relationship; the emotions and sexual attraction become very strong. And when that begins to wear off they begin to see they are not in a compatible relationship.

According to Kittrie, the danger comes when a person says, "You're the only person I can talk to"—or "I've never loved anybody the way I've loved you." She says this might seem very complimentary at first, but it shows a wish to control and pressure the other person. When the flattery wears off, the adored person may feel trapped:

> I think that the Dr. Jekyll and Mr. Hyde personality is something to be aware of because one minute they might be super nice, and then they quickly change and lose their temper. When the person is nice, you tend to forgive the outburst of temper, but it's not going to change. This is a sign that the person may have two separate ways of reacting and has not managed to integrate them in a way that is easy to live with. Also be aware if someone admits that he has had a lot of difficulties with women in the past, such as "She really brought out the temper in me." I think that's a red flag. There's a lot of projection. The person is really not taking responsibility for his behavior. He's blaming somebody else, and that's a red flag.

> Another is when a person is verbally abusive and expresses himself in a way that hurts the partner. A few examples are: "You are really not that smart" or "I don't think you can manage without me." I heard another one recently: a man told his girlfriend, "You'll never find anybody who loves you like I do."

> But you see, I don't think we can base our impression of a person on just one of these characteristics. You cannot lose the context. This person who says, "I love you very much and I cannot live without you," may be expressing a very strong emotion that he feels. That might be very wonderful. But if along with that there are other indications that this person is very dependent or wants the power and control over someone else and will try to get it no matter what, then this is a problem. He may promise the moon and the stars, but what's really behind it is a position of control.

Kittrie explains that a single insult doesn't necessarily mean your partner is abusive. Rather, she suggests looking at the whole picture and basing your judgment on an accumulation of remarks and your overall response:

> The feeling that it leaves you with is absolutely essential. One of my favorite expressions is, "A really good friend is someone who helps you feel as good as you possibly can." It's the feeling that you are left with after spending time with the person. That is a very strong indicator of how things are going. Someone who breaks things or throws

things in a fit of temper—I would want to stop and look at this and see what this is all about. Maybe next time *I'm* going to be the target.

The bottom line, Kittrie stresses, is getting to know the person well before you end up in a committed relationship.

Warning Signs of Abuse

What comes to mind when you think of the word abuse? Physical violence? Inappropriate sexual behavior? According to K.J. Wilson, Ed.D., author of *When Violence Begins at Home: A Comprehensive Guide to Understanding and Ending Domestic Abuse*, these categories only scratch the surface.

Verbal abuse and "the use of size or presence" can be just as menacing, she says. Examples of verbal abuse include: "name calling, yelling, using insults, being sarcastic, sneering, criticizing, ignoring, threatening family, friends, or children." Wilson describes abuse involving the use of size or presence as: "stalking; unplugging the phone; taking car keys, credit cards, money or checkbook; locking partner out of the house; controlling access to money; displaying intense jealousy; isolating partner from friends and family; not working; threatening to divorce or take custody of children."

As examples of sexually abusive behavior, she cites "unwanted touching, forced sex with partner, unfaithfulness, and even insisting a partner dress in a more sexual way than she wants."

Helping victims of abuse is a subject very close to Wilson, a domestic violence consultant. Dr. Wilson, herself once a victim of abuse, spends her life helping other survivors. She describes the different forms of abuse and warning signs of potentially abusive partners.

When I talk to people about abuse, the first thing they think of is physical abuse—violence in a relationship. What we know is the majority of violent relationships do not start out with violence, they start out with both emotional and verbal abuse. And over time, without some intervention, chances are great that it will escalate to physical violence.

What we experts on abuse know is that if a woman is in a physically violent relationship, she will be experiencing emotional abuse as well.

The reverse is not true, in that you can have an emotionally abusive relationship with no physical violence present.

Most people don't have a clear understanding of what emotional abuse looks like. Emotional abuse is much more subtle and insidious. A good example of emotional abuse is failure to talk to one's partner. An abusive partner could go days or weeks without speaking to the other person. That's a form of emotional abuse.

Another example is a partner who encourages his female partner to have a hearty appetite. But when she gains weight, and she's having trouble fitting into her clothes, he says, "You're really getting fat. I need to tell you this because I love you and don't want anyone to laugh at you behind your back." Even though she has been eating more because he encouraged her to.

We look at emotional abuse as a way of one person negating or ignoring someone else's feelings. One partner says something hurtful in a joke form, but it still hurts. The other partner says, "That hurts my feelings." He responds, "You can't take a joke." This is a blatant minimalization of the abuse survivor's feelings.

The use of size or presence frequently occurs before physical abuse. Physical abuse may be the last resort. Survivors of abuse become very conditioned to their environment. They instinctively look for cues that something is about to happen. It can be an action, a facial expression, a gesture. Often that's all that's needed to make the survivor behave in a manner the abuser wants. A batterer can give his partner a look, kick something, punch a wall; the implication is clear—the survivor could be next. These are forms of intimidation. We're talking about control—one person's choice of behavior in order to control another. Control is at the root of the problem.

A typical red flag in a dating situation might be: Is the man trying to control the woman in some fashion? The control is hidden behind words like, "I love you and want the best for you." That's why it is so critical for women to trust their instincts.

And it's a double whammy. As women, we live in a culture that tells us not to trust our instincts. If you're dating a batterer or potential batterer, he's going to tell us not to trust our instincts. "But I love you, don't you love me?" There are mind games and lots of manipulation.

We see many more abuse cases—95 percent—in which men abuse women. In only five percent of reported cases do we see men as the victims of domestic abuse, including gay violence or female abuse against men. But abuse against men is probably underreported.

I believe very strongly that we're talking about violence against women that occurs in a larger context—male privilege—and that goes back a long way. The key to a potentially abusive relationship can be answered in this question: is my partner able to look at me as an equal? If not, there is potential for abuse in the relationship. Are both partners sharing jointly in decision making? Are both expending the same amount of energy nurturing the relationship? These things are imperative to consider when making choices about who we want to spend our lives with. If they're missing, we may have an inequality that can become a breeding ground of violence.

My advice to women dating or in a relationship is, if you think it's too good to be true, run screaming, because it is. Perpetrators tend to be charming, charismatic people. They figure out what we like and want and they inundate us with it. They are on their best behavior. "He's perfect. He's the person of my dreams."

The bottom line is, none of us is perfect; we make mistakes. He is someone who is pushing our buttons. In essence he is trying to entice you into a relationship with him. That's how people get sucked into abusive relationships. The deeper we get into the relationship and the more committed, then more subtle forms of abuse start occurring.

In this country, we have this misconception: if you love someone, you're jealous, and jealousy means love. The bottom line is, jealousy reflects a sense of possession. So many people equate jealousy with love. Pathological jealousy is one of the red flags of an abusive relationship.

The most common question is, why do women stay? What I find interesting is no one ever asked me, "Why does he batter?" That is indicative of the problem. Instead of holding the abuser accountable, it is easier to blame the victim. In blaming the victim, we are contributing to the continuation of the problem. The misconception is that there is a certain type of woman this happens to. But every woman is at risk.

We need to know warning signs. I would look for the need to control one's partner, extreme jealousy, isolation, any history of past abuse with a partner, abusive behavior toward animals, or a partner with unrealistic expectations around children.

There is no time frame on when abusive behavior begins. My recommendation is to trust one's instincts. Know what the red flags are. If the woman sees them, her instincts will tell her something's wrong. They are there to protect us. It is absolutely critical that we pay attention. Our instincts will tell us the right thing to do. I encourage people not to care what a friend or boyfriend tells you. Trust your instincts, because they can save your life. When women are afraid of hurting someone else's feelings or making someone mad, we're actually putting our lives on the line.

Father Joe Breighner, host of the nationally syndicated radio show, "The Country Road" and author of *Stops Along the Country Road*, agrees with Kittrie when he says, "We need to replace lust with friendship. When a woman trusts and values herself, her intuition is valid. If she's not feeling comfortable, she needs to listen to that discomfort. She may not feel respected in the relationship or she may feel afraid. Maybe he's got a temper."

Father Joe suggests you try to see each other in as many different times of day and in as many situations as possible to avoid learning too late what your partner is really like: "Lunch time, after work, under different stressors. How does he [or she] react to you then?"

The Aroma of Jealousy

James P. McGee II, Ph.D., chief psychologist and director of Chemical Dependency Services at Sheppard Pratt Health System in Baltimore, and chief psychologist of the Baltimore County Police Department, also lists jealousy as a key warning sign when dating.

Jealousy may initially be flattering, but it can come back to bite you. If right off the bat the guy shows a very high level of interest in other men you're seeing, or how much dating you do, if there seems to be more than a passing interest, that would be something to cause suspicion. If you go on a first date with a guy and he's really grilling you about how many men you've dated and what happened to them, he may just be concerned about herpes and AIDS. People want to find out your track record in that area. It depends on how it comes across.

If it has the aroma of possessiveness or jealousy, be careful. The jealous, possessive guys sometimes come on much too strong early in the relationship; they're showering you with flowers and sweet nothings and cards. On one hand that's nice and romantic, but you have to keep everything in proportion. If they're becoming insistent early on in the relationship and have you accounting for your time, such as "Where were you," "I tried calling you," "I couldn't get ahold of you," and there's kind of an urgency to it, watch out. If he is pestering you, wanting to know your every move, that's a red flag for the kind of possessive guy who becomes a colossal pain in the neck. And when the girl tries to reject him, he really goes haywire.

Red Flags: Advice from Single Baby Boomers

Okay. Even if there are no experts around for you to get a reality check on the new someone in your life, you can still learn to recognize harsh personal affronts to your dignity or self-esteem. Here are some blatant red flags noted by some of the single men and women interviewed for this book:

"It's a red flag when dates tell you terrible stories about their ex-wives or girlfriends and take no responsibility for their role in the failure of the relationship."

—JANE, 46

"A classic red flag for me is lying. If a lie is done to protect someone's feelings, it's a social grace. If it's a profound lie and digs into the fundamental basis of your relationship, it's unforgivable. I hate being betrayed."

—VINCE, 43

"I think it's important that a man I meet love his parents. (Not too much though.) Because someone who loves his parents is able to love you. It's a danger signal to me if a man doesn't have any friends and doesn't get along with his family."

—REBECCA, 39

"Look at people's relationships with others in their lives. Who are that person's friends and family? Are they close to their siblings or parents? I'm close to a lot of people. I've stayed in touch with friends from a long time ago."

—KEN, 39

"One man said to me he didn't like his own child because she looked like his ex-wife and was overweight. Another man said he had grown-up twins but hadn't seen them since they were five because his wife took them to another state. I went out with another man who hadn't seen his son in 12 years. He never bothered to contact him because he lived too far away. How can you alienate yourself from your own flesh and blood? Those are unbelievable turnoffs for me. I admire a man who adores his children. I find that very attractive."

—PAULA, 45

"Listen to messages when you first meet a person. It's tough to hear these things when you're clouded by emotion. Kevin warned me from the start. One of the things he told me early on in our relationship was he always fought to win. We traveled to Scottsdale, Arizona, once a year to play golf. Driving home, we got into an incredible argument over a boy playing ball in the driveway of our hotel. We were trying to drive through, and the kid was ignoring us. Kevin had a short fuse with young punks. He got out of the car to yell at the kid. I was unforgiving of him because he got so out of control. It was a very tense day. He attacked my integrity and told me I was a spoiled brat and naive. He resorted to some very cruel words to me. Now I understand what he meant when he said he fights to win."

—JEAN, 49

"My last boyfriend had a temper. It's not that he would hit me. He would get mad at people in a car while he was driving or get irritated with service people, like waiters. His excuse was, "I'm from New York.""

—GINNY, 40

"Up until right now, I was a hopeless romantic. I would fall in love and be blind to things I shouldn't have been blind to such as incompatibility and behaviors I should have noticed as red flags and didn't. One woman constantly criticized me in public and let out sarcastic remarks that would make Roseanne look gentle. I had a Camelot view of things. When I would fall in love with a woman, I was completely committed and not practical about other things. Sex was one element. I believed in the fairy tale where you live happily ever after. Now I don't confuse love with orgasm."

—GENE, 50

"My problem is becoming involved with men who are not emotionally available, when there's no getting a commitment of any type. The red flag has two parts. The first is the guy's part, if he's evasive about the future. And the second part is my being sensitive to the avoidance because I want that guarantee of the future before I invest myself in the relationship. I have to be constantly aware of my goal: To be in a healthy, lasting relationship."

—PATTY, 35

"I've been in relationships where the sex was great and the relationship was very bad. The woman was into drugs and things I never did. Her attitude was, there was a guy around every post. I was one in a chain of people. The excitement drew me into it. In every one of my relationships I can look back and say, 'I knew there was a problem.'"

—RAY, 50

Marc's Big Question

I went through years of post-divorce, dating women who told me horror stories about how they were psychologically or even physically abused by boyfriends. After a while, I decided to ask women the question that was kicking noisily around my brain: "Why do women go out with guys who are nasty, brutish, and insensitive?" I knew that the question would hit home with many women. What I didn't expect was the response I almost invariably got. The women responded almost unanimously by smiling weakly, shrugging their shoulders, and saying something incisive like, "I don't know."

These women couldn't—or wouldn't—tell me why they were throwing themselves at bullies and punks and even fought to maintain the relationship.

Only once did I get a straight answer from a woman, a teacher in her thirties who'd never been married and had just broken up with someone. We met on a blind date arranged by her girlfriend. Around the third date I popped the question: "Why do women go out with guys who are nasty, brutish, and insensitive?" I expected a weak smile and a shrug.

Instead she told me that a lot of women don't want to grow up and do what their parents expect them to; that is, find a nice guy and settle down. Instead, they want excitement. So they go out with "bad boys." Maybe those weren't her exact words, but that's what she meant. So was it a rebellion thing? A search for excitement? A desperate stab at livin' *la vida loca*? OK, I'll buy that. But how often and long must a woman be treated shabbily before she tosses her boyfriend aside?

I was brought up by my parents to be a good person. As an adult on the singles scene, that meant I fell into the category of "nice guy." I didn't bully and humiliate and run around on girlfriends. I was still a nice guy when I hit the singles scene after my divorce.

Of course, I was still trying to grow and heal and figure out how to have a relationship. So between my own struggles and baggage and those of the women I was trying to have a relationship with, it's no wonder I drifted from person to person and from bed to bed. I'm not complaining about the sex, mind you. But the mind-bending that goes on as a relationship rolls over and dies does get tiresome.

I put up with a lot for the sake of trying to make a relationship work. After all, the most important relationship of my life, my marriage, had failed. I don't like failure. What I didn't realize is that I needed to learn how to have a healthy relationship, to work at it, and to avoid people who weren't capable of having a healthy relationship.

What I've learned over the years is that, if I want to have a good, healthy, lasting relationship, I have to be more than just a "nice guy." I've got to have the psychological and emotional tools to build that relationship and maintain it.

Introspection: Questions for You to Consider

Do you identify with any of the stories in this chapter? How?
Briefly describe your last three relationships.

Why didn't they work out?

What were the red flags in each relationship?

What were your reactions to the red flags in each relationship? How did you act on them?

What lessons did you learn from these relationships?

If you just met someone and you noticed red flag signals that make you feel uncomfortable, what would you do?

Now you have a clearer understanding of what you don't want in a relationship. Create a list of qualities that are most important to you. Rehearse what you want every day, and don't settle for less.

6

Fathers and Daughters

"Home is where we all start from. When we see where we've come from, then we can see why we're going in that direction. We tend to recreate our family of origin in spite of ourselves."

—JUDY BURCH, M.S.N.

THE RARE FISH

My steps are leaden as I pass
rows of sagging breasts,
dowager humps,
crocheted shawls
and sleepy white heads
in the green halls of Sinai Nursing Home.

I fast-forward to my golden years.
Will they be brittle and brown?
Will I rock mindlessly on a porch
with white Ionic columns?

No.
Angels will breathe light into my soul
and hold my shoulders high.
I will write poetry, paint portraits
and comfort faithless hearts.
I will wear ruby rings, red saris,
crimson lipstick

and flaming Dolly Parton wigs.
I will dance to Beatles songs
with cranky men
bobbing turtle heads on leather necks.

My time machine drops me to the present.
Urine and antiseptics marry; my nostrils burn.
But I visit Father, like King Lear's
dutiful daughter.
I've found strength and peace, but not with him.
We are numb when we're together,
connected only by blood and history.
I wear protective armor.
If I'm so strong, why does he
still bruise my inner child?

I kiss his cheek and sit beside him while
Ella sings on the radio.
With shallow breaths
I battle his indifference,
his selfish silence.

"Is your blood pressure down?"
"No."
"Are you comfortable?"
"Yes," he adjusts his hearing aid.
"Do you have enough shirts?"
"I have enough."

He eats a tasteless lunch while watching CNN.
Maybe it's Mom's death, my divorce and overwork.
Maybe it's 40 years of his calling me "young lady."
But today, as Father sleeps, my anger flares.

"It's time we talk." I tap him awake.
Fearing the smell of my anger, at first I speak softly.
"Do you know the pain you've caused me?
I tried to please you,
make all A's.
But you never felt my joy

or held me when I cried.
Why didn't we ever talk like friends,
ride bikes, and share secrets?
Why didn't you ask my thoughts
as we drove to college each fall?
I sang to the radio, organized
my purse, opened and closed
the brass button to stop the silence.
There was so much we could have
learned about each other then."

I feel the blood surface in my face.
"You had so many passions:
opera, art, the ocean's inner world.
At 10, I wished I were a rare fish
so you would take my picture
and brag to friends about your treasure.
But I couldn't even swim."
My voice crescendos as
red tears stain my silk blouse.
I turn my back to him.
"Your aim with the strap was perfect
like everything else you did.
It stung my leg as
I ran to Mother's arms."

My chest fills like a blowfish.
My shoulders shake, but I continue.
"But your belt never touched my spirit.
I rebelled.
As a child, I wished that you would die while
Mother clung to her denial."
"Your father was an orphan," she chanted,
"he doesn't know how to show his feelings,
but he loves you."
"Why couldn't you ever tell me that?"

My soliloquy ends as the sun rests.
I feel calmer, at peace.
"Father, I'm tired of your world of silence.
Please let me know you while there's time."

The sun lights Father's face like an Old Master
painting.
I lift my purse, nestled in his pillow.
Stingy tears stay balanced in his eyes.
"I'm tired Annie, but sit with me a little longer.
Please come back next week. We'll talk."

I rock in the chair and hold his hand in silence.

—JOAN

This poem reflects the deep chasm between me and my father, a brilliant scientist, who died scuba diving in Australia's Great Barrier Reef in 1984, and how I slowly came to terms with that emotionally charged relationship 14 years after his death.

Writing "The Rare Fish" was very therapeutic. Through it I was able to rewrite the script of my relationship with my father and give it a hopeful, happy ending. Now I'm grateful for the gifts he passed on to me—my appreciation for classical music, the opera, and theater as well as his strong values—integrity, honesty, commitment, and fidelity. Now when I think of him, it's with compassion and understanding.

Even though he was emotionally unavailable to me, he was the most brilliant, creative, adventurous, generous, and ethical man I've ever known. I admired his contribution to the Manhattan Project during World War II, and his passion for his work as an environmental scientist. He built the first waste treatment plant in the United States. He was a good provider for the family and never missed a day of work in 35 years at the same company.

And Dad was always there when I needed him.

One summer day when I was three, my parents, my sister, Sandy, and I spent a day at our swim club. As the pool closed, my parents dressed Sandy and me up for a Sunday dinner out. But I had other plans. I jumped into an Olympic-size pool in my party clothes, my petticoat framing my face just above the water and my black patent Mary Janes floating to the surface. I liked taking risks, even then. One beat later, my father dove in after me in his best suit. I guess we ate at home that night.

When I was 11, my cousins invited me to spend a week in New York. I should have been excited, but the sudden growth of hair under my arms embarrassed me. My father came to the rescue again. He tenderly shaved away the hair.

Even during the sweet moments, I never thought that I was good enough in his eyes: not smart enough, graceful enough, creative enough, pretty enough. I felt like I never earned his approval or his love. Perhaps my mother was right—he just didn't know how to express his feelings, especially to girls.

Ten years ago, I had an epiphany about my father when my therapist asked me if any of my boyfriends reminded me of someone else in my life. I had described a pattern: I fell in love with brilliant, emotionally vacant men who never loved me back. I sat silent for several minutes. "My father?"

"Maybe. Do you think so?" she said.

I denied the similarities and told my mother what the therapist said. My mother—who didn't approve of therapists, who once said she'd rather see me spend the therapy money on a vacation—said, "That's the most ridiculous thing I've ever heard."

A week later, I was sobbing in my therapist's office. It was true; I was dating men with many of my father's characteristics.

Awareness was the first step. I worked with my therapist on how to stop my dead-end dating pattern. It seemed so natural to get involved with emotionally unavailable men; I continued the pattern with two more men over the next two years. Now I see the warning signs and listen to my intuition.

Therapy and writing poetry helped me move past my anger at my father for not letting me know him and for his erratic, rageful outbursts. But the remaining traces of my anger dissolved only recently when I remembered his mood swings, irritability, and constant sleeping. I realized my father had many of the symptoms of clinical depression, and through heredity, he passed it on to me and my sister.

At the time that my father suffered from depression, there were fewer kinds of antidepressants on the market than there are today. And therapy was frowned upon by society. My father self-medicated with alcohol, which caused his inappropriate outbursts at gatherings with family and close friends. Knowing how he must have suffered, I was able to forgive him.

I hope this chapter will help you explore your family relationships and move forward with your lives. You are not alone if you had an emotionally unavailable father or mother. I have learned that a parent needs self-esteem to be able to pass it on to a child. My parents did the best they could.

Like Father, Like Boyfriend

While researching *Celebrating Single*, I didn't have to look far to interview single female baby boomers about their father-daughter wounds. Kathy, 47, who lives in my neighborhood, was more than willing to share her story.

> Starting in my teen years, my relationship with my father was very poor. He was emotionally aloof and absent, and it caused me to be desperate for affection from anywhere or anyone. By emotionally unavailable, I mean he worked a lot out of town and was physically not there. Even when he was there, he didn't provide any emotional support.
>
> The only way I knew how to relate to men was sexually. By 16, I was promiscuous. I wasn't interested in sex, I was desperate for affection. Being promiscuous lowers your self-esteem. Everyone in my family was taught to deny their feelings. You simply didn't talk about things. I knew my parents bickered but these and other "secrets" were vehemently denied. For instance, my father was an alcoholic, but that fact was denied and never discussed.
>
> Of the three siblings, I had the least tolerance for the tension in the house. I was often angry, which went against the household rules. Once I would get angry, everyone else would get angry. The anger and frustration was so intense. Into my early forties, I still carried this anger with me, and I couldn't understand where it was coming from. When I was an adolescent, my parents sent me to a psychiatrist because they thought I was defective. The psychiatrist asked to see the family, and suddenly I was excused from therapy. My sister did tell me that my mother said, "Kathy is crazy. It's got nothing to do with me or Dad."
>
> My mother didn't like me. She saw me as competition for my father's love and attention. For as much as I argued with my father and we were at each other's throats, he never disguised the fact that I (the oldest of his three daughters) was his favorite. Like my father, my

mom was immature. But she was quiet and withdrawn. She grew up with a very austere, cold father and that's all she knew.

It was only years later, in retrospect, that I realized how my family dynamics influenced me. I worked with a therapist. It was a slow process and yet a priceless experience. One of the most enlightening things of my life, I discovered in therapy. My therapist said that I fit the profile of someone who had been sexually abused. My father had frequently alluded to the fact that he found me attractive, and he touched me inappropriately. He grabbed or pinched me and my friends on the rear. He was a hands-on kind of guy. My therapist helped me realize that maybe it wasn't all my fault, maybe I wasn't such a horrible person.

My father, who was cheating on my mother, also introduced me to his girlfriends. I finally came clean with my mother. I told my mother about the women, and how he involved me. He was in his fifties at the time. One of the husbands of one of the women he was fooling around with called my mother and told her. My father denied it. But he had introduced me to this woman and others. I said, "Mom, you're right, Dad is seeing other women." That conversation brought me and my mother closer. She said he should never have dragged me into his affairs.

Alcoholism runs in my family, especially on my father's side. I had my first drink when I was 16 and was a heavy drinker from the beginning. It was like an escape. I had no idea how to socialize without a drink. I just assumed that going out and drinking a bottle of wine and a six-pack of beer was the way you did things.

When I was 32, I finally realized with absolute clarity that I definitely had a problem with alcohol. I almost had an accident driving home one night from a party. I must have fallen asleep on the Beltway and was heading toward the shoulder. I woke up and quickly steered back onto the road. If there had been a lot of traffic, I could have hurt someone. I decided then and there I needed help. I didn't want to cause someone else's death.

I just quit drinking. That's when the rock-bottom depression hit me. I didn't have my escape anymore. I started seeking therapy in earnest. Then the slow process of healing and forgiving began.

Even though at first I didn't really see any progress, I stuck with therapy. Then slowly it became apparent I was better than I was a year before. The relief of feeling so much better kept me going. Eventually, it helped me to forge a healthier relationship with my family.

When I entered therapy, I thought there was something wrong with me. It was a relief to know things that happened to me weren't all my fault, and that they had shaped me the way I am. When I saw more clearly what my father was like, I accepted him as he was. Bringing the family secrets out in the open helped me to feel free.

Kathy still had more work to do to recover and heal when a new man came into her life and taught her some vital lessons—how to become stronger and more independent, and how to respect herself. Rick, nine years her senior, was a doctor Kathy worked with in the hospital oncology unit where she was a nurse.

I started dating Rick about six years into my recovery. During my relationship with Rick, I was able to work on a lot of issues I had with my father. Rick reminded me a lot of Dad. No big surprise there. Like my father, Rick was controlling; it had to be his way, and his way was the only way. When Rick asked me out, I felt flattered. I never thought he would be interested in me. I was attracted to him at first because he liked doing a lot of different things. He was fun to go out with. He enjoyed dining out, going to the opera, eating sushi, traveling to Europe—things I never would have done alone. He opened my eyes to the world. When I started dating Rick, I felt that he was my intellectual superior. Now I see that even though he was worldlier and more experienced, that didn't necessarily mean that I was inferior.

Things went smoothly for about a year, then I started thinking for myself. Initially, I did anything and everything he wanted to do. My schedule revolved around his. Then I started having and expressing opinions. That's when we really got into some arguments. He wasn't very compassionate, understanding, or flexible. Rick said the problems in the relationship were my fault. That was exactly how things had been at home. I realized it wasn't entirely true in either case, and I took my share of responsibility.

Rick and I broke up after three years. I learned so much about myself—that I was a worthwhile person who could stand on her own. I knew I had choices. I wanted to be in a healthier, more nurturing relationship.

Because I learned to stand up for myself with Rick, I am much better at standing up to my father than I ever was. My father can be intimidating, and just being able to stand my ground and tell him he's wrong when he butts into things that aren't his business is validating.

My healing was largely a matter of becoming aware of how things had really been and how things had affected me. Once I was able to see things in an unbiased light, I could let them go. Once I was aware of what had caused my anger and frustration and saw it for what it was, all the anger left me. Now I can get angry and it doesn't consume me, I can just get over it.

Neither one of my parents ever meant to harm anybody. My father is not a good father, but he can be a good friend. I much prefer to be on good terms with him than to cast him out of my life.

Healing Father-Daughter Wounds

Another valuable contribution to healing my father-daughter wound was finding Linda Schierse Leonard's brilliant and compassionate book *The Wounded Woman: Healing the Father-Daughter Relationship*. I discovered it in my favorite bookstore in Berkeley, California, three years ago when I was interviewing singles and experts for *Celebrating Single*. Leonard's words soothed me; I no longer felt that I was alone, that I was the only woman who needed to heal those invisible father-daughter wounds.

As I skimmed the back cover of the book, I drank in Leonard's words like a fine merlot: "*The Wounded Woman* shows that by understanding the father-daughter wound and working to transform it psychologically, it is possible to achieve a fruitful, caring relationship between men and women, between fathers and daughters—a relationship that honors both the mutuality and the uniqueness of the sexes." I felt hopeful about healing the rift with my father and pursuing a healthy romantic relationship. Standing alone in the basement of that small secondhand bookstore, I cheered out loud. It was time to stop blaming the past—my father and myself—and celebrate the present. As Leonard said in her book, "I believe the real task for women's transformation . . . is to discover for themselves who they are."

This magical book led me to Haight-Ashbury, where I spoke with Dr. Leonard's colleague, Jungian analyst Dr. Gloria Gregg, a single baby boomer who spent several decades healing her own father–daughter wounds. Dr. Gregg's double-edged father–daughter relationship echoed into her adulthood, both in her private practice and her personal history with men.

Q: *Describe your work with women who have father conflicts.*

A: I've done many workshops with women on father–daughter issues and have also helped private patients heal their father wounds. I believe there is an answer for each woman and how she comes to terms with it. Sometimes women whose fathers have died feel helpless to change anything because he's dead. But even then you can make your relationship with your father into one you want or need, because ultimately it is an inner relationship. If a woman's father has died, she need not feel hopeless or helpless about it. A lot depends on what she makes of it and how she processes and comes to terms with it. It's what you carry inside with you that really matters.

I've had patients whose parents live 3,000 miles away, but a parent is so dominating that, psychologically, the parent is sitting right there next to the patient in the room. That person needs to do the inner work of separation in order to have a full separation from her parents. For women and fathers, getting away geographically isn't the answer, though it may help a bit.

It's also important for the patient to remember her inner relationship with her father when she has lost him through death and/or divorce, and she never really knew him in the first place. I see the issue of loss more with fathers and daughters than with mothers and daughters because children usually stay with their mothers following the divorce of their parents. Also, men generally die younger than women, and children tend to lose their fathers first. Many baby boomer women lost their fathers through World War II and Vietnam, through psychological or spiritual death such as alcoholism, post-traumatic stress disorder, and depression, or other reactions to the trauma of war including the impact of physical disabilities.

Women have to access feelings that have been split off, such as anger or sadness. Women need to get into those emotions they're not conscious of. If they are angry, they may not be in touch with the pain of the loss or abandonment of their fathers. There's also sadness when a woman has lost a good father or has never had a good father and the potential of a good relationship has been lost. With sexual abuse, there's a tremendous loss of innocence, loss of a healthy connection to a male figure. That's tragic.

Q: *How did your own father's wounds affect your life, both personally and professionally?*

A: As the result of my own family and father wounds, I did nothing intellectual with my life for 15 years or so. I stayed far away from any academic or professional setting. When I went into therapy, it was clear to both my first and second therapist that I had a calling as a therapist. But I wasn't in a position to answer that call. Although I'd had a lot of experience in psychology as a non-professional, leading human potential and women's groups, I had to do a lot of deep work before I could become a licensed therapist. At 34 or 35, I was ready. I started a master's program in counseling and did well. Then I started a practice and a doctoral program, had internships and patients, and completed a dissertation.

My own father was manic-depressive. He had been a sports writer. As I got older he was progressively in and out of hospitals. When I was 11, my parents divorced. Mom remarried when I was 12. I was in my twenties when my father died. My stepfather had serious losses in World War II and as a result of that and his own personality, developed a serious problem with alcohol. There was a lot of violence and emotional abuse in my family as a result of that. I had two father figures who were powerful intellectually, very charming, and were unconventional. For me to become a therapist was both a calling and a challenge. My own father was negative about therapists and my mother and stepfather were very threatened by them.

Q: *How did your father and stepfather shape your emotional development and your views on marriage?*

A: Their effects on me were profound. Although I'm middle-aged and I have chosen not to marry, I am still open to that possibility. One never knows what life will bring.

I've had many relationships. There is a part of me that wouldn't let any man have any power over me. My mom was trapped, but she had choices. Part of me never wanted to allow myself the vulnerability and powerlessness that I've witnessed in my mother's marriages to her husbands. I'm aware that I don't have to repeat her pattern.

There are times when I wonder if the lack of a life partner is a failure for me at this time in my life—but I haven't given up on it yet. I've had unusual relationships with men.

I have never felt the need to have a conventional structure in my romantic relationships with men; however, I have been blessed with some rich and loving relationships of diverse natures.

Ironically I have felt a certain freedom to create my relationships outside the confines of society. That has been my great strength and also the place that has brought struggle and pain to my life.

How your father relates or related to you can be healing or hurtful. Both of my fathers drank. Needless to say, I was attracted to men who drank. I was attracted to wounded men and tried to heal them. Professionally, I made major changes in my life and have been successful with that. On a personal level, the anger I felt still surfaces, but the generic anger has dissipated a lot. I cleared out a lot of the angry feelings so the feelings of love could flourish again.

Although I was in my twenties when my father died, I was so young emotionally. I wish I could have known him. He was a man of amazing gifts, talents, and possibilities. I was very wounded, but I had certain gifts and abilities, too. But I had to understand myself before I could help others.

Q: *What is the process of healing the father-daughter wounds?*

A: Either women are drawn to men like their fathers, or they project their father wounds onto the men they become involved with. Identify the patterns that become obvious after you've looked at your relationship with your father. Even if your father is deceased, you can deal with him. In dreams, your father can speak to you and you to him. A woman I worked with in one of my father-daughter groups started having dreams about her father who had died before she was born. There was dialogue, and some kind of symbolic healing went on in those dreams.

The meaning of the "good father" is within us all. We have the capacity to develop "father-like" qualities such as learning how to protect and provide for ourselves and going out into the world. Often women with poor father relationships don't know how to do this.

I think another really important piece of the process is separating one's identity from one's internalized "negative father." So often I see women carrying their father's thoughts, values, personality. It's as though you have to have an exorcism to realize this is *your* life you are living, no one else's.

I've also worked with women whose fathers were very intrusive about their daughter's appearance and, for example, made them get on the scale every week as teens or showed a preoccupation with how their daughters looked while minimizing their other qualities. This is devastating to the daughter's self-image. For a father, a daughter is himself in feminine form, especially if the daughter looks like him. A father can instill in the daughter all his images and thoughts about what a woman should be, especially if the daughter's relationship with her mother or the father's relationship with his wife isn't healthy. If there's an overinvestment in the father-daughter relationship, the father can almost psychologically own the daughter. I've seen that many times. It's very destructive. She's like a psychological prisoner.

Q: *With a father like this, what might be some of the daughter's patterns in seeking a mate?*

A: No one can live up to the father. The boyfriends are never good enough in the father's or daughter's eyes. The daughter becomes too critical or picky, or she goes along with the father's views and does not choose a man because the father disapproves.

Women can also pick men who are no threat to the father. Another thing I've seen is that a woman will pick the opposite of her father. If the father is wild and creative, fun but irresponsible, she chooses someone very safe. But she finds with time that there's not much juice in the relationship. This can be true especially with women who have alcoholic fathers. Although her husband would never play around or drink, it is possible she will find the relationship or partner boring.

Q: *How can a woman benefit from understanding her relationship with her father?*

A: For me, I had to learn to allow the "positive father." One problem you might see as a result of divorce is that the father becomes the enemy. What does that mean for the woman who is emotionally like her father? Or intellectually like her father in terms of interests? She's afraid to be like him because he's such a taboo in the mother's household.

An adult woman must realize that she is her own person. I think fathers can be really intimidating in ways mothers can't be. To be your own person in the face of a father is a real struggle.

Often women fulfill their own potential through the men in their lives rather than through their own efforts.

As a result of my natural father's influence and my own inclination, I was early drawn to men who were well-educated and bright. They were living out my unfulfilled potential. I had to learn to achieve for myself. Otherwise there's a lot of envy, resentment, and unfulfillment.

Q: *How can a woman heal the father wound and her relationships with men?*

A: By claiming for herself many of the attributes she projects onto the man. For instance, the woman who serves as a man's muse might be better off developing her own creativity. If you find you're continually being drawn to creative men and your relationships fail, it's time to look at your own potential for creativity. You yourself may be the source of creativity, and you may not need to look to another. It's claiming your powers for yourself.

A woman can also heal by the love of a good man. Despite the father wounds, one can find a good man and heal through that relationship. He can be a spiritual leader, friend, therapist, or mate. We're not just products of our relationship with our fathers. There are ways of getting positive masculine relationships in many forms. Many women are healed by a partner or therapist—or by their sons. There are other kinds of intense relationships we can create for ourselves. Many women have had healthy relationships with male figures who have made a profound difference.

If you don't or didn't have many positive male role models in your life, it's important not to retreat because of bad experiences. You can't let it poison you or leave an enduring mark.

Like a detective, I had to put the jigsaw pieces of my puzzling life together. I gathered clues as to why my relationships didn't work. For me that meant exploring my relationships with my parents and how they influenced my choice of men. After I accomplished that, I felt at peace with myself and with my past. Now I no longer dwell on my formative years; the present is too exciting. I believe a healthy relationship is right around the corner.

Clearing away the cobwebs of your past is a vital step in learning to celebrate single. With counseling and reading, you can do this, too. If journaling, writing poetry, and reading books on this subject have not helped you work through your father-daughter relationship, ask friends and family members to refer you to a therapist. It may help to interview at least three therapists to see which one you would feel most comfortable with.

I'll leave you with a thought from my friend Jane Hughes: "We can choose at any point in our lives to go forward and not have our experiences be our future or our present. Choosing to live in the past is the only way for these earlier experiences to have a toxic influence in our lives. I found it was helpful to tell my story, but I don't identify with it anymore."

Introspection: Questions for You to Consider:

For women: How has your relationship with your father shaped your relationship(s) with men?

If your father had a negative influence on your relationships, how have you worked through these issues?

7

Mothers and Sons

FAMILY HEIRLOOM

From a troubled soul
he suckles soured milk—
his formula for love.

—JOAN

"Whatever unfinished business we have with our family of origin, to whatever degree that family may have been dysfunctional or may have harmed us, then we're going to project that unfinished business, those unhealed conflicts, onto other people—onto our closer relationships."

—CHARLES WHITFIELD, M.D.

JOAN: After interviewing the men for this chapter, I feel strongly that not only is a man's relationship with his mother important in influencing his choice of women, but his relationship with his father is equally so. In order to have a healthy relationship, a man needs to look at his family of origin. He needs to understand what kind of relationship his parents had with each other and how his relationship with each parent affected him. Of course the same is true for a woman.

MARC: I agree with you. And I must say that you have a genius for finding people who have very painful stories.

JOAN: You're going to have another painful story in a minute. But the issue is not just about the opposite sex child-parent relationship. A person's relationship with each parent affects a woman or man's choice of mate.

MARC: In looking at the woman's side, I'd say that she faces a double whammy. Not only does she not know what came before in this man's life in terms of romantic relationships with women, but she also doesn't know how he's filtering his interaction with her through his sieve of memories about his mother.

JOAN: That's why a woman wants to know early in a relationship what her partner's relationship with his mother is like. Many women want to protect themselves from repeating negative patterns with men.

MARC: I appreciate the fact that they want to learn about a man's relationship with his mother early on, but does the questioning have to begin two minutes after they sit down for dinner on their first date? A man wants to be comfortable about telling personal things to a woman. He doesn't want to feel like there's an ultimatum: "Talk or I walk." The man and woman need to figure out if they even want to see each other again, much less exchange intimacies. Let them each sense whether they even want to be in each other's company a second time before spilling their hearts out onto the clean tablecloth.

JOAN: I said early in a relationship, not on a first date. When do you think it's appropriate to talk about one's parents?

MARC: Not until at least the second or third date. I'm willing to say that by the third date, she should feel comfortable enough to ask. Depending on how well the first date went, even asking on the second date might be OK.

JOAN: Certainly before they decide to get involved sexually.

MARC: Absolutely! If they're going to become that intimate, they might as well know about each other's parents.

When Doree Lynn, Ph.D., Washington, D.C. therapist and author of *Getting Sane Without Going Crazy*, was asked to comment about the mother-son relationship, she quipped, "It goes back to that saying that men either marry their mothers or spend the rest of their lives trying to turn their wives into their mothers, or they spend the rest of their lives afraid that their wives will turn into their mothers."

According to Dr. Lynn, there are typically two categories of men:

There are those men who adore their mothers. They think their mothers walk on water, never do anything wrong, and no one measures up to them. Then there are those who can't get away from their mothers fast enough, because they are intrusive and controlling.

You can't really separate a man's relationship with his mother from his relationship with his parents. What often happens in a marriage is when a mother is not getting her emotional and/or sexual needs met by her husband, she will turn to her son and make him the object of her affection. When a couple's relationship isn't fulfilling or there are problems in the marriage, such as the husband works too much, the wife may turn to her children for her emotional needs. This behavior adds to the division between the husband and wife and disrupts the family even more, because the husband becomes jealous and takes it out on the son.

It's the father's responsibility to call his wife back into the relationship. If he doesn't, the couple loses the foundation of what marriage is about, and the marriage becomes problematic. The mother is drawn to the son and there is an unconscious rivalry between the son and the father. Men who are good fathers and take on their parenting role, intercept what could become a negative relationship. For example, the father takes his son out for Little League, soccer, or other activities, and he becomes a positive role model. This alleviates the pressure of the mother and son—the potential negative bond—because he's being an appropriate parent. If the father doesn't take an active, positive role in the son's life, his relationship with his wife and son becomes troubled. The son knows he's displacing his father. He either accepts his mother or becomes a rebellious kid, running away from this mother because he's scared. It's like the old Greek tragedies. The most positive mother-son relationship develops when there is a positive male figure.

When the son has a "smother mother," he'll most probably develop in one of two ways: either he'll be afraid of commitment, or he'll look for someone who does everything for him, treats him like a child, including all of the emotional stuff and caretaking. In this convoluted situation, he gets angry if the woman has needs as well.

Women want to know about a guy's relationship with his mother, what he really thinks about his parents, divorced or not, and what his vision of a woman's role is or isn't. There are a lot of runaway lovers, men who look like they'll be great catches, and then they run when intimacy shows. Secretly, these men may think they are breaking their bond with their mother in accepting another woman, or they are feeling they'll be engulfed.

When is it appropriate to discuss a date's relationship with his mother? Dr. Lynn says if a woman wants a relationship with a man, she does not start analyzing his family right away.

First you develop a relationship with the person, and relationships take time. They're hard work. If you're in a long-term relationship, you do want to know how he perceives his parents' relationship. He will follow learned patterns from his parents, such as retreating or staying silent if something is bothering him.

If you have a relationship with a man and he backs his mother over you all of the time, you don't have a good basis for a marriage. That doesn't mean you walk away or leave. Talk about it, get help from a therapist to see if you can change it. His job is to be your supporter and partner.

The Journey from Hell

The following true story illustrates the role both parents played in shaping their son's life. It doesn't take a therapist to see why this man couldn't have a healthy relationship with a woman or even a friendship with a man.

Eric's childhood resembled a Charles Dickens novel—except he wasn't an orphan. He was the only child of two living parents. Yet he hungered for a loving and supportive home.

His early memories of Christmas don't include visions of sugarplums dancing in his head; and he doesn't have fond memories of his mother tenderly tucking him into bed. What he does remember is his mother screaming at his father, the sound of glass against the wall, the blood and horror of her attempted suicide when he was only five.

Suffering from mental illness and alcoholism, Eric's mother spent many years at a state mental institution. His father brought women home, but they were too weak and dependent to give Eric the mothering he craved. His father was too bitter and selfish to provide a loving environment for his son. Eric was passed from home to home, staying with a cold aunt or a grandmother with whom he felt no emotional connection.

This is the story of a handsome, 36-year-old real estate developer who looked for happiness outside of himself: in alcohol, an expensive sports car, a house, and a relationship with a glitzy party girl who couldn't love him back. When he felt desperately alone, he sought a therapist, who helped him understand his family of origin and how his relationships with his mother and father molded him into a man who felt undeserving of kindness and love. Eventually Eric, a love addict and recovering alcoholic, learned how to express his emotions, work on changing himself (rather than his parents), and love himself.

My mother had been married before she met my father. Her first husband had hung himself. My parents met in a bar and were married after I was born, even after a priest told my father not to marry my mother.

When I was young, my mother would break and throw stuff or hit my father. He told me she would threaten to kill herself or jump out of a car. Later when I was growing up she threatened to cross in front of a train. When I was five, she attempted suicide—cut up her throat pretty bad—but she survived. Dad started divorce proceedings after that. I stayed at his mom's house. My parents divorced and Dad never remarried.

I was never very close to my father or mother. After their divorce, Dad had a hard time trusting anything or anybody. He was distant, isolated, and didn't have any friends. He was also selfish, cheap, flirtatious, and sarcastic. I remember when I was 12, I played a lot of poker with my friends. My father played with us and took all our money. He wiped us out. He was not a generous or kind person.

I grew up pretty much alone, no brothers and sisters. My cousins are 20 years younger. I described myself as an orphan in my early twenties. I turned to women for affection.

Mostly, I was attracted to girls from nurturing families. Through these women and their families, I got a sense of how it feels to have a normal family life. But inside I felt I wasn't worthy of having someone this nice or this good to me. It was difficult for me to grasp that I was lovable. So I would sabotage the relationship, because in my heart I felt I wasn't good enough. How could they want to be with someone like me? I was like my mother, who felt unlovable and would do something to prove she was unlovable. Girls eventually left me because I proved how unlovable I was.

I never had any good relationships with men. Most men who knew me didn't like me because I was sarcastic and selfish like my father. I would hit on your girlfriend, take money from you in a sneaky way. I cheated in high school and college. I was also a bookie in college and sold drugs for a couple of weeks. I have an electrical engineering degree and I can't wire up a light. The only thing that made me feel good in college was drinking and picking up women.

My dad said, "Make as many friends as you can." Of course he wasn't a friendly person. I didn't know how to make friends. I didn't know how to share. My girlfriend, Lisa, had a white sweatshirt from The Gap. I wore it all the time. I liked it so much I went out and bought one like it in three colors. One day she put on one I had bought. I said, "What are you doing?" She was crying and couldn't stop the tears. I just didn't get it. I knew something was wrong, but I didn't know how to change it.

I was always jealous of Lisa's ex-boyfriend. Not because of his relationship with Lisa, but because he had a bunch of guy friends. I was desperate for guy friends. Whenever I tried to connect with a man, it centered around drinking and sports. I liked to drink. I was a bartender. But there was always something missing. I wasn't nice to these guys. I wasn't giving. I was a taker.

Lisa loved me so much, and she was so kind to me. She lived in another state and sent me homemade cards and pictures every day. What a wonderful girl. I regret how I treated her when I look back. I was seeing another girl named Gail at the same time. Gail was on her way to law school. I told Lisa I was seeing someone else, but Gail didn't know about Lisa. I could tell Lisa anything. I was having sex with Lisa but not with Gail. I couldn't decide between the two. I knew I couldn't be myself with Gail, but I just couldn't give her up. Gail was distant. Both Lisa and Gail tried to tell me I'm a good person; they held me up as someone to admire. Lisa's married now. My dad predicted I was going to end up with nothing and he was right.

I was in and out of therapy from the ages of 20 to 27, and in that time I had three or four therapists and was in a couple of groups. That wasn't working out too well. It seemed like I was in a fog.

When I was 25, Lisa's mom suggested I do the Forum [previously EST] and stop dating her daughter. I went. I was attracted to what they were saying. It was the first time someone was being honest and calling a spade a spade. I had gotten mixed messages from Catholic school and church, "Do as I say not as I do."

When I did the second weekend of the Forum, Lisa and her mom drove several hours to meet me on Sunday night when the program ended. They brought me flowers, and I was bawling. I couldn't believe that people cared for people like this.

After taking the Forum I was on top of the world for two or three months. I was confident, something I had never felt before. I had a few acquaintances, but I was always thinking, "What can I get from them?" "What's in it for me?"

I stayed in the Forum for three or four years, while working at a Fortune 500 company, masquerading as a systems engineer. I didn't know what I was doing and didn't care. I was just hiding out there for four years. I was good at cheating or making it look good. I was lonely and frustrated. I couldn't understand how other people could get things done at work. I wasn't willing to do the work. The people I worked for liked my personality and even created a sales position for me for a couple of years. I doubled my income with this job. I bought a house at 25, had a BMW, and I was still miserable. I would go to Happy Hour and be miserable.

After Eric's relationship with Lisa ended, he dated a long-legged model with a Porsche, jet skis, a family boat, and a house at the beach and a ski resort. Eric thought she had the perfect family, but soon discovered his girlfriend, Deb, had an emotionally abusive father and a mother who spent her life shopping.

We had known each other for two weeks, and we went away for a weekend at Deb's parents' ski house. Deb and I were riding on a snowmobile, darting in and out of the woods. We were lying in an open field. Her boyfriend had just broken off their engagement. She starts taking my pants off. I remember feeling, "I don't really want to do that," but I was taught never to turn down sex. I saw this look in her eye, like, "I got you now."

A couple of months later I moved in with her, two roommates, and two cats. I don't really even like cats. I knew I was a selfish person and a jerk, so I thought, "I'll just try to be the best boyfriend I can be." I fed those cats and changed their litter box. When I was with her parents, I had this fantasy I could take over her dad's company. I thought he was the ticket to my success. Sex was great, but we never talked. I smoked pot with her, something I never had done before, and I was still drinking. I hadn't learned any lessons in therapy. But this was the best relationship I had ever been in. And I had to smoke pot even to enjoy being with her. I thought the relationship was going fine. Then I got her into the Forum, and she ran off with one of the group leaders. I was a wreck. She said I had to move out.

I would just cry and cry to this older man, an acquaintance from the Forum. "How am I going to get her back? I don't understand. She won't tell me anything." I had hit rock bottom. This man put me in touch with a therapist and got me an appointment with her the next day, even though she didn't have any appointments available for two weeks. She was really nice and different from any other therapist I'd seen.

She asked me if I drank. I said, "Not really." She said, "How much did you have the last time you drank?" I said, "Ten vodka tonics and some beer. But that was an isolated incident. I don't drink like that every day." She suggested that I try to stop drinking for 30 days. I said, "I'll do that if you see me three times a week."

I didn't really miss the alcohol. It wasn't hard to stop drinking. The therapist was really gentle; she knew what to say, what questions to ask. She looked at me and said, "You really don't have a life." It was a relief that someone had finally said that to me. I knew it all along. I would say, "I just don't feel right, confident, comfortable. I feel unhappy." People would say, "You're good-looking, you have a house, you're personable—there's nothing wrong with you." Then I'd feel worse. I felt bad that I felt bad. Here I'm supposed to be grateful, and I'm miserable. She asked me about my family history and my relationship with my mother.

I didn't really know my mother. She was institutionalized when I was five. She never communicated with me because she's not capable of communicating. It's like she was dead.

I always wanted someone to hold me or scratch my back or encourage me or fix me something to eat or tuck me in. I never had any of those things.

I chose Lisa because she was the opposite of my mother—nurturing, generous, friendly, vivacious. And I didn't have the skills to deal with that. It was too painful to let somebody love me. I cried when someone did something nice for me or tried to love me.

Mom just blamed everybody. "Your father and grandmother are no good. You're a bad son." She'd manipulate me, "If you loved me you'd do this." Even when she was sober, she'd call me after midnight. I had to say, "If you're going to continue to talk about other people, I'm going to hang up." Then I'd say, "I'm hanging up" and do it. She'd start again. I'd hang up again. Finally I got Call Block and didn't take her calls for three or four months. She called me from a phone booth and I explained, "I asked you not to call me during those hours and talk about other people, so I got Call Block." From then on she's been respectful. She's very considerate now of me wanting to go to bed.

My mom looks like a bag lady. She lived on the street, drank a case of beer a day, drank five pots of coffee. She had an eating disorder. Insomnia kept her up all night. She has a scratchy voice from when she cut herself in the throat. Couldn't hold a job. She would call me late at night and always be complaining about her mother and brother and how everyone did her in. She was a victim to the max. My father said, "She's not going to change." I would say, "I've got to try."

In therapy, Eric worked on changing himself instead. His therapist put him in touch with a couple of men in her groups. The men would get together every week at someone's house to play cards. Eric also participated in therapy weekends, where 25 men and women would get together at a local hotel and participate in role-playing exercises. Through role-playing, Eric was finally able to face his emotional demons and move on with his life.

My therapist said, "You really won't be able to be with a woman until you can be with other men." My fear was that I would get married one day and wouldn't have a best man or anyone to invite. I couldn't sustain a relationship with a guy for more than a few months.

I started hanging out with men from therapy. I hated going to their card game. There was no alcohol. No one was paying attention to me. I didn't know any of these guys; I didn't know how to play spades. They knew each other already. I thought, "This sucks." Then we went on a therapy weekend. I didn't know what to expect. I had been in therapy with this therapist for only a month.

I go in and they're doing role-playing, experiential therapy. The therapist got me up on the stage with a girl who even looked like Deb. The group asked why Deb left me. I said, "Maybe I'm boring, not fun, selfish." The therapist had her say, "I'm leaving you. My parents don't like you. I'm going away with Geoffrey."

They coached me: "Tell her you'll try harder, don't leave." They told her to turn around and walk away. They said to me, "Tell her how much you want her." She says, "You're nothing." Next thing I know, I'm screaming, "Don't leave me." Next thing I know, I'm curled in a ball, crying and crying. Then six guys pick me up and rock me. There's music in the background. It was nice. They laid me down and patted my head.

My therapist asked, "How does it feel to have all these guys supporting you?" I said, "It feels nice." We did more of that role-playing, and it was the beginning of the healing for me.

The older man I met at the Forum let me stay on his couch. He didn't even like me. He was in AA. I started going to AA. It wasn't at all what I thought. I was also in group therapy with 15 people. They would tell me I'm a needy person, always needing and wanting attention, not able to accept or give love. I had nothing to give.

The therapist said I was a sex and love addict, and to heal, I would have to stay away from women. I would have to get rid of all the women I was dating and past girlfriends. I couldn't even flirt with a woman. I started hanging out with guys. They said I don't respect women. I said that I love women. I was mad. They said I don't love women. Slowly I began to see I wasn't capable of caring about people. Things started to change. I called people just to see how they were doing. We were hanging out morning, noon, and night. I didn't date a girl for 14 months.

I started being a nicer person. I was going to AA or SLAA (Sex and Love Addicts Anonymous) meetings every day. I did the 12-Steps; it took me a couple of years to work them. I tried to be more helpful wherever I was. I'd give someone a ride, send someone a card, clean off the toilet seat. I tried to do the right thing and not think of myself all the time. The hurt had stopped. Then I tried to work on my relationship with my parents. I told my father about relationship addiction. He met my therapist and he went to therapy with me. My father is much more generous and friendly now.

Now I'm helping a guy who's getting separated from his wife, and another guy, a heavy drinker and drug addict who'd gotten a federal indictment. I call him every day and see how he's doing. I went over his house during Christmas so he wouldn't drink around his family. People in my group told me to pray for God to send people into my life that I can help. AA meetings help keep me in touch with what's important to me.

Five years ago, I felt desperate, in pain, like I needed someone to take care of me. I wouldn't ever have thought I could feel this good about myself. I never thought I could give freely of myself; I never thought I could not be selfish or stop drinking. Today I feel like I'm a decent person. I have good friendships, and I'm able to do things for people without expecting anything in return. I feel like I'm part of the human race.

The Seduction of George

Everett Siegel, M.D., assistant professor of psychiatry at The Johns Hopkins University School of Medicine, tells the story of "George,"★ a man in his early forties who came to him for help in recognizing the patterns in his relationships with women, and over time, in resolving a love-hate relationship with his mother.

George wanted to become involved in a long-term relationship that might lead to marriage. He had no trouble finding dates, but was still looking for somebody suitable. Yet when he looked among his friends, colleagues, or guests at a party, he would inevitably pick the woman who was the coolest, the most teasing to him.

One of two things would happen. He would date a nice, smart, and—to him—"settled" woman, but he would find the relationship boring. He would fear being trapped or procrastinate about commitments and would brutally not return phone calls. In fact he was teasing the woman.

The opposite pattern emerged when he would meet a woman he found pretty, and she would show him some interest. They would flirt and go out, and then she would reject him in subtle ways. Then it was pretty clear she didn't want to date him. Although he was usually exquisitely aware of social cues, he would somehow be blind to

★The identity of Dr. Siegel's patient has been significantly disguised and his case combined with those of other patients.

her messages. He kept coming back for more and more rejections, would get angrier and angrier, and then come back once again. In this whole process he ended up feeling terrible about himself.

In a crowd of women he'd be drawn to the most aloof woman, someone to repeat this pattern with. As we talked, more about his background emerged. His mother used to be very seductive. She'd say how handsome he was and how special he was. At other times, and for no apparent reason, his mother used to tease him, call him names, and mock him. Several times she pushed him. He felt guilty, believing that he egged her on. It became clear to him that he was re-enacting his relationship with his mother with other women. He grew up swearing off any women who reminded him of his mother. But at times he identified with his mother, behaved like his mother, teasing and bating women.

His conscious intention was to find someone he loved and have a good relationship. Contrary to this conscious wish, his unconscious wishes were to repeat the love and hate relationship he had with his mother. He made the people he dated fit these images of his mother. He split them off into categories: the exciting woman who teased him and the boring, stable woman. By being aware of these patterns he's able to disengage from this habit, so he can see both sides in the same woman.

The repressive force for this patient was the guilt he felt about his behavior when he teased women. When he was the one being teased, he felt ashamed of being rejected, and both anxious and guilty because of his anger and rage. All these forces and feelings kept him from seeing the pattern clearly in his current life and exploring the past in a meaningful way. After we discussed the repressive forces, and worked through some of the anxiety and guilt, his links to the past emerged naturally. He was able to find a woman both exciting and stable, who didn't tease him, and when they argued, they could still talk together.

Through his dreams he might have seen the intense anger he feared. People have secret lives they deal with at night. He was normally polite, on the meek side, but at night he would dream he was very powerful, a killer. Those feelings are a part of him, and he had to experience them fully and live through them in some ways before he could understand the pattern and work it out. After he was able to own more of what was inside of him, he was able to see more of the pattern.

He thought he was stuck; either he would be with a woman who mocked him or a woman he thought was boring. But as time went on, he reached a new synthesis—a woman he was interested in, although he was anxious about dating her, was neither. She was stable, not aloof or erratic, but she was not boring. It was blended together, she was a whole person.

Dr. Siegel believes people can make a conscious choice to change the destructive patterns that sabotage their relationships. But he admits it's a slow process. "It takes a lot of work to be able to finally say, 'Okay, today I'm going to choose a different person.'"

Dr. Siegel advises women not to judge a man too soon, based on his relationship with his mother.

You can have someone describe their past, but really how they live it out with you is the important criteria. Someone could have had an awful past and be great to you. Describing something in one's past is very different from how it actually felt. You can describe from memory how to ride a bike. That doesn't capture how I do it, how it feels. You can describe a relationship in all honesty. That may not be how it's lived out in your mind. You don't know it necessarily. How a woman feels treated over time is more important than answers to a list of questions.

When a woman comes to a first date with a list of personal questions, Dr. Siegel explains, it reveals a lot about her anxiety, perhaps for good reasons. He suggests she ask herself the following questions instead:

What are the models you have for a healthy relationship? If you don't have a positive relationship with your father, how about with your women friends? Are those reciprocal relationships? Draw from the healthy relationships you have in your life now. Look for someone able to empathize with you, engage in dialogue, talk about his feelings, someone who's interested in your stories and who can express a range of feelings. Can the man talk about his dependencies and how much he needs you? Look for somebody who can talk about and name a whole palette of different feelings. Is he comfortable with anger, pain, dependency? Look for a relationship that's reciprocal and a man who can think about what *you're* thinking.

Couselor Jane Hughes puts it this way, "When I find a man that I have as much fun with as I do with my women friends, and who makes me feel as good about myself when I'm with him as they do, then I'll know he's the right guy for me."

Pursuit and Panic

Strongly influenced by author Steven Carter's work, Carl Robbins, M.S., a licensed professional counselor and a specialist in treating anxiety disorders in Baltimore, Maryland, says, "In any intimate relationship, there's a universal conflict between the need for separateness and the need for connection. How one navigates that or tries to integrate those polar opposites is affected substantially by a man's relationship with his mother."

> There's some tension of opposites everyone experiences. When someone has had an ambivalent or conflicted relationship with his mother, the tension and conflict tend to be exaggerated. He's either completely infatuated and wants to spend all of his time with his beloved or he feels trapped or smothered, "I have to get out of here."
>
> The anxiety and longing that come up during separation in a relationship can reawaken old feelings of abandonment and emotional or physical distance with the mother. In the same way, the feelings of panic and feeling trapped may be related to old experiences with an intrusive or overbearing mother.

In his work as an anxiety specialist, Robbins often sees a pattern of pursuit and panic in the initial stages of his male clients' relationships with women.

> Often people experience a mixture of pursuit and fleeing. This is confusing to women. "He had to talk to me every night, and then I don't hear from him for two weeks."
>
> There's an obsessive, desperate, or intense moving toward the woman, and then suddenly with the same speed, there's a panic about being trapped, and there's this parabolic exit from the relationship. This pattern is repeated over again with the same woman as well as with multiple partners.

Robbins believes it's critical for men to recognize that they're following this pattern and to take responsibility for the amount of hurt they create by acting it out. He says, "The next step is to start with a commitment to oneself to stop engaging in the pattern of pursuit and flight."

> Another useful piece of advice to men who engage in this pattern is to understand that, for them, getting close to somebody is scary; it brings up anxiety. Recognize and understand that when you're anxious, you don't have to act it out, you can just experience, tolerate, and understand your anxiety. It's important for these men to make the distinction between feeling anxious and being afraid of being anxious (anxiety sensitivity) and to allow their feelings of anxiety to be there without struggling against them or trying to make them go away.

> One technique or structure that can be helpful to a couple in an exclusive relationship is to set a date, to make a commitment to each other for a prescribed amount of time, say between six weeks and six months. When this is decided, there's no discussion about whether the couple will be in the relationship. They will just be in the relationship. The agreement is, that no matter how dissatisfied or anxious you get, the commitment is to stay together and see what happens.

Like Dr. Siegel, Carl Robbins asks the woman to look at her possible role in this dance of pursuit and fleeing. He suggests the following steps for women to consider:

1. Recognize the pattern(s) in your relationship.
2. Distinguish between your anxiety and his anxiety.
3. Watch your behavior in terms of contributing to this spiral of pursuit and panic.
4. See if the man is willing to own his part in it rather than blame it on you.
5. Take a look at your own ambivalence about commitment and intimacy.
6. Shift away from the idea of a committed relationship as a romantic salvation and see it as a spiritual path or a development opportunity.

Once a woman goes through her own process of self-examination, such as looking at her own relationship with her father, and acknowledges the ways in which she's contributing to the couple's destructive pattern, she may set the stage for the man to do the same—to look at his relationship with his mother.

After getting a handle on her own dynamics, she can help the couple slow down the process of getting close and moving away. In that context the man may be less driven by his compulsive needs. His self-exam would free him from his self-destructive behavior.

The benefit of this self-examination? According to Robbins, "If a man can come to terms with his relationship with his mother, he has the opportunity to develop a mature and satisfying relationship with a real woman."

The Epiphany

Although Frank waged a war of wills with his mother, he discovered she was not the only psychic enemy in his quest for a healthy relationship with a woman. Through therapy, spiritual practice and healing, Frank realized that he was drawn to women who were attractive, personable, unreliable, and emotionally unavailable—like his father.

Growing up in a three-room row house, Frank, the youngest of five children, rebelled against his mother's strict rules. Until he was in his thirties, Frank believed his controlling mother caused his alcoholic, free-spirited father to leave the house when he was four.

> When my parents divorced, it was very confusing in terms of who I was going to be with. My dad was independent and irresponsible; he left my mother with five kids. He came around sporadically. He liked to fish and drink and do whatever he wanted to do. I loved to be with him because it was more fun. Mom made rules and set boundaries. When I was a kid my dad and I fished and hung out. He wasn't supporting us. At home, we were eating sandwiches, and when I went out with him, we'd go out to nice restaurants. My mother was working full-time to support us. There were only sporadic contributions to my family from Dad. She'd have to sue him.

> From the beginning, I banged heads with Mom. She was dealing with five kids and working full-time, trying to keep control. I wanted to do my own thing. I was into sports. She wanted us to follow her orders, play when she told us to play, do our homework. I'm a kid,

and she's trying to run the household like a military outfit. She's in pure survival mode. I was rebellious and was like her ex-husband. She'd make us go to school, go to church, eat at a certain time. I'd say, "Don't tell me what to do. My father lets me do what I want to do when I visit him." His way was much more fun.

I left home at 16. I was doing my own thing: No rules. Going out partying, hanging out with the guys. She paid for my school, but I lived with a friend. He had an apartment. My roommate was 18. All of my siblings left the house at 16. My oldest sister moved in with my grandmother. It was a challenging environment to grow up in. Mom said, "It's my way or the highway." We all chose the highway.

She always paid for my education. It was her thing, to give her kids a college education. Now I'm glad she helped out, otherwise I wouldn't have gone to college. She put us all through school. She'd pitch in enough to get us there, maybe not the whole amount. I wasn't seeing that, or who she was, when I was younger. As I got older, I saw what it took to raise us all. I felt a change in myself. Maybe it was an age thing. I started growing up.

At 28, I was still drinking, having fun, hanging out. I started thinking, "You're doing your own thing, but where are you going to be in life?" Who was I rebelling against at this point? Only me. I settled down a lot and started looking inside for the answers. I did some therapy. It had to do with approaching 30. I was still smoking, drinking, going out a lot. I still wanted life to be like it was when I was 20. It was the beginning of my spiritual journey, of taking responsibility for myself. I started working on a book on singles and looking at getting a master's degree. I did well in college. I considered going to law school, but got into construction so I could have a freer lifestyle. I was self-employed in construction because I didn't like working for other people. I was able to buy a house.

Then I had an epiphany. I had been stuck in a lot of negative patterns back then, and I had stuffed my past, my feelings and thoughts, with drinking, women, and smoking. When I was quiet I heard a different voice. Not "Where's the next party?" but "What's your purpose?" "What are you doing?" "Where are you going to be when you're 40?" I decided to go back to school. From 28 to 30 was a growth period for me, internally, and I've stayed on that path. Life is one big habit. Do my habits help me to grow and be healthy? It's still a daily practice.

Around the time I was 30, I was going out with a girl who would always be late for dates. After three months she didn't know if she wanted to be in the relationship with me. I went to a tarot card reader and asked her how my girlfriend was like my mother. I was very attracted to this girl. The tarot reader said, "You are in a relationship with a girl just like your dad—unavailable, attractive, and not there for you at all." If she had been there for me, I wouldn't have had to look at my dad's issues. When that ended, I chose a girl who was a bartender. She was a drinker. I was not drinking at the time. I was teaching Sunday school.

This time the message was even louder. This girl never showed up. All the times my dad didn't show up came back to me. It brought up a deep, deep sense of sadness. I figured there was no way I could be this sad about a girl who could be so unreliable. I couldn't put it together; what I really wanted was to heal my relationship with my dad. This relationship got me into therapy about my dad.

I chose women who were unavailable like my dad. He was very good-looking and very personable. He could get away with coming back six months later and taking over. He liked people. In terms of raising kids, he wasn't so good. He didn't show up.

I loved him too, and I reached a level of peace about that. I stopped trying to decide which one of my parents was right or wrong. Holding on to any of that just hurts me. He died when I was 16, and I was angry about the times he didn't show up, the times he wasn't there on special occasions.

Mom was my role model for relationships with women. There's a lot I would like to have learned about intimacy, but I didn't get that bond with my mom. It's scary for me, being connected. We lived in chaos when I was growing up. It was a survival household. Mom had to drive one kid here or there, and she didn't have the time or energy. We lived in a three-room row house. Mom slept on a sofa bed. There were two kids per 10' × 10' bedroom.

Seeing a marriage that was so wrong didn't leave me with the feeling that marriage is a pretty neat thing. My parents were pretty miserable. It wasn't a model of two people happy together. I missed that connection. It was familiar to me to not feel connected.

I stayed in communication with my mother, but there was never a real closeness until I went to University of Santa Monica in California, where I got a master's degree in spiritual counseling. It was an intense program and made me do some soul searching. At that time I was 32, and in some ways I still blamed my mother for my dad leaving. The whole experience of him leaving was very painful for me. I had to blame someone. I thought, "She's the reason he's gone. I'm turning into him and she's trying to stop that." The harder she tried, the more I became like him.

Finally, I let go of all that stuff with my mother. She's the same person she's always been, and we really get along well now. I thought my mother was very controlling. I was just as controlling as she was, if not more so. I was doing my own thing. She's saying, "Don't go out"; I am purposely going out and staying out. She can't sleep at night cause I'm 15 and I'm staying out all night.

When I stopped being a victim—blaming her for my childhood and not letting me do things, not sending me to places other kids did because we didn't have money, driving my father away—I could see her perspective. I never saw what I was doing to her by staying out and not calling her. She's the mother, and she wanted my respect. I wouldn't give it to her, just because she wanted it, just to spite her. It was a test of two very strong wills. Neither one of us wanted to give. Now I give. For example, she is very Catholic. I don't really believe in any particular religion. I try to do the right thing. When I visit, she wants to put this Catholic thing on me. Now I listen and don't get into that dialogue. Before that would trigger a fight. "You should be going to church, your life would be better." Religion gives her the strength to sustain her life. Her faith got her through raising five kids. She could have turned to alcohol. Today I'll go to church with her.

If you hate your mother, you hate a part of yourself. That's the person who brought you into this world and raised you. There's a connection to your girlfriend that's not going to develop. Healing your relationship with a parent will drastically affect your other relationships. If you're holding onto all that anger and hate toward your mother, it's almost impossible not to direct those feelings toward the woman you're with. How can you distinguish the anger and hate you have toward your mother and your feelings toward the woman you're with? What you're going to do is find someone like your mom, who's going to bring out that anger. Either you go for someone like your mom or the exact opposite. It may look different, but it will still drive you crazy. It will still bring that part up in you that needs to heal. For example, your mother is very responsible, and you may be attracted to someone irresponsible. Either way you're going to get to that anger issue.

After seven years, Frank, 39, is still with Jill, a woman he met at grad school in California. Although they own separate homes, they are very much a couple. Frank describes her as nurturing, tender, and present, someone he can really talk to. At the time of this interview, although they've discussed marriage, they haven't made any decisions about their future.

When I make a decision on marriage and kids, it will be a conscious decision I want to keep, a commitment. Jill and I are great friends, we can talk about anything and we love and respect each other. It's a mature love, not a needy one.

Marc on Mothers

I don't hate my mother.

My mother doesn't hate me.

I respect my mother enormously for bearing what must have sometimes been the backbreaking load of raising seven children—cooking for us and cleaning up after us, trying to entertain us and to create upstanding and moral children. I love my mom for this and for her sense of humor, lust for travel and adventure, and her instinctively charitable character. And also because she still buys me clothes sometimes.

So I don't think that searching for a bit of my mother in a potential partner is a bad thing. In truth, I haven't always looked for that, as anyone who's read the previous chapters in this book can tell. In those early years after my divorce, I bounced around the singles' scene like an amok cue ball banging off the sides of a pool table. I seemed to have attracted women who were the opposite of my mother. And I certainly wasn't thinking about my mother during my trysts.

Nevertheless, as I settled down and learned how to have a healthy relationship, I must have integrated something of my mother into my subconscious checklist of likes and dislikes regarding potential partners.

Although I'm not looking for a woman to take my mother's place, I know what I respect in a woman. And I certainly would never mistake a partner for my mother, no matter how much I revere my mom. There's a big difference between my partners and my mother. For example, I don't even want to know whether Mom ever wore something from Victoria's Secret.

I'm not excessively attached to my mother. I do call her at least once a week, but she lives eight hours away by car. And although I admire my mother for her role as a housewife, that doesn't mean I expect my partner to cook and clean for me. I do a mean clean every week myself, including vacuuming, scrubbing my bathroom, and washing my own clothes. I also make wicked brownies. (See the Epilogue for the recipe.)

So before women reflexively slam men for wanting a woman like their mother, I'd suggest they take a few moments to reflect on what they may be criticizing. I figure my good relationship with my mother will help me create a more loving relationship with a partner.

I'm just looking for a warm, nurturing, adventurous, charitable woman to share my life with. And so what if I also want her to help me pick out shirts once in a while?

8

Asking for Help

"It's time to get help when you know there's something better but you can't get focused and clear on how to get there. There's a stigma that you are crazy if you go to therapy. This simply isn't true. You're just admitting you need help."

—RHODA POSNER PRUCE,
PSYCHOTHERAPIST

STIGMAS

"You've never been married?"
my date asks with widening eyes.
"I chose not to marry."
I flash a Mona Lisa smile.
"You've got brains and beauty,"
he leans towards me. "Why not?"
His sincerity saps my slick retort:
Insanity runs in my family
and I'm afraid to have children.
Instead I reply,
"It's longer than a tall latte story."
"I have all night," he answers.

I feel like Scheherazade.
But I am not trying to be mysterious
or entertaining.

We are like characters in a foreign film,
speaking lines in words
and thinking truths in subtitles.
How do I tell this handsome stranger
my stories from the dating front:
the insufferable choices I made,
the patterns I repeated,
the instincts I ignored?
My brain's broken tape spits out
Mother's slow Southern lilt,
"You always talk too much."
"Play hard to get."
"Why should he buy the cow
when you give away the milk?"
It's not that it was free, Mom,
it was always the wrong flavor.
Don't worry, I don't give it away now.

How can I tell him about my past
when I don't even know his middle name
or if he voted for Jimmy Carter?
How do I tell him I chose brilliant men
who majored in emotional unavailability?
They loved the arts and other women.
How do I tell him I chose men like Ted,
who criticized me in front of his friends,
and moved in with his best friend's wife
while I thought we were still dating?
How do I reveal the pain of being left
for a younger woman?
How do I say I stayed in relationships too long
when I knew they were over?
Do I tell him I sought
charming scientists like my dad,
for the love I never got from him?
Perhaps I could share the story of Chad,
a man I dated for 10 years.
I could recall,
during one of our brief breakups,
he had an affair.
Then he grew depressed

and we grew closer.
Chad peeled back layers of intimacy
like an onion.
When sheets veiled our bodies,
he said he loved me.
He just forgot to say she gave him herpes.

For years I wore a black dress
and a crown of thorns.
"Enough,"
I begged the air.
"Please, let me learn from joy, not pain."
I booked a cruise for my spiritual journey,
a quest for truth and love.

An ancient sage said, "When you are ready to learn,
your teacher will appear."
Like Sleeping Beauty's prince,
authors, friends, and gentle therapists
awakened me from numbness—
my senses sharp,
my purpose clear,
my passions freed.
Now I find approval from within
and optimism without expectation.
With self-love, my faith in others has returned;
my psyche is repaired.

My date's beeper returns me to reality.
He leaves to use the phone.
In the distance,
he speaks to a striking woman.
I notice his broad shoulders.
He brings me a surprise latte.
"That was my therapist," he apologizes.
My heart tap dances on the table.
An aware man?
"Insufficient data," my brain answers.
Mistaking my pleased shock for disapproval,
he explains,
"I needed help breaking patterns and

learning from joy, not pain."

I reach for his hand across the table.
Screw the rules.

—JOAN

JOAN: I never realized something about that poem until you just read it out loud, Marc. The stigma isn't just attached to a person who's never been married; there's also a stigma attached to someone who seeks therapy.

MARC: Those people who don't seek help don't know what they're missing. It's a whole new world when you get beyond depression—or whatever else drives you to therapy. (Now if we could only get insurance companies to do a better job covering such treatment!)

JOAN: Like many single women I interviewed for *Celebrating Single,* my pattern was being attracted to unavailable men. However, when I stopped sleeping and eating after these relationships ended, I saw a therapist. I discovered part of the problem was an undiagnosed depression. Once she treated the depression, we focused on breaking my dating patterns. And by the way, this poem isn't just about my experiences, it's a compilation of stories from single people I met around the country.

MARC: I like your statement about learning from joy rather than pain. To me it means that first you've got to move beyond pain and know yourself—your faults, weaknesses, strengths and issues, like family of origin issues. Then you're ready to begin a lifelong process of learning through the calm, educated eyes of someone who has a healthy context for interpreting and reacting to the good and bad things life throws your way. You think about those things, weigh them, instead of reacting reflexively to them in the context of pain, anger, and bitterness. If I'd known a decade ago what I know now, the 1990s would have been the new millennium for me.

Marc's Maxim

After hitting the singles scene in my early forties, after stumbling through the smoke and flames of betrayals, lies, broken promises, and dreams, I formulated Marc's Maxim: In the world of single baby boomers, there are two warring armies of hurt people—men and women.

These men and women are struggling to rise to the surface of this maelstrom, hoping to find some peace of mind and a nurturing relationship. Instead, their emotional baggage drags them back down into the fray. At the edges of these armies are single baby boomers who've healed with the help of some form of therapy, the passage of time, and much honest self-examination. Unfortunately, the ranks are continually replenished by new troops facing the same tasks.

I was one of the boomers carrying the extra challenge of clinical depression, and consequently the frustration of not always being emotionally available to my kids. That was a special incentive to ask for help. Somehow, I found the stamina and common sense to get into therapy.

I learned to identify my pattern of being attracted to women who were in an emotional free fall and needed a life preserver more than they needed a relationship. Sometimes I didn't see—or I ignored—the signals that a particular woman just wasn't a wise choice for me. And sometimes it was simply a case of the emotionally blind leading the emotionally blind.

Through no form of magic, I worked on healing and learning how to have a healthy relationship. Now with the battles behind me, I'm enjoying the present as a happier single baby boomer.

The Journey to Personal Growth

Whether you need advice about stumbling blocks to dating or you suspect you may have a more serious problem in finding or maintaining a relationship, psychotherapy can be very helpful. It could even save your life or the life of someone you love.

Anne Stoline, M.D., a psychiatrist affiliated with the Center for Holistic Healing in Bel Air, Maryland, talked with *Celebrating Single* about stumbling blocks in relationships, the benefits of therapy, and the signs and treatment of clinical depression.

Q: *How might single people benefit from therapy?*
A: If a person wants to be in a relationship and has had opportunities that haven't worked out, a series of dialogues with a therapist may help a single person identify his or her personal stumbling blocks, understand the root causes of those blocks, and explore strategies to overcome them.

Relationship stumbling blocks can occur at any stage of dating—from trouble meeting people, to maintaining stability in an established relationship, to reaching mutual commitment. Single people needing guidance to answer the following questions would benefit from therapy; the process can help them understand more about themselves and the origin of their limitations.

How do you meet potential relationship prospects?

How do you evaluate a potential date?

Do you have expectations? If so, are they realistic? If not, why not?

Do you stay in a relationship too long because you don't want to be alone?

How do you decide to stay in or get out of a relationship?

Have you noticed a pattern in your past relationships?

Are you the one who is consistently let go, or do you end dating relationships?

Q: *How and when do you know if you need to be in therapy?*

A: Most patients seek out mental health professionals when they are experiencing some distress. The level of distress such as unhappiness, anxiety, frustration, inhibition is a good indicator. That is, the greater the disparity between what you want and what you have, the more therapy may help. Although on the surface this may be difficult to distinguish, it's important to make a distinction here between a person who needs therapy to explore patterns and stumbling blocks in dating, and a person whose relationship difficulties stem from an underlying, untreated depression.

The key symptoms of depression include a pervasive sense of sadness for a period of two weeks or longer; disturbances in sleep, appetite and energy; recurring thoughts of suicide; impaired self-esteem and/or self-confidence; a loss of interest and pleasure in usual activities; and loss of sex drive.

A person with these symptoms needs to be evaluated by a doctor. Depression, like other diseases (diabetes, high blood pressure) is treatable. In most cases, depression is responsive to psychotherapy and medication. There has been a tremendous increase in the number and variety of medications for depression which are safe and well-tolerated. Sometimes psychotherapy or counseling alone is effective.

A condition like undiagnosed depression can sabotage a person's success in finding and maintaining a relationship. It goes back to that classic chicken and egg question: am I depressed because I'm not in a relationship or am I not in a relationship because I'm depressed? Sorting out and understanding this puzzle with professional help can be critical to effective change. The value of such personal growth is priceless.

Almost everyone wants the magical secret to finding true love and happiness in a relationship. Although there is no magic formula, asking yourself the following questions and listening to the answers before committing to a serious relationship may change your life.

Why am I contemplating involvement with this person?

How do I feel when I'm with this person?

How do I feel when I'm not with this person?

Are there things I would like to change about this person? (This can be a red flag for dysfunction. People don't change and it's seductive to think they will. Love does not conquer all.)

Are we headed in the same direction in life? Are our goals compatible?

Do we both want marriage, children?

Are our priorities and interests the same? (You don't have to share all the same hobbies to have a good relationship, but something needs to keep you under the same roof—it could even be your commitment to making your marriage work.)

Go West, Young Dog

This is a story about Kurt, a man with great courage, who turned to a therapist for help because he didn't like the competitive, hard-edged man he had become. Kurt says therapy helped him become aware of his spiritual side and understand how his childhood relationship with his parents, and their relationship with each other, influenced his choice of partners as an adult.

I began my spiritual search in 1989 when I got sick with mercury poisoning. Getting sick definitely served me well. I wasn't living a bad life, but I was intense; I knew I had to change that and become more laid-back. I was the typical jock who had to win at all costs, except cheating. But I was a bad loser.

Then I got sick. I sold my business, bought an RV, and decided to go West for five months. I took off with my dog, a Great Dane I found in an alley. She's been there from the beginning. Right before we left, my neighbor threw a scrapbook journal with pockets for photos into my RV. I wrote in the journal every day. After a few months, I thought, "Wow, this journal is boring as hell." Then I added photos of the dog and redid it, telling the whole story from a dog's perspective: what a dog thinks of America.

After this trip I got into therapy—the best and worst thing I ever did. I was finally able to become the Kurt I always wanted to be. But with that growth came a lot of pain. I had to reopen the wounds from my childhood. My therapist helped me see that my parents were not happy in themselves or in their marriage. They have been fighting since I was born. My mother blames my father for everything, and it's my father's fault for letting her do that. My parents have a terrible marriage. I took in my surroundings and learned from them; it helped me to figure out the kind of relationships I *don't* want.

Now I see they did the best they could. And they did teach us right from wrong. My two brothers and I never got into trouble. But when it came to relationships with girls, that's where what I brought from childhood came up short.

I was good at being controlling. I always wanted my girlfriends to be with me at all times. There were never threats, yelling, or screaming; my relationships were just too intense. They were high-maintenance relationships. Eventually the woman would leave me, or I would leave her. At the time, I felt disappointed at not being able to settle down. But with all things said and done, I'm glad I didn't get married then; I would definitely be in the divorce category.

Like a lot of men in my generation, I had trouble at first learning to show my feelings. When we were boys, we were taught to be cut off emotionally. When I was six or seven, when I was bad, my parents would pack me up with an empty suitcase and bring me to the bus stop. One time they even got me out of the car. I was crying frantically. My therapist helped me see that this kind of parenting is worse than physical abuse. It molded me into a very dominant, controlling person.

Through therapy I now know I have a lot more to offer in a relationship. Now I meet new people all the time, have a new challenge in my career. I want to help people. I've learned to accept people just the way they are. I believe you have to accept who you are and what you are, and whoever or whatever is attracted to that is your destiny, is what's supposed to happen.

If I hadn't gotten sick, I would never have sold my business, bought an RV, or found my dog. Now I'm getting offers to write the screenplay of my dog's life. Now I'm a writer-producer. Another thing I did when I got sick was form a group of clowns, musicians, and jugglers that went around to hospitals. I got recognition. I was on television twice, learned leadership skills, and ended up giving someone else my organization. How much better can life get?

Learning to let go of control and learning to accept and love yourself is not something that happens at the snap of your fingers. If you're happy with yourself and grateful for what you have, everything around you will turn to gold. My prescription for happiness is accepting life as it is. The more you try to control, the more energy you're wasting. Letting go is the most important thing you can do in your life. Just say, "It's OK."

Asking for Help

Rhoda Posner Pruce, L.C.S.W-C., a psychotherapist in private practice, offers these thoughts on how to determine when it's time to see a therapist.

It's time to call a therapist when you're spending unreasonable amounts of time wondering if there is something wrong with you, spinning your wheels thinking the same thing over and over again, and friends, colleagues, and family members are tired of hearing about it.

It's time to get help when you know there's something better, but you can't get focused and clear on how to get there. And it's OK to talk to a therapist about what therapy could or couldn't do for you. There's a stigma attached to therapy; people think that you are crazy if you go to therapy. This simply isn't true. You're just admitting you need help.

There is some evidence that some people's problems are not based on family history or events in their lives, but on their brain chemistry. People sometimes think there is something wrong with them, and it may not be something they have control over. Sometimes they need medication to balance the brain chemistry, and then therapy can help them learn the new behaviors they need to overcome some of the effects the untreated illness left behind.

People need to be more concerned with how they personally relate to the therapist—how well they feel the therapist understands them, rather than if the therapist is a psychologist, clinical social worker, et cetera.

Finding the Right Match

What should you look for in a therapist? Charles Whitfield, M.D., author of *Healing the Child Within*, says it's important to find a therapist who is a good match for you, a therapist who has "some openness to let the person go at their own pace and find their own way." He suggests that you question whether the prospective therapist seems locked into only one way of assisting you in recovery.

Does the therapist have humility, is he or she open to other ways of helping you find your own way? Is she or he willing to make a comment instead of always saying, "Why do you ask?" and never answering the question? Is the therapist going to do more than prescribe a drug or two?

If it's not a match—and you really have to have a match in which you can trust the therapist and feel comfortable enough that you can be real with him or her—it's not worth going with that therapist.

Marc on Love and Basketball

Success in therapy doesn't come overnight. You've spent a lifetime creating and/or integrating unhelpful or downright destructive patterns of thinking and behavior. It takes time to sort things out and revise your emotional map.

But then there are those epiphanies you have at the hands of a competent therapist. One of my epiphanies, with my Ernest Hemingwayesque psychiatrist, came after I won a basketball game.

During a discussion with him about my relationships with women, I veered off into a recounting of my triumph in a three-way basketball game. The game, which had the strange name "Ice," required two players to compete against whoever had possession of the ball. So the teams continually changed as this fast-paced game raced toward its conclusion. The end came when someone scored a certain number of points.

I wasn't familiar with the game and followed the lead of the other guys. I guarded the man with the ball, and dribbled and shot around the other guys when I had the ball. The two other guys in this pick-up game were significantly younger than I was. One was significantly taller. I played my heart out, even falling to the floor as I raced for a loose ball—and recovered it.

The game bounced along for about 15 minutes. Then suddenly, the two other guys stopped playing and started walking away. I stood still and said, "Why are we stopping?" The tall one turned his head briefly as he continued walking and said, "You won."

I stood there basking in a wondrous glow, feeling good about myself. Some days later, I proudly told that story to my psychiatrist. Then I raised my index finger and stabbed it gently in the air for emphasis as I said to him, "It's been a long time since a woman made me feel that way."

My psychiatrist looked me in the eye and responded, "Marc, women aren't supposed to make you feel that way; basketball is."

The moral of the story for me was that I needed to learn the way to feel good about myself for who I was and what I could accomplish—whether on the basketball court or in my profession. I shouldn't lay that responsibility on a relationship I simply jumped into for the sake of having one.

That lesson, to play with a sports metaphor, was a slam-dunk revelation I could take home with me.

There are many sources of help for problems that single people face. Dr. Charles Whitfield suggests turning to a Higher Power, a counselor or therapist, a self-help book, or a best friend; going to a 12-Step Program, like AlAnon, AA, or Codependents Anonymous; or writing in a journal.

Not all single baby boomers need therapy. But if you think you have clinical depression and could benefit from professional help, see a psychiatrist. If money is tight or you don't have health insurance, community health clinics offer a sliding-scale fee based on your income.

Remember: asking for help shows courage, not weakness.

To find out more about depression and how to find a qualified therapist in your area, call DRADA (Depression and Related Affective Disorders Association) at the Johns Hopkins Medical Institutions in Baltimore at (410) 955-4647.

Introspection: Questions for You to Consider

How do you meet potential relationship prospects?

How do you evaluate a potential date?

Do you have expectations? If so are they realistic? If not, why not?

Do you stay in a relationship too long because you don't want to be alone?

How do you decide to stay in or get out of a relationship?

Have you noticed a pattern in your past relationships?

Are you the one who is consistently let go, or do you end dating relationships?

Why am I contemplating involvement with this person?

How do I feel when I'm with this person?

How do I feel when I'm not with this person?

Are there things I would like to change about this person?

Are we headed in the same direction in life?

Are our goals compatible?

Do we both want marriage, children?

Are our priorities and interests the same?

Part II

Celebrating Life

9

The Journey to Wholeness

"Being whole is the essence of celebrating single."

—SHANA BENDER, ACUPUNCTURIST

My heart hardened in my youth,
defied the ache of inner truth.

Yet I felt the empty spaces
that I filled with hot embraces.

Now I fill my own dark places
with inner strength and God's graces.

EXCERPT FROM "NEW BEGINNINGS"—JOAN

"The path to love is not a race. It's a lifetime process of discovery."

—JOAN AND MARC

We believe that one of the most important tasks facing many baby boomers today, whether you're in a relationship or not, is to become self-actualized—to know who you are and to accomplish your life's purpose. The experts and singles interviewed for this chapter agree that the search for meaning in life and in love begins within—often with the help of a therapist and the belief in a higher power.

In an interview for *Celebrating Single*, family counselor and author John Sanford of San Diego states, "We avoid the beginning of self-knowledge because it is usually the destruction of the ideas about ourselves that we have carefully cherished all our life. We might have to own up to some negative things about ourselves. Yet often when we hold these negative traits up and accept them, we can let them go much easier."

So how do you begin the journey to healing and wholeness?

Angela Graboys, a rabbi practicing in Columbia, Maryland, suggests taking a moral and spiritual inventory of yourself.

When you go on this spiritual quest, the relationship you're trying to create is not two needy people leaning on each other, but two whole people who can be interdependent as opposed to codependent. The mistake is to look at the time you are single as a waiting period. It's like working all your life and looking forward only to the time you retire. It's important that you feel good about yourself and what you do every day. Nothing in life is a transitional line to the next thing. There's not a great finish line when we get there. Life is a series of experiences rendered holy and sacred, so the pilgrimage is sacred. It's not, "I've got to get this single part over with."

"Our society has more single people than ever before," says Carolyn M. Ball, M.A., author of *Claiming Your Self-Esteem, Blessings in Disguise,* and *Meher Baba's Next Wave.* She suggests we consider what is causing this superabundance of singles.

Single people are struggling because they tend to look to resources outside themselves. People sometimes go through relationship after relationship without being able to feel settled. This is a phenomenon going on in our culture now. That forces a person to say "Why is this happening? Why me? What did I do to make this happen?" The search for the answer is important—the search itself. The process of looking is what brings us into relationship with the Self. Yet, this seeking gradually leads us to the awareness that the answers in our search for love do not come from outside of ourselves, but from within.

Father Joseph Breighner, host of the nationally syndicated radio show "The Country Road" and author of *Stops Along the Country Road,* reminds us of Socrates' wisdom: "The life which is not examined is not worth living." According to Father Joe,

> It's not just an intellectual exam, but an examination from the heart. Where am I looking to complete myself? As long as you look outside, no man or woman will be a perfect or complete person. If I don't love, honor, and cherish myself, I will never love you. I will try to control or manipulate you. I think we share manipulations in the name of love. Very few people are that fully developed that they can want what's best for you.

Carolyn Ball says she is grateful for her failed relationships. Instead of blaming others, Ball realized she needed to take responsibility for her own issues. She recalls her journey to understanding her Self:

> After I went through my second divorce, I thought it was time to create a *real* relationship. When you go from one relationship after another, you say, "Okay, that one didn't work. I'm going to find one that does." Whether you go through three or 30 or 300, you will eventually ask the question, "What am I doing to set this up? And what am I doing to keep the relationship I think I want from happening?"
>
> When it doesn't happen, first we look outside and we want to blame other people. But after a person has had a certain number of relationships or experiences, the common denominator remains your own problems and issues. You are forced to look at the fact that the answers are inside you. I am now finally very grateful for the growth my own failures have given me; now I love myself, and I also am a much more loving person to others.

But what are those things outside people that draw so many of them into destructive or dead-end relationships? Family counselor Judith Burch, M.S.N., of Baltimore, Maryland, has seen countless examples of the quest for those empty values. "Many people have a tendency to go outside to find what's important. They think everything is outside of themselves: money, other people, power, social or corporate climbing. Bigger, better, more. The best way to help people is to help them go inside themselves. We don't take time to get to know ourselves."

Twentieth-century Indian spiritual teacher and yoga master, Paramhansa Yogananda explores the concept of looking within in the following passage from his book *Moments of Truth:*

> People everywhere
> in their quest for
> happiness outside themselves,
> discover in the end
> that they've been seeking it
> in an empty cornucopia,
> and sucking feverishly
> at the rim of a crystal glass
> into which was never poured
> the wine of joy.

YOGANANDA, PARAMHANSA. *Moments of Truth, excerpts from The Rubaiyat of Omar Khayyam Explained,* © J. Donald Walters, Cystal Clarity Publishers, 1995. Nevada City, CA, p. 11.

The Journey into Love

Clearly there's a spiritual side to any journey to self-awareness. Let's take a look at what spirituality and the term Higher Self mean and how these terms relate to your life.

Psychotherapist Dr. Marilyn Mendoza, from New Orleans, Louisiana, defines spirituality as your personal relationship with God, Buddha, spirit, and/or The Higher Self.

It's not about going to church or temple, it's about your belief in a just and kind spirit who wants you to be happy and content, coming to believe that every life has a purpose, and understanding what your purpose is. Finding that helps your sense of self-esteem. Your life is more than this job or this relationship, which nail polish you put on or what you wear. There's a broader perspective than that. A good sense of self-esteem is about being comfortable with who you are, all aspects of yourself, no matter what other people think.

The path to healing and healthy relationships begins within. And while the term "spirituality" may mean different things to different people, the sense is pretty much the same: relating to a higher power and appreciating the vastness of the world and the wonder and glory of being a part of it. Spirituality is about finding your purpose in life—taking the time to stop, take a deep breath and figure out what's important to you.

Author Jalaja Bonheim, Ph.D., a counselor in private practice and a workshop leader based in Berkeley, California, uses the tools of healing—spirituality and counseling—to help her clients find their own paths to inner peace and purpose.

Q: *The concept of "a spiritual journey" in relation to love sounds intriguing, but what do you mean by that?*

A: It's about the journey into love. Many people in our culture have no spiritual path. We are looking for a sense of connection and love in our relationships, which rightfully comes from our connection with spirit. We are trying to make our marriages a substitute for spiritual connection and it doesn't work.

The solution lies in recreating our spirituality, which more and more people are doing today. We are acknowledging a yearning within us for spiritual connection. Whatever form it takes, Christian, Buddhist, et cetera, we are part of a greater whole that has an intrinsic meaningfulness. Strengthening our spirituality, strengthening our communication, acknowledging the value of friendships—all these things help us to put a relationship in its proper perspective.

Q: *This all leads to another concept, "the Self." What is the self and what is self-love?*

A: The 14th-century German mystic Meister Eckhart said, "Just as nut seeds can grow into a nut tree, in the same way, a human being can only grow into the Self that lies innate within them." There is this mystery of each one of us being a manifestation of the divine. In Hindu tradition, we are all cells in the body of God. The Self is that part of us that knows its identity with the divine.

We need to remember that we are born loving ourselves. Self-love is a remembering of something that has been covered up in our socialization. It's already within us. I believe strongly that just as there is a healing mechanism striving to return to wholeness when we are physically hurt, there is also a movement to return to self-love.

I believe in Joseph Campbell's words, "Follow your bliss." I think desire has been maligned in our culture. I believe that when we cut off our desire, we cut off our lifeline to a sense of meaningfulness. It is possible for desire and passion to function as spiritual guides in our lives.

Q: *How can a person find passion in life?*

A: Take that question as a mantra. When we get a glimpse of our true desire, we need to ask ourselves, "Can I find the courage to act on it?" So often we resign ourselves to meaningless lives because we don't have the faith to go after what we want and really get it. We live in a society addicted to speed and filling up every little space. We are terrified of emptiness. Part of what I do in my work with people is create a space that is slow and empty. It is only in that kind of space that we can really discover our true desires.

To listen to the voice of the soul, we need to listen to the spaciousness, to create the spaciousness within which the voice of the soul can be heard. It could be dancing, telling stories, meditating. I developed a kind of work I call Circle Work. The work evolves out of being in the moment and listening to the energy of being in the circle. It's unpredictable. It might lead us into meditation, walks in the woods, telling jokes.

There have been amazing journeys of transformation. I've seen participants coming into a place of authenticity, where what they do—from how they make their living to their relationships—is in alignment with their integrity, with who they really are.

One woman was a corporate lawyer. When she first came, she was very unhappy. Now she's given up her job and is working for environmental causes and has blossomed amazingly. She was in the center of Circle Dancing and she started saying, "I can't do it." She was in despair. A shift happened from "I can't" to "I can." This spirit burst through her. It was one of those little moments of magic. A true transformation occurred. Ever since she has been living from "I can."

Spirituality and Healing

Atlanta-based therapist, Charles Whitfield, M.D., author of *Healing the Child Within*, incorporates spiritual practice into his work and his relationship with his wife, Barbara Harris Whitfield, on a daily basis. He says, "The beginning definition of spirituality is that it has to do with relationships, and the relationships are with Self, Others and a Higher Power."

Q: *At what stage does spirituality become part of someone's healing process?*

A: The first stage is healing the basic physical or primitive psychological problems, such as if a person is alcoholic or has a physical disorder. That's stage one recovery. (Stage zero recovery means no recovery.) Stage two is the deeper trauma healing. Stage three is spirituality.

Just as spirituality includes and supports and nurtures religion and at the same time transcends it, stage three recovery includes, supports, and nurtures stages one and two and at the same time transcends them. Spirituality is a part of stages zero, one, and two. It just gets easier the farther along we get in the healing process. As people reach stage two and move into stage three, they begin to realize, "Now that I know the real me, now I can know the real God better or my real spirituality better."

Q: *How can you tap into your spiritual self?*

A: Spiritual practice. First of all, a good stage one and two full recovery program, then eventually regular spiritual practice. Preferably daily, like daily meditation, prayer, reading of holy books, reading of spiritual books, other kinds of spiritual practices of your choice.

Q: *How does one learn meditation?*

A: Through a meditation teacher, or you can read about it in any number of books. I have a one-and-a-half page description of how to meditate in *A Gift to Myself*. Meditation is easy, it's free. It just takes discipline. The book uses general language that shows the person how to do the healing.

Patty F. Cummings, L.C.S.W-C., founder and director of the Mindfulness-Based Stress Reduction Center of Baltimore, supports Dr. Whitfield's theory of daily spiritual practice. Mindfulness, the technique Cummings uses in her practice, is rooted in Zen Buddhism. She credits Jon Kabat-Zinn, Ph.D., founder and director of the Stress Reduction Clinic at the University of Massachusetts Medical Center, for bringing mindfulness to the Western world and integrating it into a medical model for mind-body healing that is now being embraced by the medical community.

Q: *What is mindfulness meditation?*

A: The practice of mindfulness is moment-to-moment or present-moment awareness. It's an approach to life that enables us to liberate our True Self from the False Self. Then we can be who we truly are. Generally, most of us live in the past and stay with the familiar, what is known to us.

What mindfulness allows us to do is focus our minds in the present moment and to let go of whatever thoughts we've become attached to unknowingly. When we're focused on the present moment, we're watching how our mind works. Instead of getting lost and carried away by our thoughts, we can come back to center and observe them with detachment.

For example, somebody thinks he or she's not good enough to be in a relationship and feels inadequate. But when he practices mindfulness, he becomes aware that these are just thoughts. As he starts observing, the mind corrects that destructive thought. It's probably the hardest thing people can do in their lives. And the payoff is incredible. If you make decisions out of the clarity of that present moment, you will be in a relationship that's healthy. This heightened awareness is very empowering.

Q: *What are some of the other benefits of mindfulness?*

A: As a person practices mindfulness regularly, we see the symptoms of depression lessen. He or she becomes more integrated on all levels—body, mind, and spirit—and learns to self-regulate his or her behaviors. A woman will say, "When I went into a relationship before, I wanted someone to take care of me, to be the breadwinner." Once healed she says, "I'm free to be in a relationship of my choice. I won't let it control me. I'm going to choose out of a different framework, out of what I want."

Many people are in relationships because they feel they need another person to make them happy. They don't feel complete unless they are in a relationship. If that relationship is threatened, they feel they are nothing. Consequently they give their partners power over how they feel. You'll hear, "He or she is my life. I can't go on without them. I don't know who I am without them. I feel empty without them." So they aren't aware of their wholeness. When we practice mindfulness regularly, it helps us open up to who we truly are; it creates an awareness that we are already complete, whole, and happy.

Q: *What is your advice to single baby boomers?*

A: Learn how to be more gentle with yourselves, how to accept who you truly are and to love yourself. This may require brief solution therapy or supportive counseling. Get yourselves out of relationships that are not supportive of your growth and get into a mindful community.

Holes in the Whole Theory?

Many experts would agree it's valuable to work on self-esteem issues before entering a relationship. But how much self-esteem do we really need? Do we need to be whole before we get into a relationship? And if so, just how whole do we need to be?

Judy Zerafa, a national public speaker on self-esteem and author of *Go For It,* says, "The only time when two halves do not make a whole is in relationships. Two wholes make a whole in relationships and two halves make a disaster."

Deborah, 46, a never-married teacher, supports Zerafa's theory.

In relationships we allow ourselves to lose something of who we are. I did that by compromising to make a relationship work, and I forgot who I was. I put on hold a lot of things I wanted to develop about myself. I lost myself. I believe we're all whole people. If we depend on another person to be our other half to make us happy, then when that person leaves, through death or divorce, we're miserable because we depended on that person. I look for someone to enhance my life, to complement my life. If your ultimate goal is to look for another half to make you whole in order to be happy, then that means you cannot be healthy or successful until you have that other half.

Sarah, 50, a twice-divorced marketing specialist, feels confused about how much self-growth is necessary before entering a relationship.

When someone asks me about being a whole person before being in a relationship I think, "Oy. I'm trying to do that desperately because I know that's the right thing to do." That's why deep down I think it's too soon for me to get involved. There needs to be more room in my life for personal growth. If I get that under my belt, that can only add to giving and receiving love. I think that's important, but who the hell wants to do that? Whatever growth or wholeness a person needs, it never ends. So it's not a question of getting to the end, because you never stop growing. You can't close that book and say, "Now I'm going to get married." I don't know how you can control it. If the right man came now, would I say, "Would you call me in a year because I have to grow a little more?"

Psychiatrist Mark Komrad, M.D., of Sheppard Pratt Health System, a psychiatric facility in Baltimore, Maryland, suggests it is not necessary to be healed and whole before launching into a new relationship.

I actually don't think it's necessary to become whole to enter into a relationship. I happen to believe that being in a mature, intimate adult relationship is one of the paths to wholeness. One of our "missions," so to speak, socially, psychologically, biologically, is to be in relationships. This goes all the way back to Sigmund Freud, who, when asked the definition of being mentally healthy, said "The definition is to be able to work and to love effectively." Ultimately, the question the person in a relationship has to ask is "Does this work for me?" And "working for me" does not just necessarily mean, "Am I getting my needs met?" That's actually only half the story. I think the other half of the story is, "How am I doing at recognizing, identifying, and helping my partner with the needs he or she has?"

Neither partner will be perfect and neither can fulfill all of the other's needs. But at the very least we have to know what those needs are; at the very least we have to know what's being asked for.

In some ways, being whole is the optimal way to enter a relationship, Dr. Komrad says. "But I've also seen people who, by virtue of their relationship, are able to experience a level of self-esteem that not only wasn't available before the relationship, but even endures after the relationship ends and is not just a function of the relationship. Relationships are among the most healing experiences that we have as human beings."

Dr. Bonheim of Berkeley agrees with Dr. Komrad. "Wholeness is not a static condition we reach once and for all. There are many layers of wholeness. It's a never-ending journey. So relationships are part of our path of growing into ever deeper areas of wholeness. It's through relationships that we grow into wholeness in many instances. This also means we have to let go of our desire for the perfect relationship. Sylvia Plath said, 'Perfection can't have children.' Perfection can't have marriage or a relationship."

"You need to find ways to make yourself whole regardless of whether you're in a relationship or not," says psychotherapist Marilyn Mendoza, Ph.D., of New Orleans. "You need to work to create some in-depth insights of yourself. Confront your shadows and have a very strong spiritual component, a sense that you're connected to something greater than yourself that's always with you. To have good self-esteem really requires a lot of work."

Dr. Mendoza also suggests that single people look at the old myths they've grown up with. "We buy into the tribal belief that a woman is not complete without a man. A lot of people try to fulfill that belief and not what's right for them. Put aside those myths that don't fit. Really understand yourself and feel good about yourself, regardless of who you are, what you are. It's not about being critical of yourself or others. The best thing you can do is to know yourself. The better you feel about yourself, the better choices you can make. You always have a choice."

The 20th-century Indian mystic Osho sums up the theme of this chapter and of *Celebrating Single*: when you learn to find meaning in your life and to know and fall in love with yourself, life will prepare you for love with another.

"Find ecstasy within yourself. It is not out there. It is your innermost flowering. The one you are looking for is you. You are the traveler and you are the destination. In experiencing the ecstasy of your own being, you have achieved the final goal."

—OSHO © OSHO INTERNATIONAL
FOUNDATION, WWW.OSHO.COM

To Be or Not to Be Whole

During our six-year friendship, Marc and I have exchanged numerous stories about dating and tips about getting along with the opposite sex. We've also had a few healthy disagreements about topics like spirituality, sex, and should you be a whole person before getting into a relationship. Here are Marc's thoughts.

I have a fantasy that there is a vast graveyard containing the psyches of baby boomers who once were unable to maintain a sane relationship because they were just too screwed up. These souls depart the bodies of baby boomers after they reach a certain undefined point of healing from their former relationship traumas, families of origin, and other damaging life events. These old souls, not very merry, depart for eternity to the nether world beneath the unkempt grass of Acme Cemetery.

In place of the old souls are healed, or at least healing, souls that can face the world of dating with some sense of fortitude, rectitude, and all the other "tudes" it takes to avoid falling into relationships with overtly appalling members of the opposite sex out of some sick need for validation, reassurance, or just plain nookie.

I imagine myself walking into that unkempt cemetery of old souls in search of my own old soul as it was during the Dark Ages after my divorce and entry into a singles' world, a time in which I was restarting my career, leaving my daily contact with my children, and beginning an uphill fight against financial insecurity and battered ego.

As I trudge up a small rise in the cemetery and stumble gingerly across a field strewn with yellowing grass, empty beer cans, crumpled cigarette packages, and condoms, I see my name on a crumbling tombstone. I've come back to make peace with my former, very unsuitable self, who drifted cluelessly through my early post-divorce dating years.

I approach and bend slightly to read the tombstone. I squint and look at the words beneath my name, words that make up the epitaph of my former psyche, which for so long plagued me during my attempts at healthy relationships. My epitaph, the terse sum total of who I was to women in those early, dark days, and what I tried to accomplish in my faltering attempts at establishing a long-term relationship, reads: "At least he meant well."

Joan: The Blind Date

It began like most blind dates. The phone call. "Hi. My name is Wayne. My dental hygienist gave me your number." An hour later, he confided, "I need to tell you that these past few months have been rough for me. My wife left me for another man. We'd been married 25 years. I'm doing a lot better now that I'm in therapy." Therapy is good, I thought, but he's not even divorced yet. The red flag alerts sounded in my brain.

We talked more. I found his sense of humor and honesty appealing; we had wonderful phone chemistry. We delighted in one another's words. We made each other laugh. He suggested spending our first date together at a museum. I suggested meeting for coffee. Phone chemistry can outweigh physical attraction.

I thought he was adorable in person, but the chemistry didn't work for him. I let that wound my ego for a little while, but what he said when he walked me to my car stunned me. "You're too healthy for me." I shook his hand, started the engine, and laughed all the way home.

Yes, I feel healthy. I've worked hard to get here. And the man I seek now will have worked through most of his emotional baggage, too. He'll be optimistic and want to share his life and joys with me.

Now I'm clear about who I am and what I want: A man who shares my goal of making a difference. I'm not looking for a perfect mate. Just someone who accepts me as I am and supports my spiritual growth, as I would support his.

Am I completely whole now? No. Will he be? No. But I no longer look to a man to complete me. I am my own knight in shining armor.

Becoming a whole person is a lifelong process. Nurture yourself every day; get to know yourself one pure petal at a time and you will discover the love within. You will fall in love with yourself.

WHOLE

I sheltered soulless warriors in my womb,
their strength restored.
They sucked my power from once ripe breasts.
Yet I preferred the sour taste of shame
to the shadowless silence.

I greeted each stranger with scented oils,
sweet cakes and
champagne baths.
While candles flickered
my soul's lamp died.
I grieved over lost soldiers
and witnessed the death of Self.
From a seed, a fetus slowly blooms
as nature planned, like love.
Now I unfold like a rose,
one pure petal at a time,
my fragrance proud and strong.
My body is a sanctuary,
a stained-glass tree of life,
restoring each branch with renewed passions.
I am my knight in shining armor—
healing my wounds with forgiveness,
protecting my borders from rippling red flags.

I am whole—no more pretense, no charades.

Now he leaves his sword outside
till we have waltzed,
and laughed
and cried.

—JOAN

Marc: On the Road to Whole

Before I was able to learn the lessons life could teach me about healthy relationships, I had to begin my own journey toward wholeness and stop being at war with myself.

After years of emotional disarray, I finally told my psychiatrist that I was "burned out on relationships." Relieved, he sighed and said, "It's about time." Not that he wanted me to be alone. But rather, he wanted me to find happiness in my own personal life, aside from romantic entanglements. I'm no paragon of virtue in that regard. But I have learned some valuable lessons about neglecting the search for wholeness while spending precious time and emotional energy trolling the singles' scene.

For example, I once briefly dated a younger woman I'll call Jody, whose husband had disappeared, leaving her alone with her young daughter. I met Jody at a singles dance club one Saturday night. We went out dancing several times, sometimes staying on the dance floor for a half hour at a time. I loved dancing with her.

There was no sex; we barely kissed. I figured, give it time.

One night after I treated her to a dinner I couldn't afford, and she lit up a cigarette, which I abhorred, she convinced me that we should go to a singles' dance at a local nightclub. I agreed. We arrived at the club and I paid the cover charge for us both. We walked in—I ready to dance, she with something else on her mind.

Jody turned to me and announced that we should each go in search of someone to hook up with. And off she went. I walked around, slightly stunned, for about 20 minutes. Jody and I ran into each other. She hadn't had any luck; me either (almost everyone was clearly younger than I). So I took Jody home.

On the way home, Jody told me she didn't want to go out with me anymore. Seems like I was too tall; she was kind of petite. It didn't work for her. I dropped her off and figured that was that. A couple of months later she called me at work and asked, in a somewhat whining voice, "Whyyyyy haven't you called me?"

I actually took her out once more. Then she apparently met someone else and didn't have time to talk with me on the phone. But why in heaven's name would I have even gone out with her after that singles' dance stunt she pulled on me?

Why indeed?

Probably because my psyche, ego, self-respect—whatever—was on hiatus or just moribund. I surely needed to get healed and get my head on straight. If both Jody and I ended up with each other, then we'd be out of circulation and in a sad relationship hardly based on love or mutual respect. Such relationships aren't illegal or immoral, but they are really a waste of two peoples' potential for a healthy relationship. And they certainly are not the type of relationship I would ever want for myself or my sons.

I've learned that there are no bright ribbons with colorful balloons and a John Philip Sousa march playing in the background when you reach wholeness. It's a gradual journey; it's a melange of maturity, awareness, and some fond and not so fond memories along the way.

Joan: **The Finish Line of Love**

While we're on the subject of becoming a whole person and not rushing to the finish line of love, I thought I'd share my thoughts about finding joy in dating—cherishing the moment, learning something new from a stranger, making a friend, treating another human being with kindness and compassion—even when the person may not be "the one."

Rush, rush, rush. Get involved. Push intimacy. Have sex. Fall in love. Not always in that order. This is Hollywood's portrayal of love. The reason for this fast-paced formulaic writing is that story spinners only have 120 minutes to weave their tale. Unfortunately, well-meaning men and women imitate this larger-than-life art, and in the process, they race to cross the finish line of love.

I predict that in the not-too-distant future, single men and women will drive up to a window to pick out a mate on a menu, like placing an order at McDonald's. This futuristic company, "Match Made in Heaven," will offer the "perfect" mate at the Spiritual Partner Window, with a fully-equipped chemistry car in which the couple can test sexual compatibility. The marriage ceremony, with witness included, will follow at the Eternal Bliss Counter. Heaven's Gate is the last stop, where the newlyweds can pick out their burial plots together. "Match Made in Heaven" will promise fast service, no lines, and an opportunity to appear in a television series.

I'd like to know what happened to "take your time and get to know someone." In *Future Shock*, author Alvin Toffler predicted 30 years ago that as people "move further from their parents, further from the religion of origin, and further from traditional values . . . as human relationships grow more transient and modular, the pursuit of love becomes, if anything, more frenzied."

Toffler's prophecy came to mind recently while I was reading an article in *The New York Times* about a frenzied social gathering for singles called "SpeedDating." It was created by an international Jewish educational resource center to "discourage intermarriage and preserve Jewish heritage" and to provide an alternative to painfully long blind dates.

It is innovative. It creates excitement. It brings people together who might not otherwise have met. But when I finished the article, I felt a vague annoyance.

At first I didn't know why—it's just an innocent icebreaker. Single men and women have eight minutes to get acquainted, then a hotel desk bell alerts them to switch partners. The bell rings again and the participants change partners again. The process continues until all the attendees have met.

Call me old-fashioned, but SpeedDating is like a fast-forward game of musical chairs. It may be democratic—all participants get to decide if they'd like to see the person across the table again—but in the rush, someone is likely to select a shiny fake and overlook the slightly imperfect diamond. It promotes the frenetic pursuit of love that Toffler described.

Perhaps I'm overreacting, but I believe that SpeedDating is a metaphor for the current trend in living and loving too fast. Almost all a person can determine in eight minutes is the quality of a person's resume, if there is an instant chemistry, and who has the slickest answers. These factors are not usually indicative of love.

And yet several women whom I interviewed for *Celebrating Single* said they know in one or two dates if the man is "marriage material." Unless they have x-ray vision into his mind and heart, I would question their judgment. No wonder the divorce rate is so high. I've also heard both men and women say that if after three to five dates they haven't had sex, the chemistry just isn't there.

What happened to enjoying the moment, having fun and learning something new from someone, whether he/she becomes a friend, a mate, or a memory?

My most memorable dating experience was with a man whose warmth, generosity, and creativity made up for our cultural and educational differences. We didn't share intimate personal histories or a toothbrush.

Dan's construction business was shutting down after 20 years and he was looking for work; however, that didn't stop him from showing me a wonderful time. Instead of bringing me expensive gifts that would have been inappropriate, he surprised me with coloring books and stickers on my birthday, our first date. We colored and painted together like schoolkids and rewarded ourselves with Chinese carryout and peanut butter ice cream. I had confided in him that I wanted to do something daring on my 39th birthday, like get a small rose tattoo just above my heart. He knew I never would, so that night he bought me one that washed off after three weeks.

On our second date, we splashed down tacos with Mexican beer at his friend's house. By midnight Dan said, "I don't want this date to end. Would you like to go out for breakfast?" We ate scrambled eggs and greasy potatoes at a 24-7 diner. At 1:30 A.M. he said, "I don't want this date to end, would you like to do something else?"

I said, "What do you have in mind?"

"Do you trust me?"

"Yes," I said.

He stopped at a 7-11 and came out with two gigantic mugs of steaming coffee and a box of chocolate donuts. We drove to his row house, where he gathered two blankets and a boom box and led me up some creaky steps to his rooftop. We danced to Jimmy Hendrix, Cream, and Ella Fitzgerald, and gazed at the skyline while the sun painted the white sheets on his neighbor's clothesline pink.

Eventually, Dan and I went our separate ways. I still play those innocent evenings back in my mind, especially when someone says there are no nice men left or all the good ones are married. I met Dan by chance in a parking lot through a mutual friend. I doubt if I would have gone out with him if we'd met at a SpeedDating encounter. In eight minutes I would have seen his resume and not his heart.

Introspection: Questions for You to Consider

What is your opinion of the whole person theory?

What steps towards self-growth are you taking?

What steps are you taking to find your purpose and to become a whole person?

What would you do with your life if money were no object?

Now ignore the voice that says "I can't," and write a simple plan.

Another exercise to help you focus on finding your purpose, and no it's really not morbid, is to write your obituary. Be as creative as you like.

10

On Purpose

"When you have a sense of purpose it drives you to pursue your goals and it doesn't allow you to accept failure or a mediocre lifestyle. Aspire to be everything you know is in you."

—CHERYL, MEDICAL STUDENT

SHOW ME

Hold me now.
Don't let the
lonely wind
seep into my bones
through the leak
in my spirit.

Cradle me
for I lost the
sunflower dreams
of my youth.

I dig the earth and
plant my seeds
but where is my purpose now?

Breathe your light
into my soul—

and show me how
to serve you.

Amen

—JOAN

JOAN: Many of the baby boomers I interviewed for *Celebrating Single* are looking for meaning and purpose in their lives—in their work and relationships. They're examining questions like "Who am I?" and "Why am I here?" Of course these answers are different for everyone, but they lie inside of each of us.

MARC: Like your friend Dorothy from Oz.

JOAN: Yes.

MARC: So how do we tap into that power?

JOAN: We just need to ask for guidance from a friend, a therapist, a minister. I asked for guidance through prayer and meditation, and lines of poetry came to me like dictation from God. Often, when I was driving, I had to pull off the road and write on tiny scraps of paper the poems and parts of chapters that appear in this book.

MARC: So your purpose is to help single people navigate through healthy relationships and to inspire people to find their passion.

JOAN: Yes. I think it's especially important for single people to understand their purpose, so they can live their dreams and find a passion besides romance. What do you think your purpose is?

MARC: To plague you.

JOAN: Well, you've mastered that art. What's next?

MARC: To get my kids through college.

JOAN: What about for yourself?

MARC: That's a tough question because for 10 years all I wanted to do was survive and get by. I remade my career (from unemployed freelance writer to a manager in an international public relations company). I didn't have time for more spiritual pursuits. My goal now is to get to a point where I can answer that question you just asked with a heartfelt response. I'm still working on it.

To find my purpose, I'd have to take some serious time off, away from phones, faxes, and cell phones and have little to do except enjoy nature and confront myself. I'd have to do a spring-cleaning of my soul. I do have some initial thoughts though.

JOAN: You bring up a good point. We're so busy today "doing" that we don't have time to ourselves for just "being"—being alone, being quiet with our thoughts.

MARC: My purpose in life? I like to think that I have a purpose besides trying to make a living and seeing to it that my children are cared for. And yet I haven't fully thought through the question. I do know that I want to be someone who shares what he has with others, without wasting my time simply being taken advantage of. I want to encourage people to stand up for themselves without being belligerent; and to insist on being treated with respect without being arrogant. (Although when pushed sufficiently I can be pretty tart.) I want to be a refuge for those who truly need support during tough times and a lifelong friend to those with whom I'm able to create a special, mutually nurturing bond. In other words, I want to be the kind of person my children can be proud of, my family can love, my friends can think of with joy and that people I meet who wish me well and not ill will remember, however fleetingly, as a good person. And if all else fails, I want people who knew me to be able to say, "He made a hell of a brownie."

In addition to prayer and meditation, therapy can also provide insight into your unique meaning or purpose. Psychotherapist Marilyn Mendoza, Ph.D., from New Orleans, Louisiana, says, "Prayer, meditation, and therapy are similar in that they help you to focus and look inward to get the answers that are already there." Therapy, she adds, is particularly important if people have depression and unresolved issues, which can block their dreams and passions.

If you are mired in depression and trauma, it's hard to see any meaning or purpose in your life. You're just dealing with the pain. Once you are free from carrying the burden that held you back, then you can move on into something more meaningful and realize your potential. Then you can look at your life in a different way; you don't have to focus all your energy on healing your pain.

Finding your purpose often involves an innate intuition. Sometimes people are lucky and know what their purpose in life is. Sometimes it takes them a lifetime of discovery to find what that purpose is. People's purpose in their early adult years may be different than in their later life. A person in his fifties may say, "Been there. Done that," and move on to something else.

A therapist helps people clarify what their values are. What has value for you at this time of your life: raising kids, making money? As you get older, what you value changes and your focus changes. In therapy we help people to recognize what their focus is and how they are changing. And that it is OK to change. Some people get stuck, like women with children. They are supposed to raise them. They can get tired of that. But they feel that's what they have to do. A therapist's role is also helping people understand they have multiple purposes in life, not just one thing. Our purpose may change as we grow as adults. What therapy does is help people clarify where they are in this particular time and what may be missing in their lives. It's also about asking, "What—in your gut—do you want to do? If you could do whatever you wanted to do in this part of your life, what would it be? How do you put it into action and realize that?" What I end up doing is encouraging them to take some steps in that direction.

For example, I have a patient who's been in the oil-field business her whole life. Her passion is to teach. That's what she has always wanted to do. It's about helping her find the courage to change her life. That would be a very dramatic change for her. Therapy involves helping people realize their potential and become more self-actualized.

Joan: Learning Through Loss

Dr. Mendoza suggests looking at personal crises such as divorce, the loss of a job, or the death of a loved one as a chance to grow, an opportunity to reevaluate your life and move into something different and to change in a positive way.

When I turned 39, I became a blonde (from a dark brunette) and left my job as a mall marketing director. The first change was my choice. The second was not. I was fired when a new mall manager took over. Not only did I lose my income, but I lost my self esteem. To add to my problems, society and my mother were telling me it's time to get married and have children—when I didn't even have a boyfriend. I thought I had hit rock bottom. A friend referred me to a therapist. In therapy I discovered I was clinically depressed because I wasn't accomplishing my spiritual goals. I didn't know what my purpose was, but I knew it wasn't encouraging people to shop. Looking back, I now realize that losing my job was the best thing that ever happened to me.

Therapy helped me clarify my goals in life and forgive my past relationships. My spiritual journey, which guides me daily, helps me define how I can share my purpose and passion with others.

My passion is to teach and inspire—to help others breathe in their purpose. This passion led me to write this book and create Celebrating Single®, a series of workshops I teach on creative writing and cooking, designed to help single men and women enjoy their lives. If I had stayed at my mall job, I'd probably have a steady income with benefits, but I wouldn't have taken the risk to create the life I had always wanted.

In this chapter you will meet three special women who found answers from within and were determined to lead rewarding lives. For them, pain or loss of love and youth encouraged them to find their purpose. Cheryl is one of these inspirational women who entered my life and infused me with her joy, determination, and accomplishments.

Cheryl

Some girls who become pregnant in their early teens resent giving up their adolescence: parties, dances, dating, sleepovers, spending free hours daydreaming about their future and just hanging out with friends. At 14, when Cheryl found out she was pregnant, she didn't waste time thinking about missed social opportunities. She was determined to be a good mother, make good grades in high school, and go to college. Her mother helped with babysitting and eventually Cheryl graduated from high school and college with honors.

Early motherhood thrust this remarkable woman towards her purpose: going to medical school to become an obstetrician or a psychiatrist so she could help other pregnant teenagers. She worked in a psychiatrist's office to learn more about the field and to earn money for medical school. She will start next year.

For some, the revelation of their calling, destiny, or daimon, occurs in childhood. For others it happens later in life.

"A calling may be postponed, avoided, intermittently missed. It may also possess you completely. Whatever; eventually it will [win] out. It makes its claim. The daimon does not go away."

—JAMES HILLMAN, THE SOUL'S CODE

If you haven't found your purpose yet, it will find you. Listen to the whispers in your soul as Cheryl did. Try to find meaning in life's challenges.

Two other dynamic women, Rebecca and Christine, tell their stories about sacrifice and disappointment. At first, they spent many years in abusive, dead-end relationships because they thought women had to work harder to make relationships work. They ignored their instincts about their own dreams until they could no longer deny their callings. As it turns out, when they found that seed of purpose within and took action, love blossomed, too.

Rebecca's Story

Some guys I've been deeply involved with were very self-centered. There are warning signs when it's bad. Don't ignore them; it's easier to walk when you first see them. You will know because you are feeling insecure and neurotic. There are big warnings that don't go away. Move on before you really get involved and hurt. Don't be needy.

Believe me, I've been there. In my last major relationship, I was a classic doormat. I knew I was putting up with something bad. I was disgusted with myself. He would belittle me. He was never sure I was "the one" even after a year. He never liked the clothes I wore, my hair, my body. He never exercised and he would pat my stomach and say, "Maybe you should do a few more sit-ups." I was always doing for him, he didn't do for me. It looked good on paper: marry a doctor. That's the way we're raised, to get the prize husband.

Finally I told the doctor it was time to commit or move on. My friends said I was crazy, and I'd be miserable if I married him. He bought the ring, brought it home, and put it in a drawer. He took it out to show me once in a while, but wouldn't give it to me. It was a control thing, and I put up with it. He always wanted what he couldn't have and when he got me, I was never perfect enough. It was sick. I was so disgusted with it afterward.

I hung on to that relationship so long, so I wouldn't have to make decisions. When he ended it, I had to make those decisions. I made them and it wasn't easy. I dated but didn't have a serious relationship for four or five years. I took a risk, quit my job as a Navy dentist and went back to specialize in endodontics. I gained a lot of confidence by doing what I was afraid of doing.

I was going to marry the doctor and not have to worry about money or what I would do. I had worked so hard on that relationship, and when I could finally let it go and put half as much energy into my own life, I propelled myself way ahead of where I was, professionally and personally. I felt happy and free. I wasted so much effort on something so bad.

Changes were so painful. I stayed in that relationship to avoid making my own decisions because I was afraid of making the wrong decision. Sometimes just making a decision is good. It's so frightening to take risks, just closing your eyes and jumping. Just ask yourself, "In 20 years do I really want to be in a mediocre, or worse, an indifferent relationship?"

Rebecca could have settled, but she listened to her instincts. Her love story follows in Chapter 11, The Healthy Relationship.

Christine's Story

One of the things that attracted me to my boyfriend initially was that he had volunteered as a doctor in Third World countries like Africa, India, and South America. I thought that would be something we could do together. But he was tired of traveling and didn't consider that a possibility.

He was charming, articulate, handsome, well-built, the bachelor around town. I knew there were a lot of single women in this town who thought he was a real treasure—another reason I thought he was a catch. I thought, "My God, I should thank my lucky stars that I have him."

But from the beginning of our relationship, he wanted to change me. First, it was my appearance. I'm a doctor and he would dress me in trampy clothes. That did a number on my self-esteem. He bought me spiked heels and miniskirts. I'm conservative in my appearance. I wore classic, preppy clothes. I was like Mary Richards. My hair was dark and I wore it in a page boy. He insisted that I get it cut really short and dye it platinum blonde. It just wasn't me.

That was the hardest thing for me. I felt as though I had to do that or he would no longer be attracted to me. In order to make this work, I had to go along with it, even though it was humiliating to me. I remember going to see patients at the hospital the day I got my hair cut. The back of my head was shaved. I was thinking, "It's not me, but it's what he wants."

It goes back to that unwritten law—in order to get married, have kids, do all the things you have to do as a woman, you have to have a man. You're already late when you're in your thirties. I felt this was what I have to do as a woman. My mother, who was from Europe, always told my sisters and me that the woman has to work harder than the man to make the relationship work. The pressure was on me to make it work. I was an avid anti-smoker and I even smoked with him. My behavior was so uncharacteristic of me. When I came home with this hairstyle, my sisters knew something was not right.

There were many other red flags, but Christine ignored them. At parties, her boyfriend flirted inappropriately with other women and criticized her in front of other people. He asked her to give up a pediatric cardiology fellowship because he wanted her home at night. She agreed to this and worked as a locum tenens, a traveling doctor, and commuted several hours a day to her temporary assignments.

A few years into the relationship, Christine came home from work one night and found her belongings strewn on their front yard. The man who thwarted her career and cheated on her in her own bed was screaming from the front porch that he wanted her out.

After we split up, I looked into going abroad. I found ways to make my schedule more flexible so I could volunteer. First I was in private practice and then I took a job in an emergency room. Then I went overseas with Doctors Without Borders. That started a whole chain of events. I was in Thailand on the Cambodian border for six months. In the beginning I really didn't think I could live without a curling iron. I was more afraid of that than of contracting a disease.

This amazing woman followed her passion and volunteered to go to Africa. During this assignment, Christine met a manager at the site and eventually fell in love. Last I heard, she moved to Europe to be with him and work in Third World countries. She found her purpose and a man who shares it. Christine explains why she loves Claude.

> One of the things that endeared me to Claude is he's so kind and very gentle. It's something I wasn't used to. When we started getting involved and I asked him to use a condom, there was no issue. My last boyfriend said he couldn't wear condoms; years later I discovered he was cheating on me. With Claude my wish was respected, no questions asked. Since then, he has respected any request I have ever made.
>
> What I've learned is self-respect goes above everything else. I don't care how much you think you love this person. You have to love yourself most, first.

Joan's Creative Visualization Exercise

When I present Celebrating Single® workshops on enjoying the single life, I am frequently asked how I found meaning in my life. My answer is, "I pray a lot when I drive. Then I listen."

When I'm unclear about my current purpose, sometimes I imagine myself 10 years into the future and ponder what regrets I might have at that time. "I had the energy then, I could have. . . ." "I could have made some extra time to. . . . " "I could have taken the loan Aunt Hilda offered." Then I snap myself into the present and write down the things I could have done.

If that approach doesn't work, I picture myself with one wrist resting on my forehead, like an aged Collette, and the other hand fanning my face. I lean toward the dramatic in this visualization. Of course I'm wearing a satin nightgown cut on the bias. "I'm too old now, I have congestive heart failure." (Sputter, sputter.) "If only I had. . . . " Then I write in my journal until my hand hurts.

In the next visualization, I die and go to heaven. An angel greets me. He looks like John Travolta. He has the nerve to ask me how I'm feeling. "I don't feel anything," I snap.

"I need to ask you a very personal question, Joan."

"Go on," I say, "I have nothing to hide."

"All you ever wanted to do since you were x-years-old was to. . . . Why didn't you do it?"

Before he lets me answer, he takes out a digitalized master video of my entire life and shows me the times I could have. . . . ”

Then I fall asleep with my pen in my hand and the journal flopping over my wrist.

The next day I feel the energy to start building a master plan and implementing it.

⊗   ⊗   ⊗

Try the above exercises, and fill in your own. . . .

11

The Healthy Relationship

A NEW ATTITUDE

I will drink from the urn of love
before I drown in the River Styx.
No more Cyclops lovers,
angry and lopsided,
unsure of their affections.

I will read lines
from my own play,
resist the Satyr's lure
and ignore a well-intended
Greek Chorus.

I will make angels in fall leaves,
shape teapots in warm, wet clay
and sing "Ave Maria" with
my window open.
I will sit and be
proud of the me I am.

—JOAN

MARC: It seems from this poem that you've drop-kicked your old habits with men right out of the stadium.

JOAN: Yes, and it's very liberating. I'm looking for completely different things in a life partner now than I did six or seven years ago. I've cooked up a whole new recipe for a healthy relationship.

MARC: I like your cooking. Go on.

JOAN: It has to be reciprocal. If it's a one-sided, unbalanced relationship, it's not going to work. The person needs to be emotionally present and available. He's also got to be my friend before we're lovers, so I know I can count on him during the good and the bad times. And of course, there has to be a physical attraction. OK, your ingredients.

MARC: Honesty, a sense of humor, generosity of spirit, passion about things she cares for. I have to be physically attracted to her as well. Like in cooking, presentation is important.

JOAN: Good list. For me learning to celebrate single means being happy spending time alone. I need someone who enjoys time alone and supports me when I require that as well. I feel like a relationship for me now would be like fudge icing. I already have the well-baked cake.

MARC: My cake's not quite ready for *Bon Appetit*, but I'm working on it. I noticed the texture improved when I learned how to own my own stuff. I first knew that I was owning my own stuff when I decided that anytime a relationship failed because I thought the woman failed me, that it was probably 90 percent my fault anyway. That's because I missed or ignored the red flags that were telling me the woman wasn't capable or healthy enough to have a long-term relationship with me.

JOAN: Bravo, Marc. Speaking of cake, let's tell our readers that our famous brownie recipes, the ones that originally brought us together, are coming up in the Epilogue.

MARC: You just did.

Healthy Relationships 101

Wouldn't our love lives be easier now if Healthy Relationships 101 had been a requirement in high school?

Probably, but maybe not if you believe that it is your destiny to learn and grow from every relationship, even the most painful ones. Eleanor Roosevelt said, "Nothing we learn in this world is wasted and I have come to the conclusion that practically nothing we do ever stands by itself."

But without a positive role model or an understanding of what a healthy relationship is, many of us continue to dabble in dead-end relationships. Where to start? According to psychotherapist Rhoda Posner Pruce, L.C.S.W-C of Baltimore, a healthy relationship begins within oneself.

> Know yourself and what you are looking for. Because in order to find a relationship that will suit you, you have to know who you are. If you are confused about yourself, never thought about your needs, have no idea what will work for you or what your own potential growth areas are, you may cause avoidable problems in a relationship.
>
> Also, you have to be brave enough to cut loose from a relationship when it's not working and not get bitter, which is hard. You need to see it as a learning experience—What can I learn from past relationships that don't work out?—without getting discouraged.
>
> Instead of saying the glass is half-empty, you can say, "I've had eight relationships and I've learned more about what I want and about myself." It's a type of faith, believing that it will happen if it's supposed to.
>
> You also need the self-confidence to know you will survive if you don't find a partner. It takes a confident and strong person to say, "I'd love to have a man [or woman], but I can survive and thrive if I don't."

If you're not sure what a healthy relationship looks like, this chapter offers advice from other experts and an inspiring story about a never-married baby boomer who found the courage to pursue her dreams and stumbled upon love at a Happy Hour.

Happy Hour

After being on the receiving end of several broken engagements, at 36, Rebecca, a slim, blonde, wholesome girl-next-door type, says she is in her first truly healthy relationship. If she knew you well, she would confess that her current relationship was destined. She tells most people, with an embarrassed laugh, "It was just dumb luck."

"My last two long-term relationships were so miserable," Rebecca shudders, "that I had given up hope of ever getting married or even meeting someone I could be compatible with."

Then a series of coincidences changed her life.

I was new in town and out at a Happy Hour with a woman I work with. She was telling me I don't have good taste in men, that I was attracted to flashy, good-looking guys. She pointed at a man I wouldn't have looked at and said, "That's the guy you need to meet." It was eerie—she kept getting a strong feeling I should go out with him. "You're afraid to trust and get involved. Give it a chance. He's nice and he's the one you're going to marry." She coached me to keep my defenses down, to be real and not play games.

So she brought me over to talk to him and his friends. It turns out Jason lives in another state and was visiting some married friends for the weekend. His friends were very nice to me and we exchanged cards. They knew Jason wouldn't ask for my number even if he wanted it; they said he was burned out on dating and tired of women.

That weekend, I bumped into Jason twice when I was out walking through the city. And Baltimore is a big city. When I told my friend I saw him accidentally, she urged me to call his friend. A few days later, I called and asked if Jason was single. The friend realized that I was expressing an interest. He called Jason, gave him my number, and told him to call me.

Jason called. The first night we went out he apologized for not asking me for my number. We've been together every weekend since, and we've been honest with each other from the beginning.

I know this relationship is right. It's healthy because I'm not neurotic; I'm content. In the past, either there were things about people that would irritate me and I would try to change them, or they would do the same to me. I don't think we irritate each other. We're both easy-going, and we can give the other space. I can be myself. We enjoy the same things and it's easier. We're both pretty outdoorsy—we enjoy boating, gardening, hiking—and we like to play in a lighthearted way.

We're able to talk about issues as they come up. Communication is key. Last weekend, he was very proud of what he had accomplished during the day. Without saying, "That's great," I quickly said, "What about the other things you said you'd do?"

He took that as nagging, which I probably was. I never realized I was doing it; next time I would catch myself. He said his fear was being with a woman who nagged him. I shared my fear: that I would work 40 hours a week, come home, and still be the one who cooks, shops. I was afraid of falling into those patterns. It's OK on the weekend, but not during the week; I could just picture if we were married, this would be the daily routine. We can talk about anything.

We can be real in this relationship. For example, I was falling into a pattern of nagging. It's easy to do when you come from that kind of family. But neither of us got defensive because there's enough trust and respect. There's a respectfulness of how the other feels. We care enough about the other person to work on it.

He always tells me "thank you" if I cook or clean up or drive him somewhere. We both like to feel appreciated. I've never had that before. He gives me a hug and says, "Thank you, I appreciate that you do all this for me."

There's still romance, partly because we mostly see each other on weekends and occasionally during the week. We live about an hour and a half away from each other. I've been clear with Jason that I don't want to live together before marriage. It's not easy when two people have been single so long. He's 35 and I'm 36. I would get too attached and become neurotic without a commitment.

If you make a commitment to each other and to making a relationship work, then it should be because you get married, especially when you give up your space, time, and independence.

Part of a successful relationship is meeting the right guy at the right time. If you go into a relationship without a sense of neediness and huge expectations, then if it's right, it has a chance to develop without you forcing it or pulling back. Before, I tried or they tried to force it and it wasn't right. I tried to force one relationship. I was crazy about the guy, more so than he was about me. I made it easy for him, although instinctively I knew he had womanizer tendencies. I ignored it. I never would question him about our relationship, even after a year. I never brought it up and he never did; I didn't want to know the truth, although deep down I knew.

This time, after six months, Jason and I both agreed that if one of us felt this was not going anywhere, we would tell the other person. At this age, I will not spend more than a year with someone if there's no possibility of a permanent commitment. We'll go our separate ways.

Jason always said he wouldn't consider a permanent commitment with someone he hasn't dated for a year.

Last week, at our 12-month anniversary, my deadline, I told Jason I had big decisions to make—whether to buy a house, buy into a dental practice—and up until now I had put my life on hold. I asked him if he thought anything would happen with us. He said, "How do you think it's going?"

The "m" word hadn't come up in a year. We tried to enjoy the moment and get to know each other. I said, "I think it's going good. How about you?" He said, "Do you think this is something we could make permanent?" I said, "Yeah, I think so." We were circling the issue. Neither of us wanted to show our cards totally, yet there has always been a strong undercurrent of love.

I trust him because he has integrity. I like the way he treats other people, the way he conducts himself in his business. He doesn't want to just make money; he wants to do it till he gets the job right. If he says he'll do something, he always does it. He's generous, never cheap. He always offers to pay. I pay, but it's never expected. I just insist.

He's also generous with his time. Even though he's busy, he always makes time to be with me. If he's with his friends, he reaches out and touches me; he doesn't ignore me. I went to a party at his house two weeks after I met him, and he introduced me to his parents. Jason gets along well with his parents. They have a good marriage, and they're excellent role models. I would say he's closer to his parents than I am to mine. He lives close to them. He says his mother is his favorite woman in his life. He and his dad are really close. He calls him for advice; they talk on the phone a lot.

This relationship is different because I had spent five years without dating anyone seriously. I was working on my goals. When you're coming from a point of strength, feeling you don't have to be in a relationship, then you're not so accepting of people when they don't treat you right.

Do what you like to do, be open to meeting new people. Life is a wonderful thing, live it. Maybe you will meet a wonderful person. I had given up on it, then I met Jason.

Memorial Weekend was cold—outside and inside Jason's sailboat. Rebecca and Jason's plans fell through; a couple they had invited to join them on the boat for the weekend canceled at the last minute. The boat rocked on choppy waters and a dreary downpour dampened their holiday spirits.

Rebecca felt disappointed, but not about the couple or really even the rain. She had set a goal for their relationship. If Jason hadn't proposed in a year (the deadline passed in March), she would have to break off the relationship. Here it was, already May. Seriously considering ending their relationship on that stormy day, Rebecca held back tears. She felt Jason seemed very tense that weekend.

Jason found her wrapped under a blanket reading. He smiled nervously, opened a ring box, and popped the question. Rebecca's tears of frustration mingled with tears of joy.

They were married in December, 2000, in Key West, Florida.

The Lesson

Rebecca learned an important lesson: when you're coming from a point of strength, feeling you don't have to be in a relationship to be happy, then you're not so accepting of people when they don't treat you right.

Author Dr. Jalaja Bonheim's words echo Rebecca's message.

People need to know they are loveable and worthy of love, they can survive on their own, they do not need a relationship. It helps if they have a very practical and realistic knowledge of who they are and what their needs are and what their limitations are. That grounded self-knowledge will help a lot. They need to know that a relationship is a path. It's a very demanding path. If they expect it to be all milk and roses, they are in for a nasty surprise.

Of the couples I have interviewed in vibrant, alive relationships that have lasted many years, every one said that at some point they had to make a choice between their own growth and the relationship. They had chosen to go with their own growth; paradoxically this choice had been what had caused the relationship to thrive.

Jesus said, "What does it profit you if you lose your own soul and you gain the world?" We need to stay true to ourselves even if it's scary and it looks like we're losing the relationship. That's when ultimately the relationship will thrive.

I'm working with a couple now. The woman feels she needs to retreat and devote a large chunk of time to her work. Her partner feels very abandoned, yet this is what she needs to do for herself. She's not saying "I need to leave you." Her partner's expectations and needs are in conflict with her goal. He's trying to understand that his partner's turning away is not a rejection of him; he's trying not to take it personally. It's prompting him to look at some very deep issues in his own life. He's gradually moving from seeing it as a threat to seeing it as an opportunity.

Mark Komrad, M.D., a psychiatrist at Baltimore's Sheppard Pratt Health System, says that a good indication of a healthy relationship is being able to say, "This is my stuff and my problem and I take responsibility." Dr. Komrad says the most common problem he sees in intimate relationships is blame—being more attentive to what's wrong with the other person and not taking responsibility for your own issues.

People should ask themselves, "How typical is it for me to go to my partner and say, 'I saw something in the way that I related to you that I don't like about myself and I apologize for that. And it's something I've seen is a pattern for me and I want you to know I'm going to take some responsibility to try to work on it.' That kind of statement is a sign of tremendous health in relationships; that ought to be a goal. How often have you said that in a relationship as opposed to "you" statements: "You did this," "You're wrong," or "I hate this about you?"

I think that a barometer of relational health is marked by people being able to say "me" statements. There are two kinds. Examples of the first kind are: "What I need from you now is just a hug." "What I need right now is for you to listen to me, not to try to change me." "What I need from you is to just love me, don't judge me." Give your partner the chance to hear it by articulating. You need to be clear with how you want to be treated and tell the other person.

The second kind of "me" statement is being able to say in a relationship, "This is about me, not about you." It's identifying your own stuff. If one of the partners hears "This is about you" all of the time, there's something wrong with the relationship.

Psychotherapist Rhoda Posner Pruce says one of the key aspects of having a healthy relationship "is the ability to be fully yourself while being connected to your partner."

It can be unhealthy to be too connected to your partner. The opposite—if you're only concerned about yourself and you can't be connected—is not healthy either. The ancient Jewish scholar Hillel said, "If I'm not for myself who am I, and if I'm only for myself what am I?"

You have to have the capacity to be fully with yourself and fully with the other person at the same time. Those are the sweet moments; they happen only once in a while. You need to be able to move back and forth between those two positions easily, based on what's happening in your lives. If your partner wants to be alone, you need to move away, more into yourself, and have interesting things to do. If your partner is away or wants time alone, can you enjoy being fully with yourself? And when your partner needs you, can you give up a little of being fully yourself?

You also need to be able to communicate. Relationships require the ability to communicate in an honest way about your deepest feelings, your wants, your hopes and dreams. It's a higher level of communication, not just the ability to be understanding during a didactic presentation. It's intimate communication.

An intimate relationship is one in which you are so safe that you're bringing all of yourself—including your deeper parts and your shadow side. The more intimately you communicate, the more you'll become aware of differences between you and your partner.

Every couple has a different kind of relationship, so every couple needs to find their own way of navigating the differences. If it works for the two people and lets each of them be who they want to be, then it's a healthy relationship. If you're truly in the relationship fully, then you're going to hit these difficult times or emotional roadblocks. There will be times when there's a lot of conflict and a lot of stress. That's a sign of really dealing with the issues.

If you have the commitment, trust, and skills to look at the issues that come up, then the relationship becomes the best vehicle there is for personal growth.

Friends and Lovers

Father Joe Breighner, national radio host and author, has counseled hundreds of couples in relationship distress. This is his take on what a healthy relationship is:

The healthier we are, the more self-aware we can be. The more we are in touch with our family of origin, the more we know what we are looking for and what we are recovering from, the healthier the relationship will be.

Our society is big on romantic lovers. They always look sexy and have wild romantic times. That level can't be sustained; it lasts six months to two years. That's when you have kids and/or the infatuation is gone. You wake up suddenly and say, "I have kids?"

Friendship needs to be the foundation. Friendship includes a common vision about the purpose of life and values. It's not about how you spend your recreational time, but what you want for your kids. That's what reflects what you really value.

If you don't discuss questions like what faith to raise your children in and what kind of education you want for them *before* you have a child, then the differences are going to have to be worked out when the child comes along. Couples tend to gloss over bigger issues when they're caught up in the romantic stage.

The romantic fantasy is, "I make your needs more important than mine." After time that builds resentment—giving more and not getting anything back. There are so many relationship pitfalls. Look at our role models. If we didn't have a good relationship with mom or dad, or they didn't have a good relationship, then what does it mean to be married and committed?

A working definition of love is wanting the same good things for another that you would want for yourself. There are so many layers. There's the theological layer, the belief that God brought us together, that this is the person I'm committed to before God. In a healthy relationship, we keep our promises to be committed, to do things in the Judeo-Christian sense—that is, doing for others what we see God doing for us, i.e., forgiving us.

The next layer is why people get married. People are looking for happiness, looking to be happy. We go into a marriage for conscious reasons, we get married, and suddenly we get into unconscious reasons. "I expect you to be the one who takes care of my needs now that we're married."

It's a beautiful dance about what we're looking for on the conscious level and what we're really looking for on an unconscious level. The unconscious level may say, "Look for someone you can't please."

Then there's the physical layer that tells us to procreate and educate our child.

What I haven't worked out I will act out. If I haven't done my growth work, I will attract people on an unconscious level for reasons I don't understand—people who don't call me back, people who leave me or treat me abusively. The unconscious immediately filters in at every level.

People need to do growth work, like group therapy for singles, ahead of time. A lot can come out in a safe environment. People can interact and learn about themselves. Single includes so many categories: widowed, separated, divorced. Each group has different issues, but they also have commonalities such as trying to raise children on their own. Typically, single people are more likely to make bad decisions because they're looking for stability, such as a father for their children.

In a healthy relationship there is the capacity to enjoy each other, to befriend each other. My favorite definition is, "We don't belong to each other, we belong with each other." It's not ownership, it's friendship. You make a conscious choice to be with the person who will bury you or whom you will bury, whom you will be with until death. Friendship bodes best for the success of the relationship.

To determine if you're in a healthy relationship, Father Joe suggests asking yourself these questions and paying attention to the answers:

How spontaneous can I be with this person?
Do I leave dates feeling anxious?
Was it fun? Or was it hard work?
Am I trying to impress this person or is he/she trying to impress me?
Is he or she controlling?

He also suggests that you listen to your instincts. Then after you've dated for an extended period of time, ask yourself:

How do I feel?
Do I feel good about myself when I'm with this person?

Do I have to compromise my values or do what he/she wants to do because I want him/her to like me?

These little tips may indicate that this person might not be good for you, Father Joe explains. Or he/she might be very good for you, because you feel really good, and it was fun, not hard work.

In addition to friendship, another component of a healthy relationship is the capacity to laugh together. A sense of humor is healing. I don't mean put-downs or sarcasm. Just being able to laugh at our foibles and not take life so seriously. It's so much fun to laugh. When people can laugh and not get mad at each other, it does wonderful things.

Kindness

Barbara Harris Whitfield, author of *Spiritual Awakenings,* says that kindness is the glue in her relationship with her husband, Charles Whitfield, M.D., author of *Healing the Child Within.*

Healthy relationships are not necessarily finished relationships, unfortunately. We are still two individuals struggling to learn more about how to live together and work through what issues are left lurking in our shadows. We are still doing that dance of learning about ourselves and each other.

There are times I'm not sure which end is up—who is "right" and who is "wrong." Black and white have turned to infinite variations of grey. We've agreed to give up "either/or" and hopefully in the middle of a conflict remember that there is "both/and."

The bottom line for us is, only kindness matters. Charlie and I face each other and see our Godself and our shadows with that in mind.

Ingredients for a Healthy Relationship

Dr. Charney Herst, an author-therapist from Encino, California, says a healthy relationship means:

Having absolute and never-ending respect for each other.
Agreeing to disagree.

Forgiving and letting go of any ill will.

Working through one's own hostility and unmet expectations so as not to project them upon a mate or date.

Regarding one's significant other as a best friend and confidant.

Trusting that this person will never hurt you deliberately.

Measuring one's honesty so as not to harm the other, yet informing them of shortcomings and asking for change, not demanding it.

Realizing that there is no perfect relationship (so stop looking for it).

Picking your fights about things that really matter, not the small stuff.

Having a great deal in common, or the willingness to share and learn commonalties, i.e., religion, cultural aspects, sports, entertainment, travel, or pastimes.

Agreeing on basic values and principles: i.e., truth, honesty, integrity, loyalty, freedom.

Never trying to control the other. Rather, each always stays true to the self.

Not expecting the other to be a clone or mirror of you, but a complement to you.

Loving, cherishing, and adoring the person you are with in all ways.

Realizing that sex is a plus factor in a relationship but not a good basis if it is all there is that you have together.

Not complaining about his or her family since there is no way a child can change their parents, no matter what the age.

Always working assiduously on your relationship and *never* taking it for granted.

If you can accomplish at least 10 of the above, you will probably have a good relationship. Pick your priorities carefully, pray a lot, take two aspirin, and call me in the morning.

Joan: What Do *I* Want?

Part of becoming healthy, if your goal is to be in a healthy relationship, is knowing how to spot inappropriate partners sooner rather than later.

I met Dan, a twice-divorced, charming, handsome law enforcement agent, on a blind date two years ago while I was researching *Celebrating Single* in California.

To me, a special agent conjures images of espionage, adventure, and danger—sheer machismo. Something about a man carrying a Glock made my knees weak. Anyway, we dined at romantic bistros for two weeks and shared a bottle of wine on the beach on my birthday. He bought me flowers and whispered, "You're beautiful." I felt like a character in a screenplay.

The next month Dan took me to The Metropolitan Opera, while he was on assignment in New York. I had always dreamed of seeing an opera at The Met, especially since I saw the movie *Moonstruck*. I wept as Placido Domingo sang an aria from "Carmen." Dan reached for my hand.

Although I felt safe and protected when I was with Dan, I was able to see through the romantic fog. I sensed there was no substance beneath the veneer. We didn't connect on a spiritual or intellectual level. We didn't share the same values or interests—not a good way to start a relationship. For example, he said he would be in Washington for a meeting the following week and made plans to see me. He didn't call when he said he would, and he left me hanging about when to pick him up at the train in Baltimore. Actually I never heard from him that weekend. He didn't return my call for several weeks.

During my love-addicted days, I would have felt crushed. Soon after our affair, I brushed it off as a wonderful memory and a great time.

When Dan finally did return my call, I told him I didn't appreciate being treated disrespectfully. "You could have called me from your cell phone to let me know you weren't coming to Baltimore."

Then almost two years later, Dan called me while I was scrambling to finish the manuscript for *Celebrating Single* and asked if I ever read my e-mail. I laughed and told him I had gotten his message and had meant to answer it—along with about 50 other messages. He asked me to accompany him to a weekend of parties in New York for agents in his division. I accepted.

Two mornings later I woke up thinking, *Why* am I going to New York? Because I remember his Glock fondly? Because I yearn for excitement and adventure after spending my Saturday nights working on the book for the last three years? Because my life lacks romance? Not a good enough answer, my heart replied. Why would I want to see a man, even for a weekend, who never called when he said he would and stood me up for a date he initiated?

And having sex with a man I didn't trust would be dangerous and irresponsible, I realized. Especially since he had lived overseas since I had seen him last.

The final answer was, I just didn't feel comfortable.

That afternoon, I e-mailed Dan that I couldn't meet him in New York. I also left him a message at his office and house. It was the first time in my life I had canceled a date. It was such a relief.

I sat on my balcony and smiled at the birds and my garden, knowing I did the right thing.

After calling Dan, I wrote the following poem to celebrate the joy of living in the moment.

PEACH SOUP

The blender pulses and
juicy peaches swirl
into clouds of cream,
cool and sweet
like ambrosia.

Surrounded by strawberry plants
and lavender,
I prop my feet on jewel-tone cushions,
smack my lips for the last lick
and suck the mint leaf garnish
while the pink and orange sky
melts into midnight blue.

—JOAN

Marc: **What *Do* I Want?**

In my opinion, it was Rachael who made the first move. If, in fact, it *was* a move on her part. Okay, so it might have been merely my fantasy.

We had made a nodding acquaintance professionally the previous week. A few days later she walked up to me and introduced herself.

This time she suggested we have lunch some time. She was very bright, attractive, energetic, and already quite accomplished. And about 22 years younger than I.

A week later we did lunch in a small restaurant. Rachael and I got to know each other over a meal. We talked about family, interests, background—the usual.

We took a walk after lunch. As we ambled through the early afternoon sidewalk traffic we talked about relationships, including her ex-boyfriend.

Suddenly Rachael's voice took a slightly high-pitched quality as she sprung an unexpected query on me.

"Can I ask you a personal question?"

"Sure," I said.

"Are you dating anyone?"

I quickly threw my brain into third gear and rammed the throttle. My mind raced through a giant database of phrases, syntaxes, metaphors, aphorisms, and dependent clauses. My left hemisphere frantically responded to the sudden vocalization emergency and within several microseconds tossed the first draft of a response into my right brain. Zoom! Right back at ya, left brain! Another few microseconds and my mouth was moving, air pumping up from my lungs and through my trachea, trilling the flaps of my eager voice box as I turned to Rachael and said:

"No."

Okay, it wasn't Chaucer or D.H. Lawrence or Percy Shelly or even Rod McKuen. But it was real. It was raw. It was me.

As I hung over the precipice of a highly anticipated incredible move on her part, she said—nothing. We continued walking and talking. I slammed my brain back into second gear and then eased it down to first, pulling back the throttle and drawing myself back off that precipice.

We became friends and that's where it stands as of this writing. We eventually coordinated schedules and went out to dinner. I like her because she's bright, friendly, artistic, and has an impressive resume at what I consider to be a fairly tender age. And there's no getting around the fact that she's very pretty and I enjoy looking at her.

Around this time, however, there arose in the deep recesses of my mind a gnawing question: "What does she want from me?"

I pondered this question seriously on and off for a few weeks. Then one evening my subconscious finally gave up a response to that question. And wouldn't you know it? The response was another question. The real issue was not "What does she want from me?" it was "What do I want from her?"—well, besides the obvious.

I realized that my common sense and hard-won good judgment in these matters had tempered my natural tendency to pursue with abandon this potential relationship and perhaps make a fool of myself in the process. This predatory dawdling on my part had given me time to think about the bigger, although not more enticing, picture. Any relationship with Rachael would have been a passing fancy between us, given our different ages. It could be a good experience for both of us, if we handled it right. It could be good for me, my ego, and my general state of mental health. But it was not the relationship of my dreams, however fuzzy they are.

Rachael could give me some of the things I want in a relationship if she had the mind to, but I realized there are some things only an older woman could offer. It's nothing personal. Just chronological and experiential.

Although I put the brakes on my intentions toward Rachael pretty quickly, I had found myself in an old familiar state of mind for a while: head down, full speed ahead at the first inkling there might be something worth pursuing. As it turned out, she steered the relationship toward one of mentorship. So I became her advisor and confidant. Meanwhile, she pursued a romantic relationship with another older man (eight years younger than her mentor). So goes the story of my life.

My dawdling also gave me time to think about my previous full-fledged relationship and how I'd entered with my eyes half shut.

I knew going into the relationship with Jenny that she was just coming out of a marriage. She was looking for a man she could enjoy being with, plain and simple. Jenny was even pretty blunt with me about her not wanting to be alone. Red flags? Sure. But hey, I had nothing going on in my life.

So I moved too quickly into this relationship with Jenny, treating her like a princess—wining, dining, and romancing her to a pretty fine degree. But it ended darn suddenly when we realized that our individual goals for the relationship just weren't in sync. Jenny wanted me to spend a lot more time with her than I thought I had to give, considering my scattered and busy life and the moderately long distance between us.

Although I tried to explore the possibility of our staying together, the odds were against it. Neither of us was going to compromise on our respective positions. I was disappointed, but not because we had had a world-class relationship. Actually, although I liked her a lot, we simply hadn't known each other long enough to nurture a world-class relationship. She wasn't in a healthy position, squeezing her way out of a marriage. And I wasn't in a healthy position, trying to make my round peg of a lifestyle fit into her square—well, we'll leave that one alone.

In any case, I wasn't devastated by the breakup. And that's because I knew from the start what I was getting into. So when the relationship hit a wall, I had no one to blame but myself.

The point is, it's easy to fall into an unhealthy relationship when to do so makes you feel good, at least for a while. Hell, lots of people would probably feel good living on a diet of pizza and beer, and that wouldn't be healthy for them.

Nowadays, my appetite for pizza and beer isn't quite as hearty as my appetite for a full, meaningful relationship. It wasn't always that way, and that's no slam on any particular woman I've dated in the past decade. It's simply a capsule summary of the story of my journey from trying to gorge on relationships while I could, to learning how to step lightly toward them, and draw back in grace when they fail.

Oh, I'm sure I'll stumble some more, but at least I'll recognize what's happening a lot sooner than I used to. And I'll recognize when I get foiled it's probably because I've tried to gorge on pizza and beer instead of enjoying a satisfying, warm, and healthy home-cooked meal.

12

True Destiny Stories

"I believe that finding a special soul-mate is fate. You can't go looking for it. It's just going to happen."

—SHELLY

THE CIRCLE OF WIDOWS

Hadassah arms flap in delight
as the circle of widows inspects its prey.
Before the mesclun salad is served,
before the best man taps the crystal,
Mildred smiles into warm, chocolate eyes
and pats the Brooks Brothers wool.
"Are you here with your wife?" she coos.
"No, I'm divorced," says the charming, dark victim.

Mildred whispers towards the girls,
"This one's for dear Julie;
may our Rose rest in peace."
The silver, blue and purple heads bob in unison,
their turkey necks tanned from a game of nine holes.
"Are you family or friend?"
Hieroglyphic creases stretch across her face.

"I went to med school with the groom.
My name is Paul Field."

Mildred's gnarled fingers warmly embrace his beefy
hand.
"A doctor?"
"Yes, an internist."
The ladies squeeze hands under the peach floral cloth,
glancing away with delight.

A pastel swirl with raven tendrils floats by their table,
across the dance floor.
A silver-haired man holds her delicate shape firmly.
"That's my niece, Julie, dancing with her father,"
Mildred taps Paul's pinstriped arm with a manicured
claw.
"She looks like a Russian princess," he sighs.
Julie kisses her aunts' upturned, translucent faces.

"Dear, this is Paul Field." She touches Julie's flushed
cheek.
The middle-aged strangers smile at each other like
adolescents.
Silently, the circle of widows adjourns to the powder
room.
Each member lifts her champagne flute to the brass
chandelier.
"To Rose . . . a match made in heaven."

—JOAN

JOAN: Marc, do you believe in destiny?

MARC: The only destiny I truly believe in is having to pay my taxes.
As far as destiny in meeting people, I think of the old expression,
"Chance favors the prepared mind," but in this case, chance favors
the prepared heart. If you have a prepared heart the chances of finding someone are probably increased so much that it seems like destiny. I don't believe that you're destined to meet that one person,
you've got to be prepared for it.

JOAN: Don't you believe that it's destiny that you and I met and became close friends?

MARC: I think it was just great good fortune.

JOAN: I do believe in destiny. It's as natural to me as breathing. Every person I interviewed for this chapter would agree that destiny played a role too dramatic to be mere coincidence.

Food for Thought

On her way to meet a group of girlfriends at Clyde's, a popular bar and grille in Northern Virginia, Debbie, an attractive divorcée, felt a strange floating sensation while driving to the restaurant. She was consumed by a feeling of inner peace. When she arrived before her friends, she sat at the crowded bar next to a tall, dark, handsome stranger, whom she thought was foreign at first glance.

"Are you Jill?" he inquired, without a trace of an accent.

"No, I'm Debbie," she smiled.

"It seems as though my blind date stood me up," the hunk named Roy said. "Would you like to join me for dinner?"

Now they dine together every night. The couple has been married more than four years.

My Baby Wrote Me a Ticket

A young woman, speeding to get to work on time, saw flashing lights in her rearview mirror. She whispered obscenities under her breath as a handsome state trooper stood by her door.

"Ma'am, you were doing 60 in a 40-mile-per-hour zone." He waited politely for her license and registration and smiled into her auburn eyes.

Shawn grabbed the ticket from his hand and drove off. Daniel, the trooper, called that night and asked her out.

"I wouldn't go out with you if you were the last man on earth." Click.

Several months later she fought the ticket in court, but there was no one to fight with. Her state trooper didn't show up and she won the case. He called her that night and asked her out again. "I wouldn't go out with you if you were the last man on earth. And besides that, where did you get my phone number?" Click.

Several months later, Shawn, covering for a secretary at the front desk at work, was held hostage at gunpoint by her colleague's disgruntled boyfriend. A co-worker called the sheriff's office, but they were not prepared to handle a hostage situation. Not knowing the identity of the damsel in distress, Daniel, trained in hostage negotiation, heard the call and freed Shawn from her captor.

"Would you go out with me now?" he inquired.

"Yes."

At last account Shawn and Daniel were planning their wedding.

A Second Chance

They were college sweethearts, a ballet dancer and a football star. He married someone else. She would always love him. Even after an ill-fated marriage, a beautiful child, and a divorce, she still wondered, "What if?"

PAUL: I dated Terry's roommate and she transferred. And I began dating Terry. We went together for two years at Bucknell, and unfortunately I married someone else. And that didn't work.

TERRY: I adored Paul. He wouldn't tell you but he was a college hero. Three sports he starred in. He was gentle, intelligent, empathetic, a scholar, so incredibly handsome. He did go off with someone else, and not only did he do that, he remained at Bucknell to do graduate work. He was a year ahead of me. It was very difficult because I was still there for my senior year. I got sent to Europe for four months, the proverbial trip to forget him. I never forgot him.

My brother, James, had transferred to Bucknell from Cornell. Paul had kept him under his wing. This was pertinent many years later.

It took me a relatively long time, for those years, to marry after Paul got married. And I might not have, but I really wanted a child very much. I got that one child and that marriage didn't last. I was unmarried for many, many years.

PAUL: And Terry was always in the back of my mind. . . .

JOAN: So you had thought about Terry through the years, and you, of course, had thought about Paul.

TERRY: Too much. And I talked about him. My daughter knew, when she was grown up enough to know, that there was somebody who was the great love of my life.

PAUL: Then, I was listening to Larry King one night and James, Terry's brother, was being interviewed. He had written a historical novel. I teach history so I was very interested. And I had used the first book that he wrote for my class.

So I heard him being interviewed and I tried to call him. The way it worked then, if you didn't get through, they just cut you off. I'd wait a half-hour, call again, and then I'd get cut off and call him again. This was two o'clock in the morning. I read the book, partly because of the interview. I was very impressed with it. So I decided to write him, and it wasn't easy because the publishers don't give you the address. I had to write the publisher and they forwarded it to him. James answered it and I sent him a book my students and I had written. This was just an approach to teaching, to get students to work as historians, no great literary accomplishment.

TERRY: James called me and said, "I'm going to read you parts of the letter and you guess who wrote it."

It was a beautiful letter, the parts that I heard, and I said, "I don't know, a writer friend of yours?"

And he said, "The letter is from Paul Spencer and I'm going to answer it. He didn't ask about you directly, but would you like me to add something about you in my letter to him?"

I was stunned. I said, "James, no. And if you and Paul correspond, I don't want to know about it."

PAUL: Neither of us knew that the other was not married.

TERRY: Three months went by till I saw my brother. I borrowed Paul's book from James and read a good part of it.

"Are you going to write to Paul ?" my daughter asked.

"Absolutely not."

The book was so extraordinary. I became aware that Paul was an incredible teacher. In any event, I assumed he was married. I wrote just a short note saying I liked your book. And then we started to correspond for a period of months.

PAUL: One day I telephoned and that began a series of phone calls, and I invited Terry to Baltimore.

TERRY: Before I came, I said, "Paul, after 42 years, how do you know I'm not a 400-pound mama?"

He said, "I don't care, I know what's inside."

Somewhere along the way we were talking about something and I said, "I never stopped loving you." So that came out without control. I normally would never have said anything like that. A 1950's person doesn't. After that, we exchanged photographs. I don't even remember that first visit, to tell you the truth.

JOAN: What was it like seeing each other after so many years? What were your first thoughts?

TERRY: On the train I really hyperventilated. I was trembling like a leaf. I could barely get up the stairs in the train station. I was paralyzed with fear.

PAUL: The first thing I thought was that Terry looked awfully nervous. I had her brother's book under my arm. I thought that I hadn't really changed in 30 years or so. I just happened to carry the book. I thought she would just recognize me right away.

[Paul pulls out pictures of Terry in college. She has a glossy ponytail and her bangs frame an Audrey Hepburn face with flawless skin. She was petite, fawn-like, with a superstar quality.]

TERRY: After an hour with Paul, I felt I still did love him. After so long, you wonder, "Is it a fantasy?" But with all of his qualities, it was real. After spending that weekend with Paul, I had a hard time working. I became flighty and goofy. I'm usually super-reserved, serious. I finally had to tell my boss. Fortunately, I had a wonderful boss who understood.

JOAN: When you first saw her that day at the train station, did the feelings for Terry flood back for you like they did for her?

PAUL: It was slower. After we got married, my love became stronger.

Joan: What is it you love about Terry?

PAUL: In addition to her looks, she's the most decent person I've ever known. Even here, at school, with people she doesn't know and students she doesn't know, she's so kind and gentle and so thoughtful. I even have to tell people, "Look, she's really that way. She's that way all the time."

JOAN: And tell me what you love about Paul.

TERRY: The same things that I loved when we were together in college except they are more pronounced. He is the most gentle person. He has a container of quarters on his desk if his students need to make a call or need anything. They love him. He knows who they are, what they need.

JOAN: Why do you think your being together was destined?

PAUL: In a way because we were in each other's minds.

TERRY: I had become happy on my own. It took a lot of work and self-education but I had gotten to a point where I would not go out. I liked my life; it was rather complete. I liked my job. My family was loving. I wouldn't consider marriage, even a date. I never entertained the idea of being together with Paul. He was the only man in the world for me. And if that isn't fate. . . .

JOAN: You spoke about projections, seeing people the way we want to, not as they really are.

PAUL: At first, I think I wanted Terry to be the Terry of 40 years ago. That slowed things up a bit.

JOAN: How?

PAUL: Terry had changed. She wasn't 21 years old anymore. She had always viewed me through rose-colored glasses and was very subservient. And when we got back together from time to time she was no longer subservient, and that would kind of shock me and scare me a little bit.

JOAN: Well obviously it didn't frighten you too much. How did you work through that?

PAUL: That's a good question. I think that at 69, I grew up a little.

TERRY: You're pretty formed at 65, and you have to accept the other partner for who he or she is, which doesn't mean there isn't a wish and an ability to accommodate. You are two fully formed individuals.

JOAN: What's your advice to singles on how to connect with each other?

TERRY: I have friends, male and female, who desperately want to be linked, as opposed to those who have found a piece of happiness in this world alone. I say, go back over your past contacts. Who were your friends? We were friends in college. And the loss of Paul, my friend, was as devastating as the loss of Paul, my first love, and as it turns out, my only love. There is something about friendship—I think more of it now when I see these college friends, who are all in their sixties, who still are my friends.

PAUL: The title of the history book my students wrote was *What If*, and I think some of these people might go back and see what if. What if I had married x? What if x and I had been closer friends and had communicated? And I think they might find an awful lot in their past.

JOAN: Some people say you can never go back.

PAUL: You can't go home again, but to some extent, I believe you can go back. And I guess I believe you should.

JOAN: What advice can you offer singles on their search for a mate?

PAUL: Avoid someone who is self-centered, who just talks about himself. In spite of what Terry tells you, there were some times when I thought I was doing a lousy job of teaching. I remembered listening to some successful teachers at a conference and every single one of them said, "Be human." And that's what you should look for in a person. Is this person human or is it all a facade? When I started being human, my teaching improved.

JOAN: What do you think about the concept of wholeness? Do you believe that before you connect with another person, you need to be a whole person or be working toward being a whole person?

TERRY: Knowing myself, I don't think we would have made it had we married 40 years ago. I don't think we would have survived had we married the first time.

JOAN: Why?

PAUL: I was very immature.

TERRY: So was I. I think I was so insecure that my ego wouldn't have enabled me to rise with any ups and downs or beyond my shell and insecurities. It was difficult. Paul took things very seriously. Before a football game, I would have needed his undivided attention.

PAUL: And I wouldn't have been able to give that.

TERRY: My self-esteem was fragile at the time.

JOAN: How did you get stronger emotionally?

TERRY: First of all, my parents didn't like the person that I married. I was disowned for marrying him. I had grown up very comfortably, and suddenly I had to work very hard to have enough to eat. And I had this baby, who I didn't want to suffer because of my supposed transgressions. I simply had to grow up. I had this little life. I simply adored this child. And she went away to college, which took me three jobs to accomplish.

I was not a smashing success in my career. I didn't have a certain kind of drive. I was terrified by the thought of living by myself. And then I found out, over the course of the years, that it was OK, and I began to like it. That took many, many years. So by the time I met Paul, I was OK on my own.

JOAN: It's like you were preparing yourself to be ready for Paul.

TERRY: I've found that marriage is better this time around, better than it was in my younger years, because I've learned who I am. I wouldn't have traded those more difficult years for these years. I'm just afraid I'll wake up. I still am. I still pinch myself every day.

Larry King Plays Cupid Again

Destiny works in mysterious ways. At times it's quick like a cupid's arrow. Other times it happens gradually over many years, as with the love story of Barbara Harris and Charles Whitfield.

In 1985, Barbara was a researcher at the University of Connecticut Medical School. She was in the Department of Psychiatry for six years, researching the aftereffects of the near-death experience. That year she spoke at a meeting in Washington, D.C., at which researchers discussed, with congressmen, funding sources to study consciousness. The meeting was the beginning of her love story, which she wrote for this book.

> I was speaking the last day and Charles Whitfield, an author and physician, was in the audience. He introduced himself as soon as the conference was over. I don't remember what he looked like but I remember meeting him and thinking this man had kind and gentle energy.
>
> After that first meeting in Washington in 1985, I went back to the University of Connecticut and continued working and healing from my divorce. Charlie would call me one or two times a year to chitchat and ask me research questions. I would send him an article on what we had discussed and with it a brief note. This went on for five years.
>
> In 1987 Charlie sent me a copy of his first book, *Healing The Child Within,* and I didn't read it at that time. I just put it on the shelf with a lot of other unread books. Many authors sent me new books in hopes we would review them in our publication, the *Journal of Near-Death Studies.*
>
> In 1988 I was in Washington, D.C., speaking on the near-death experience, and a dear friend of mine, Kay Allison, from Charlottesville, Virginia, came in to hear my talk. She has a New Age and recovery-oriented bookstore and knows many in the field of personal growth. We were having dinner after my talk and she asked, "Did you know that Charlie Whitfield is really sick and in the ICU?" I said, "No." We both stopped eating and there and then we prayed for him.
>
> My first book, *Full Circle,* came out in April, 1990. I was going to be interviewed on "Larry King Live" to introduce it. On the Friday

night before my appearance on Larry King, as usual, I lit my Sabbath candles. I was living in a little 650-square-foot flat with my two sons, who were 18 and 20 at that time. Usually they both stood by me while I lit the candles but this particular Friday evening they weren't home.

I was standing alone after I said my prayers. I remember looking through the two flames and for the first time realizing that this was a direct line to God. I had always said prayers asking for my children and my family to be healthy and safe and that was it. This time I looked at the two flames and thought, I know if I speak, this will go directly to God. That was just how it felt to me. I knew it in my heart.

Writing my first book, *Full Circle*, had really opened me. It is the story of my life, my near-death experience (NDE), and its aftereffects. I went from being an atheist to knowing there was a God in a fraction of a second. I also had what we call a "Life Review," where my whole life had flashed in front of me. Writing about all this opened old wounds from my childhood. Since my divorce I had been involved in a few relationships that were abusive, so I stopped dating, focused on my writing, and got back into therapy. I took a year-and-a-half to heal and to clear the air.

So I looked between these two flames and I said, "Okay, God, this is it. Please send me. . . . " My mind went blank, and then I said, "Send me someone who is intelligent. Someone as smart as I am." I was getting really tired of dating men with whom I had to hide my intelligence. "Dear God, send me someone who is as intelligent as I am, someone who is kind and gentle." Then I took a really deep breath and said, "Send me someone I deserve." That was really scary to say—"someone I deserve." I was scared but I had faith that I was ready for someone I deserved.

Monday afternoon I flew from Hartford to Washington, D.C. The evening I was on "Larry King Live," Larry's wife started working there. She was in the control room, and I could hear her voice in my earplug. She and Larry were talking back and forth when we were off camera, and they were speaking with great affection. They had only known each other four months and had just gotten married. It was a whirlwind romance, and they were so loving toward each other. I was getting really lonely. I remember telling both of them how envious I was.

While I was on "Larry King Live," Charlie was coming home from his office and flipped on the TV and there I was—on his TV set. He said to himself, "Barbara Harris, Barbara Harris," and he realized that he was going up to Hartford the next weekend to speak at an ACoA (Adult Children of Alcoholics) conference. He thought, "I'm going to give her a call and ask her out for dinner."

Charlie called me Wednesday evening. I was praying only the Friday night before. And I thought, "Can this work this fast?"

I had a cancer patient I was seeing every evening that week for energy work after her chemotherapy, so I told Charlie I couldn't meet him for dinner. I asked him if we could have brunch the next morning [after his speaking engagement]. He agreed to that. Then I called my friend, Kay Allison in Charlottesville, and asked her if Charlie was married. She told me he wasn't, and she said she really liked him and his work. Friday morning my patient called to tell me that her chemotherapy treatment had been canceled. I thought, "Well this is pretty interesting." I called Charlie in Baltimore to let him know I could meet him for dinner, but he had already left for Hartford.

I hadn't been able to reach Charlie so I showed up at the hotel Friday evening unannounced. I went to the desk and asked where I could find Charlie Whitfield, and they gave me directions to the ballroom. I walked in and there were 800 people sitting and waiting for the conference to begin. Here I am at my first ACoA conference with all these people and so excited to talk to Charlie about his book and tell him about our research. Someone asked me where my name tag was and I told her that Dr. Whitfield had invited me to attend his talk.

There were seven or more men sitting on the podium and I kept wondering which one of them was Charlie. I just couldn't remember what he looked like. Most of them were older, stodgy, and had big bellies. Finally, they introduced Charlie and his talk, which was going to be on feelings. He had been meditating in his room and walked in from a side door. The first thing that struck me was he had to be a runner, because he was built like one and obviously in great shape. He talked for an hour and a half about feelings, and I just sat there in awe. After his talk, people were lined up halfway around the room, waiting for him to sign their books. Right in the middle of signing a book, he paused and looked in my direction. He put down the pen, got up, and walked over to me. He took my hand and said, "I'm so glad that you could come." Well as soon as he took my hand I knew that this man was going to greatly influence my life. I knew that right away.

We ended up having dinner in a beautiful restaurant in the hotel, and we talked until 1:30 in the morning. Charlie had even remembered what I had worn when we met in Washington five years earlier. He said I had worn all red. I agreed to return the next day for lunch and then I would take him to the airport.

Charlie called me at 8:30 the next morning and asked me to meet him for breakfast. I was there in a half-hour and I was wearing all red. He immediately commented on what I was wearing. We talked until 2:30 in the afternoon, when I dropped him off at the airport. And that was it.

I thought about him a lot that week and wished he would call me. Finally, Thursday evening I called him. His machine picked up, and I started to leave this really dumb message. But in the middle I said, "Charlie, I'm going to cut the crap and say what's on my mind. I really enjoyed being with you and I'd like to see you again." He didn't return my call on Friday or Saturday. By Sunday I felt like I had probably made a fool out of myself. And then he called late Sunday evening. He had been in California all week and knew when he came home he was going to call me. And there I was on his machine, saying what he was going to say to me. We made arrangements to meet the next weekend in Pennsylvania, where I could attend two of his workshops, "Healing the Child Within" on Saturday and a workshop on spirituality on Sunday.

Charlie told me when we were together that weekend in Pennsylvania that he had been praying for a good relationship just before he saw me on "Larry King Live." It turns out we had been praying at about the same time.

The next year was a whirlwind romance; either he was flying to Connecticut or I was driving down to Baltimore. We were together more than we were apart, and at the end of that year we moved in together in Baltimore.

We lived together for three years and then we got married. It was a wonderful wedding down in South Florida. We checked into a hotel on South Beach with our kids and their mates, our one grandchild, our brothers and sister, a few other relatives, plus a few dear friends. We all got dressed up Saturday evening and went over to Unity on the Bay Church in Miami for the wedding ceremony.

It was beautiful and totally unrehearsed. My daughter, Beth, was my attendant and my son, Gary, "gave me away." Charlie's daughter, Kate, sang the love song from the *Phantom of the Opera* to us. Her voice and the words were so beautiful we all cried. The minister blessed us as they do in the Christian tradition, and then Charlie broke the glass and we shared a glass of wine as we do in the Jewish tradition. It was a beautiful blend and what made it so spiritual was that we were surrounded by the people who love us and everyone's heart was open. Then we drove back to the hotel and had a huge Cuban dinner.

Charlie and I believe that we are all really "spiritual beings" trying to have a human experience. We were spirit before we inhabited these bodies, and we will be spirit again after we leave. While we are here we want to contribute as much as we can to this wonderful home we call "Earth."

The writing that we do we share with everyone. But we start off by sharing it with each other, and the synergy between us is incredible. One and one doesn't equal just two anymore. He gives me ideas and I give him ideas. We ask each other questions and that spurs us on to write more. We sometimes teach together and that's good, too. I think that the time has come on this planet for couples like us to find each other and get together not only for us personally, but to help work with and heal the collective community.

Love is completely different for me from what I had once believed before my NDE and my journey of healing. Love used to be what my ego demanded from others. It was like, "All right, I will love you, and in return you have to love me back the way I believe love should be!" Real love is different than what I used to think. It's different from Hollywood's fantasies of enchantment. Love turned out to be real. It turned out to be what I am inside. It is the core of who I am and the core of who you are. No one can love us the way we want to be loved until we first learn to love ourselves in a healthy way.

Love Late in Life

This is a story about hope, courage, and love—a love destined for Katie and Bob at the autumn of life.

At 83, Katie London is still hungry to learn. "If I see a bug," she quips, "I want to know what kind it is. I research it in the library. But at my age, I quickly forget." It was this determination to learn—about her past relationships—and "sheer desperation and frustration" that led Katie to seek the help of a therapist at the age of 79.

> I think if you need therapy you should get it. Finding Judy, my therapist, was a kind of miracle. I was feeling so hopeless about life that I called a number from a program I had seen on public television. I was hospitalized for 11 days. Then I came home without support. When I got home I knew I needed follow-up care. I went to every support group I could find that had anything to do with my problems. I went to 17 meetings in one week. I met my therapist, Judy, through my friend Roy at one of these meetings.
>
> Judy turned my life from upside down to right-side up. Now I try to live very much in the present, as best I can. I've been with her for four years. I've become much more aware of the world around me, the people around me, of myself. Where Judy leaves off and the world begins it's not possible to say. Awareness is a big thing and living in the present is a big thing. I think that it was through my times with Judy that I really learned to love. I really never was in love until Bob. Maybe I wasn't ready for it. If it hadn't been for her, I might not have been ready for it when he came along.
>
> There is a French saying that the end is nothing, it's the journey that counts. When we leave this earth, we will definitely know still very little. People, when they start in therapy, are always wanting to know when they are going to get there. There is no such thing as "there." You never get there, you are always traveling and learning.
>
> I wasn't looking for love at all. I have had a need all my life to help others, and I think that need came from my needing help and love that I didn't get from my mother. I had a very good father, a wonderful man. He was very strict. Many were in those days. His integrity and determination enabled him to do what he believed in. He was very single-minded in that. But the woman he married caused him great and continued pain. He never said that. I didn't know it. My mother caused everyone in the family sadness and pain.
>
> Whatever my mother thought, that was right. He prized education, and church and God went along with it. Everything he did was for the children and the family. He also believed he had to be true to my mother. She didn't treat him well.
>
> I believe in the importance of forgiveness, and that's difficult. If you don't forgive, you are in very serious trouble, and you won't get out

of it until you learn. I made a trip to Wisconsin, where I grew up, to find out what I could of importance. I had to do that by myself. I found out things happened when my mother was a very little girl. Although I had no proof of it, discovering that was what helped me to forgive her.

Before meeting Judy, I was without hope. Now I'm never hopeless. I saw no reason in living. Now I'm much stronger. No matter how bad things get, I can't imagine feeling that way again. I know I have value. It is never, ever too late. We're here to develop and grow. As long as you have life in you, get on with it, do it. I do think some single people have problems that make it difficult for them to keep their perspectives healthy. They can only make better choices when they grow. You have to take some risks; you have to make the best choices you can make.

Realize that you really have to be happy about yourself, and pursue your interests. Make your life as full as you can, regardless of whether you are attached or not attached. I've seen a few people go hunting and say, "That's all I need, if I had somebody like him or her, I'd have everything." It isn't true. You have to grow yourself and feel good about yourself. The way to do that is to grow and develop.

I think that you're never too old to love. Bob and I met in the dining room at our retirement community. It wasn't love at first sight or anything like that. He and I had a wonderful time. We just enjoyed each other's company. I only knew him for about three months. The first few times I met him, I ate dinner with him. He was in the Health Center permanently. I visited him. He got so that he really looked forward to my coming. If he saw me in the distance his face would light up. He was very successful, a well-known person in his own right.

We met when he was 90 years old. My first impression of Bob was of the great strength in him, not flabbiness. Then it got to the point where he wanted me to have dinner with him every night. We saw more of each other, and I got so that I came over after dinner and sat with him a while. I was very taken with his integrity and his really first-rate mind. I had many questions for him. We could discuss anything. We could disagree or agree. It didn't make any difference. He was very wise. He had been the head of a large law firm in New York that he had built from the beginning. He was always looking at all sides of an issue, to the best of his ability. I was used to people who were so categorical in their decisions. He was a delight to me. We just got along well.

One Saturday, I took him to the theater. It was a horrible play. We had to get out at intermission because he had to smoke. We sat in the coffee shop and sipped coffee and had a lovely time. But the play really was bad so we didn't go to the second half. The next week we went to the symphony and had another wonderful time. We got back to the Health Center late. He and I were outside after they locked the gates. I didn't realize we couldn't get in. Boy we had a time. We were like two teenagers missing curfew. I forced the door open. Actually there was a bell, but I didn't ring it.

A funny thing happened one day. My younger daughter was coming out to see me. Bob said, "I want to meet her." I told her and she said yes. She probably knew I was spending evenings with him. I took her over to the Health Center. She was in our company for no more than a half-hour and she helped him into his wheelchair and wheeled him out. I sat on one end of the bench so she could sit next to him and talk. He had a few cigarettes. We went back in and said good-bye.

She said, "My life will never be the same."

For the longest time I tried to figure out what they had talked about. It was just being with us and realizing how important we were to each other. That was like a miracle, too. It meant so much that she was there and saw us together.

To me, love is a very steady, miraculous thing. Our love for one another made all the difference in the world to me. It's brought me peace and joy and love and gladness and all good things. And a connection with the universe, I guess. It helped a lot when he died because he stayed with me. And he'll always be with me, no matter what I do or where I'll go. It's a lovely thing to have.

First Impressions: One Man's Insight

Josh, a divorced ad writer in Manhattan, put a "personal ad" in *The New York Review*. Gail's friend brought her the ad and insisted she answer it. She still remembers fondly what it said:

Nice-enough looking, flat-bellied, likeable achiever. Fond of idea-candling, ["He was looking for a brilliant woman and I knew what it meant," Gail says.] nose-rubbing, beach hikes, travel, Manhattan, cooking, art, honesty. Looking for spunky woman of quality, 49 plus, previously married, for the real thing.

This ad brought them together, but Josh's first impressions of Gail, based on a photo she sent him, almost nipped their romance in the bud. Fortunately, he had the wisdom and maturity to see beyond the surface.

She looked like somebody who was trying to impress me with her style. She was wearing sunglasses. Silly, since the picture was supposed to show me what she was like. I discounted it because I didn't ask for a picture. You have to meet a person. There's a very wide range of acceptable looks: beautiful, pleasant, so many acceptable forms. What is not acceptable is a dishonest, difficult, or shallow person.

As Josh got to know Gail, he learned that the woman behind the sunglasses had "great depth and intellectual honesty" and that he "could talk to her and know who she is and test ideas on her."

I think there is a lack of flexibility in men. Women are more flexible and understand better what is important in life. I can't tell you why men are looking for poster girls, and I'm inclined to think they are. Everybody needs somebody else. It's the need that pierces the veil of requirements. A strong need sees beauty even where it isn't obvious.

When people talk to me about doing personal ads, I tell them they have to park their expectations, and understand that if you don't reveal yourself honestly you'll run into problems later. That's why I said "nice-enough looking" in my personal ad. If you look at ads, people say stunning, highly attractive. That raises a hurdle. I suggest people be very honest with their requirements and their picture of themselves. It's so much better for a person to come into a situation where the other person has relaxed expectations, instead of expecting a Hollywood star, and is pleasantly surprised.

Our story is so good that a lot of people have retold it and have asked me for help with writing an ad. I find that they don't want to face themselves honestly or understand they probably have something highly valuable that may not be a high degree of beauty or brilliance. Maybe he or she is simply a decent person who is accepting of another person with his or her own faults.

The following is a letter Josh sent me several days after our interview.

Joan,

About a year before I met Gail, my son, who lives in Hawaii and doesn't see my day-to-day life, asked me what I was doing to get a life partner. I told him that after 10 years of trying to do that, I wasn't sure I would ever find that person. I think in retrospect that the pain of my divorce had kept me in a defensive mode, and it was comforting in a sense to say to myself that permanent pairing wasn't for me. My answer to him also showed a yearning . . . the need I spoke to you about.

That yearning or need is what allowed me to poke through the defenses I had built up. So when Gail turned out to be too stylish for me, my needs asked me to put that aside and look for something about her I really did want. And it was there in spades, once I allowed myself to see. I think I sensed in her stylishness an inclination for fun in life, something I hungered for despite—or perhaps because of—my natural seriousness. Gail bursts with enthusiasm. I do not, but I respond well to it in her. I dressed in conservative, somber tones; she explodes with color. I think I knew that we were a good fit if I could overcome my fear of being overpowered.

Little by little I learned to handle what I first thought of as outrageousness, but which was nothing but spirit. And that is the lesson I would offer your readers. In pairing, I am convinced, what we all look for most is comfort and approval. The old, "I'm all right, you're all right" feeling. We want to be accepted, ideally without question. Because when someone makes us feel comfortable, we want to be around them. So being gorgeous, being rich, being famous, being widely admired—all these attributes may suggest that a person is a highly desirable mate. But they also might mean someone who has no reason to approve of others, especially me, a normal person who is not nearly as charismatic.

A prospective partner with great credentials may seem like the bargain you're looking for. But the biggest bargain is a person who allows you to feel good about being yourself. Those people are much more available than the bargains.

Josh

Josh and Gail are married and living in Key West.

Going Back

I ran across the following destiny story in *The New York Times'* wedding announcements. I knew I had to include it in *Celebrating Single* to give other 40-something singles hope about finding their soul mate. So I tracked down Andy Matlow from the information in the article.

Andy's wife, Peggy Cullen, author, expert on chocolate, and baker extraordinaire, wrote her poignant love story for *Celebrating Single:*

In Hebrew, *bashert* is the person who is your destiny—your fate. I found my *bashert* when I was young. After a brief time together, destiny tore us apart. Twenty-five years later, we found each other again—reunited by the grown daughter we had given up for adoption two and a half decades before.

The first time I met Andy, who was my good friend Judi's housemate, he had just returned from ice fishing on Lake Champlain. The kitchen sink was filled with fish. There were buckets of fish everywhere. He proceeded to clean and fry dozens of perch for dinner. The three of us stood over the stove and ate them with our fingers, right off the bone. I was struck by Andy's bold spirit, contagious laugh, and dark good looks.

It was the early '70s. We were all students at a college in Vermont. The day after I met Andy, I left for a seven-month journey to Peru, part of my required off-campus studies. Andy was very much on my mind.

When I returned we saw each other again, and it was wonderful. Shortly after that, however, I had to leave for another trimester of off-campus study. Our budding relationship was interrupted, but we decided that when I returned we would rent a house together, along with Judi.

A few months after I came back to Vermont, to the house we shared, I realized I was pregnant. At that point we didn't have the history in our relationship, the commitment, or the skills to handle such a profound event. Scared and overwhelmed, Andy withdrew from me. I didn't understand him—I thought he was cruel and heartless. I became angry at his seeming indifference, which made him withdraw even further. We stopped speaking. When our lease was up, we all went our separate ways.

I didn't even know where Andy went. I went to have a baby. With a broken heart, I gave my baby up for adoption. I didn't have the financial resources or emotional support from anyone to keep her. About three months after she was born, I was up in the attic of my apartment looking for something. I happened to peek out the little round window and saw Andy's car, piled with his belongings, at the gas pump across the street. I knew he was leaving Vermont, and that I would probably never see him again.

I never got over giving up my baby. She was always in my heart. But I put Andy completely out of my mind. It was too painful to think about—being pregnant and abandoned by someone I cared for so much.

Eventually, I moved to New York City to pursue my career as a baker, writer, and candy maker. While my life was relatively full and happy, my relationships with men never lasted more than a year and a half. I never married or had other children. I dreamed of the day I would finally get to meet my daughter.

Twenty-five years passed. Then one day, when I had almost stopped hoping, I received a letter from my daughter, Raychel. She said she was coming to New York from Los Angeles, where she lived, for 10 days, and would I like to meet her? The sadness that had surrounded me all those years lifted immediately. I walked on air in anticipation of seeing her.

Our first meeting was both awkward and joyous. It was like being with a stranger I'd known all my life. During the evening I mentioned that I'd help her find her father if she wanted. While I secretly hoped she wouldn't want to meet Andy, I felt that she was entitled to know her birth father. After thinking about it for a day, she asked me to find him for her.

It was easy to track Andy down through our mutual friend of long ago, Judi. She told me he was married and living in the country, in a house he built himself. I called him late that night.

That evening we had the conversation that we should have had 25 years before. He spoke with an open heart about his sorrow and pain over what happened to us. He explained that my anger led him to believe that I wanted nothing to do with him—so he stayed away. I told him how I felt so utterly devastated and abandoned by him. We had so hugely misunderstood each other so many years ago.

We talked, laughed, and cried on the phone into the wee hours. It turned out he had divorced a few years before. When I hung up the phone, I thought, "I'm home now. I don't have to go any further. My daughter is in my life, and Andy Matlow is single and looking for love."

Andy came to New York that weekend. The three of us—Raychel, Andy, and I—met together for the first time over champagne and homemade pizza. Despite the anticipation and excitement among us all, there was a level of comfort and familiarity that was undeniable—a feeling of home. We were like a little family. We were a family.

Raychel returned to Los Angeles, and we continued to talk. Andy returned to the Berkshires in Western Massachusetts, and he and I continued to talk, too. We started seeing each other almost immediately. Our courtship had all the joy, thrill, and delight of any two people falling in love with each other. But then, out of nowhere, I would be triggered by a painful memory, and we'd have to travel back to the past—to those terrible times—to sort out our feelings. It was almost like there were two relationships going on at once.

But we always went forward. I never had one doubt that Andy was the one for me. I had waited my whole life—I was 46—to feel that way about someone.

We were given a second chance. For us, falling in love in our late forties is so much richer than it was in our early twenties. We have our priorities straight. We don't get bogged down in petty issues. We are each happy with ourselves—so we have more to give to each other. A deep appreciation of the fact that we have found each other again permeates our life. It's a dream come true that I never dared to dream.

A little more than a year after our first date, Andy and I were married. Raychel was the maid of honor. Her adoptive parents were at the wedding. It took place on Sukkot, the Jewish holiday that celebrates and gives thanks for the harvest. In keeping with the season, we were reaping the joy that grew from seeds sown long ago.

Andy believes that he and Peggy were destined to be together. He talks about finding love later in life and offers advice to other single baby boomers.

I believe we were meant to be together. It's perfect now. Who knows what it would have been like 27 years ago? The beauty of this is, it's great to fall in love at 50; it's better than at 20. You've got the brains. We make a lot of mistakes in our twenties, thirties, and forties. I worked out childhood stuff from my first marriage. At 50 you have your priorities straight. I'm not going to argue over something that's not important. Life is too precious.

The best time to meet someone is when you're happy with yourself, not desperate. When that happens, you meet someone when you least expect it. When you're looking and looking, you're not paying attention to the moment. Not that I didn't spend time looking. When I think about my significant relationships, I met the women in an "unlooking" way. Look how I met Peggy. I was watching TV, and I got a call from her.

Joan: The Lecture

I sat with 200 women in the lecture hall, cast by her spell. Marcia spoke about her best-selling book at a woman's networking dinner. This 50-something author had it all: radiance, beauty, energy, creativity. I wanted to be Marcia when I grew up.

We had a common friend, so I gathered my *hutzpah* and introduced myself after Marcia's lecture. We exchanged cards and occasionally chatted by phone. She gave me the names of several agents and publishers for *Celebrating Single*. I gave her names of people to interview for her upcoming book. Then I shifted the conversation to a more personal level.

"Anyone special in your life?" I asked.

"No," she answered.

"Same here," I said. With the determination of the quintessential matchmaker I said, "I'm going to find you someone. I know a very handsome divorced dentist. . . . "

Through the years she became an important role model and mentor to me. No, the dentist didn't work out, but this special woman was too busy living her life to worry about that or a new wrinkle. She never lost hope about meeting a special man. And eventually destiny took care of that for her.

Although I don't discount destiny, I'm not a major believer. Jay and I sometimes talk about this. The forces that connected us after so many years were so convoluted, one has to think there was some greater power involved.

About three years ago, in the fall, I gave a speech on one of my books in Fairfield, Connecticut. My speeches are attended mostly by women. When I looked in the audience, there was a very attractive man. I wondered who he was and why he was there. After I finished, he came backstage and said, "I bet you don't remember me."

I hemmed and hawed. Jay told me his name and I said, "Oh my God, how are you?" He lived across the street from me when I was a baby in Philadelphia. I knew his family. Our parents had been friends. He had moved to another town when we were in junior high school. He was a year younger than I. He knew who I was and I knew who he was, but we never had much interaction. He did go on some double dates with my sister in high school; he was friendly with someone she was dating. I very quickly told him I was newly divorced. He knew. He had a cousin in Philly.

He said he was married and gave me his card. I thought to myself, I wonder why he came to the speech? That was that. I put his card in a drawer and forgot about it.

Fast-forward to two-and-a-half years later, to the fall again. I was at my sister's house for Break the Fast on Yom Kippur. First, a little background: The mother of my sister's best friend was very friendly with Jay's mother. There was a third woman in the community where I grew up who was friendly with these two mothers. Her daughter had attended the same private school as Jay's sister.

For some reason, I'm not quite sure what, that daughter had gotten in touch with Jay's sister and had picked up Jay's e-mail address. She then sent an e-mail with New Year's greetings to everyone on her list, which included my sister's best friend. My sister's best friend then e-mailed Jay to say "hi." He sent an e-mail message back to her, bringing her up to date on his life—and mentioned the fact that he was divorced.

After we broke the fast on that Yom Kippur, we were all sitting around in the living room. I complained how bored I was with everyone I was dating and how tiresome dating had become. My sister's best friend mentioned that she had gotten an e-mail from Jay and that he was divorced. "He's not divorced," I said. "He was married three years ago." She said, "Not anymore."

I remembered how cute he was and said to her, "Why don't you e-mail him and tell him I come into New York a lot." He lived in Connecticut and I lived in Philadelphia. I said, "Tell him I'd be happy to meet him for a drink." She contacted him the next day, and he told her in an e-mail that he'd always had a crush on me. He called me that night. We talked a long time, and we spoke again the next night. I went into New York that Saturday and met him for lunch, and it was like we'd been good friends since childhood, even though we hadn't been.

The connection was so immediate, so strong. We've been seeing each other ever since. It was immediate and powerful. We're very much in love, happy, and totally connected. I'm 60. People say, "When are you getting married?" I say, "We're waiting to see if I get pregnant."

We spend every weekend together and vacations. He calls me every night before I go to bed. He says, "Sweet dreams." They're certainly sweeter because he's in my life.

If it hadn't been for the e-mail that came from that convoluted chain, there's a good chance I would never have learned he was divorced. I asked Jay why he never called me after we ran into each other. He said he thought about calling me, but he met a woman. We refer to her as the transitional relationship. When you are an attractive single man, there's always someone nearby. He was separated from his wife the week after he saw me. He came to my speech because he saw it advertised in the newspaper and remembered me. When my books got successful, he would say to friends, "We grew up together and I used to know her."

You just never know. Life is remarkable. We look at each other in wonderment at the forces that brought us together. A lot of forces converged for us to reconnect, and the connection was instant because of the history we share. We know so many of the same people. While we're lying in bed, we'll say, "So who was the principal of our junior high?" The older you get, the more important it is to have people in your life who knew you when you were young, and we provide that for each other.

My advice to single people? First, never lose hope. People used to say to me, "You're going to meet someone when you least expect it." I always thought, "Baloney," but that happens. When you're single you're always expecting to meet someone. I never walked into a room without doing my fast x-ray scan to see if there was anyone who looked interesting. Then he pops up out of nowhere!

You think the older you get, the less your chances are of meeting someone. I was 55 when I got divorced. I thought, "I should have done this 209 years ago."

Second and most important, you must create a life that satisfies you whether you're with someone or alone. I had a rich life, although I wanted someone to share it; my life was never diminished because I was alone. You need to create a life that gives you satisfaction. Then if you do meet someone, that's the icing on the cake. You can't live with the hope of finding someone to make your life better; you have to make it better yourself, and that in turn, I think, makes you more attractive to someone else.

When I had my 60th birthday last year, I said that in every decade of my life, I had literally everything I dreamed about: getting married the first time, then children, career, success of my books in my fifties. I was planning to dedicate this decade of my life to finding somebody to share my life with and make me happy. Six months later, there he was. His blond hair was gray, but the twinkling blue eyes were still blue.

Selma and Howard

Selma thought her fate had been sealed. World War II had just ended, she had a loving family, and a good job, and her fiancé was driving from California to Baltimore to plan their wedding. The rest of the love story reads like a Cary Grant/Irene Dunne comedy.

Selma and Howard Berman sit in their eggshell-blue living room. After 45 years of marriage, they still share a mutual respect and attraction for one another.

SELMA: I was single and about 20 years old. One of my girlfriends kept saying to me, "I have a cousin Ben and he wants to fix you up with a friend of his." It's not that I was the most popular girl in the world, but I had a lot of dates. I didn't have to go looking for blind dates, so I declined.

Four years prior to this, I had fallen in love with a neighbor's friend. He and his family moved to California. We kept in touch. He kept writing to me and vowed he would come back some day so we could become engaged and get married. The controversy was whether to live on the East Coast or the West Coast and where the marriage would take place. He wanted it in the middle of the country, and I said my parents would never hear of it. Anyway, he was driving from California to Baltimore on a weekend, and we were supposed to re-new our love.

Meanwhile I was staying at my friend Florrie's home, and she took me to her cousin Ben's place. We were just talking to Ben and his wife. He left the room and came back and said, "Someone wants to speak with you on the phone." I picked up the phone and it was Howard. He said that Ben suggested we get together for a date.

I didn't want to tell him that I was getting engaged, so I said I was busy that weekend. He said, "How about Thursday, before the weekend?"

So I said, "All right I'll go out with you Thursday for just a little while."

My sister, who's older than I am, had gotten married about five years before. I adored my brother-in-law. He was my confidant. He drove me to work in downtown Baltimore every day; I was a legal secretary at the time.

One day on the way to work I said, "I'm so upset, I have a blind date tonight and I really don't want to go on it. I don't know anything about him except he's a friend of my girlfriend's. My boyfriend is driving back from California and we're supposed to become en-gaged."

"Well who's your date?"

And I said, "I don't know, Howard or something like that."

"What's his last name?"

"Berman."

He pulled his car over and parked it.

"Open up your wallet," he said.

"Why should I open my wallet? I'm going to be late for work."

He said, "Open up your wallet."

I had forgotten that years before I had asked my brother-in-law for his picture to carry in my wallet.

He took the picture out. I didn't even remember it was there because it was folded. He unfolded it and said, "There's your date for tonight." And I looked at him.

HOWARD: It was taken at Tamarind; a group of us guys used to go up there in the summer in the Poconos.

SELMA: My brother-in-law had been away with Howard the year before he gave me the picture. He was kind of good-looking.

So that evening Howard and I went out. The minute I got in his car, I thought, "I really like him, he's nice and intelligent."

I remember coming home that evening and awaking my mother. My parents had twin beds and I remember walking in between the beds. I said, "Mom, I met the man I'm going to marry."

And she said, "Is Jerry in from California already?"

"No, this is somebody else, my blind date."

"But Jerry's coming back."

"Mom, this is the guy, I know it."

And so it was.

Joan: On Destiny

Marc and I frequently disagree about issues of the heart. I am a believer in destiny; he is not. I savor the following story because, if it were not for this book, the couple I'm about to describe might not have found each other.

I made two decisions in November, 1996. One, to write this book, and two, to learn all I could about managing my finances. I met with five financial mavens. One was single, so I also interviewed him for my book and asked if he knew of any other single subjects. The first on his list was Ted, a handsome attorney in his mid-thirties. During our interview, Ted seemed quite nervous, perched up on his bar stool, pulling his stiff white collar and jutting his chin. Three drinks and 40 minutes later, his story came to life. He had studied in the seminary, changed career paths, and switched to law.

"What are you looking for in a woman, Ted?" I inquired.

"A woman, who when I look into her face, I see the eyes of God," he answered without missing a beat.

I found his answer odd, but my response was even more bewildering. As he elaborated on his ideal woman, I thought of an angelic-looking blonde woman I had worked with on a video project several months earlier. "Yes," I thought. I stroked my chin and smiled.

The next morning, I called Lorraine and asked if she wanted to meet a cute lawyer. She said she trusted my instincts. Then I called Ted and asked if he wanted to meet the woman in whom he'd see the eyes of God. He couldn't resist. The rest is history. They got married in June, 2000. I rest my case.

13

Celebrating Love

BEATRICE

Sterling bangles
click and clang
about her wrist,
as strong hands
breathe life
into wet clay.

An elegant Bohemian,
she dons silk saris,
sheer negligees
and dangles a
shapely leg over
a velvet couch.

Dancing eyes
sweep me into
her soul.
I swim in her
mystical potion
so I can
build
and play
and love
when I'm 100.

—JOAN

JOAN: Well, Marc, we've come to the end of this journey together.

MARC: And we still haven't killed each other.

JOAN: Yeah. (Laughing) What strikes you about the stories in this chapter?

MARC: What strikes me is the power that these women were able to generate within themselves. Sara's story is probably a model for women who have their backs against the wall but are determined to succeed. Not just survive, but to make their life flourish. Having breast cancer, no job, and no husband would seem like the end of the road. For Sara, it was the beginning of a new and better life. That's why it's an awesome story. Talk about turning lemons into lemonade.

JOAN: What do you think the message is for our readers?

MARC: That the raw material for the new and better life that they want for themselves is within them.

JOAN: These women have found that being single is fulfilling, regardless of what society tells them. For some of them, single is a happy ending.

MARC: This book is for women who want to create a rewarding life that suits them, and for guys who are intelligent and sensitive enough to appreciate women like that.

JOAN: OK, what's our next book?

MARC: *How to Get Marc a Date.*

Joan: Sayonara Stigmas

I grew up with the myth of the post-menopausal crone—wise, asexual, and unproductive—the Norman Rockwell painting of an old woman rocking on the front porch. Fortunately that myth is drying up like the unappealing picture it paints.

When I read *Playing Chess With the Heart* I felt inspired. I had found another vibrant, accomplished mentor, who had better things to do than wait around for romance and life to happen. Beatrice Wood, 100 at the time the book was published, jumped off the pages and into my heart. Her thoughts on love, life, and sex were sprinkled among black-and-white portraits shot by photographer Marlene Wallace. Wallace captures Beatrice Wood's sensuality, passion, sense of humor, beauty, and spirit—the very essence of woman.

This chapter is dedicated to women who, like Beatrice Wood, dispel the myth of middle-aged women as crones and single women as spinsters. "Celebrating Love" spotlights vibrant women who are making a difference and living their lives with purpose and passion, with or without romance.

Each of the women you will meet in this chapter has discovered that single isn't a stage you're trapped in while you're waiting for life to happen. It's not a race to the finish line of love. It's a fluid state that you can change whenever you choose. And when you learn to embrace it like a lover, often a lover appears.

Part of celebrating single is living your authentic life, the life that only you can create, and having the courage to make challenging choices. It's about fulfilling that acorn, the daimon (Greek for call in life, your soul companion) within you that is your purpose. Like a thumbprint, the daimon is different in every person. Yet no person can deny it when they hear its call.

The Gift of Love

Patricia, 45, a divorced computer consultant, felt her calling and listened to the hunger in her heart. The decision she made in 1997 brought more joy to Patricia and her family than she could imagine.

I had debated becoming a mother for years. When I got divorced, I kept telling myself I could adopt or have a child on my own. At 40, I seriously started thinking about it. At that time I didn't see myself doing it on my own. When I turned 43, being childless wasn't an option. At that point I was able to deal with enormous amounts of fear and anxiety: How am I going to deal with this myself?

The turning point came at my friend's daughter's third birthday party. The little girl, Leighton, chose me to be the one to open her presents with, and she wanted me to hold her on my lap. I realized I had a hunger and passion inside. I wanted a child. It was not an intellectual thing. My analytical side said this couldn't and shouldn't be done. My heart correctly took over.

I went through a long thought process about the way I wanted to become a mother—adopt or have one on my own. There was a lot of soul-searching along the way. When I came to a decision about adopting, then there were more choices. If I chose an international adoption, for example, then what country?

Through research I learned there were impairments and developmental delays in institutionalized children, especially in babies from Eastern Europe. That raised a whole host of fears for me: What if something goes wrong and the baby's sick? Am I able to deal with unknown problems? At the time research also indicated there was a higher percentage of fetal alcohol syndrome in Eastern Europe.

Although my heritage is Eastern European, I began to consider adopting a baby from China. I had reason to hope that the care given children in some Chinese orphanages, and prenatal care in general, was better there. In China they can have only one child, so if an infant turns out to be a girl, parents sometimes make the gut-wrenching decision to give up their daughter for adoption in the hopes of having a son.

Adoption is a leap of faith. After a lot of thought I decided to adopt a baby girl from China. After a long process of applications, paperwork, and certification, I got a referral. Getting that referral was unbelievable. When I got the news I was with my girlfriend Liz. I couldn't believe I had the referral. I had to get the nursery ready. Then, when I heard I could go to China, the Chinese government was in the process of restructuring their adoption process. No one knew how long it would take. To make matters worse, there was flooding in the province where Grace, the little girl I would adopt, was living, and a lot of people were getting sick and dying in that orphanage. This is typical of the international adoption experience. I've heard of people landing in another country to find out that the country had shut down their international adoption process.

I said, "Liz, I know I want to go to China, but I don't know if I can do this by myself." She said without hesitation, "I'll go." Then my father and I were kidding around and he said he'd like to go, too. It was unbelievably precious to me that Liz and my father volunteered and went with me to China. At times it was still overwhelming, especially without an interpreter. I was on tenterhooks until we got through every last step and we were finally on the plane back to Los Angeles.

Grace brings me more joy than I ever would have been able to guess was possible. The joy you feel when you see your child growing, happy, and learning something new is not a sensation I can describe easily. It happened about four days into our life together. When I got her in China, she was nine months old—she was sick, unhappy, and very scared. She was terrified when they put her in my arms. Then four days later she reached over and gave me a hug and a kiss. Parenthood is all about that experience of joy in that kind of moment. Your heart melts, basically.

One of the joys I didn't anticipate is the amount of happiness Grace would bring to so many other people besides me—my family members and friends. My father, who is not an overtly demonstrative man by nature, although he has become more so as he's gotten older, breaks into a grin when he sees her and stays grinning the entire time. The same is true for all of my family. I expected them to be happy, but I didn't realize how much joy they would get from Grace and how much joy I would take from their pleasure. I love seeing my family with her; it's really neat. She means the world to them and that's wonderful. The nanny loves her, too.

Patricia offers the same advice others gave her about adopting a baby. She urges people who are considering adoption to be realistic, not just about their financial resources—the money for adoption—but about the other resources needed to raise a child. "If you have financial resources, you can get help—and you will need help. If you've thought about the practicalities and you have resources (family that can watch the baby) then adopting a child can be the most important and joyous thing you'll ever get to do. Run, don't walk, to the nearest adoption agency. Know, too, that it is the hardest and most demanding thing you'll ever do, and it's an unending job."

Although her life is full and she loves being a parent, Patricia still hasn't ruled out marriage in her future, if she meets the right person. Divorced 10 years, Patricia quips that her days of having a passionate fling are over because she doesn't have enough energy. "If my energy would go to that, it wouldn't go to Grace." As she looks back over the past year, she realizes she's had little opportunity for a romantic life.

I was briefly involved with one guy, but I told him I couldn't have an intense, all-consuming kind of relationship at that point in my motherhood. I don't know if that will always be true, but it was true at that moment. My professional life has been tremendously stressful and demanding over the past few months. My employees are doing their damnedest not to get divorced over it. I'm just grateful I don't have a relationship right now. My guess is I'll meet a man in a very different environment, maybe something to do with kids. Maybe I'll take my daughter to the playground one day and I'll meet a single father and his child.

I've thought about how I would feel about being alone, without a mate. I know I feel a lot better with Grace than if it were just me. For the first few years after my divorce, I had a great time. Then the novelty wore off and my work was becoming less fulfilling and more demanding. I was finding it harder to meet anybody interesting. At the same time I was feeling something of an ache, an emptiness, a loneliness, and I was trying to sort out if it was due to my lack of a relationship or my lack of a child.

Although I would like to be in a relationship, the lack of one is a far less emotional issue to me than it was before I became a mother. Having a family really means so much. I have several employees, all married, all with kids. Until a year ago, I was unlike them in both respects. They'd talk about their husband and kids; I'd talk about dancing lessons. Now I'm a mother, and I don't envy them their husbands. A husband would be nice, but not all of them are happily married. When I hear about some of those relationships, I think my nanny does a better job than some of those husbands, except for the sex part. But every once in a while I get a little yen to dress up and have someone find me attractive. Then I look at Grace's face and think, "I am so lucky."

Joan: Single By Choice

Over a dozen years ago, I produced television programs for a nonprofit organization in Baltimore. I worked with a woman named Rachel, a writer in the communications department, who was about 70 at the time. She'd never married and never retired.

I'd never met an unmarried career woman before. There was my Aunt Yetta, but she didn't have a career or a job. She lived with her mean sister, Fanny, and Fanny's husband. Rumor had it that Yetta's family thought she was mildly retarded. She seemed fine to me; I always liked her. Later I theorized that she had been hidden from society like a leper not because of her I.Q., but because she was considered homely.

Rachel was different from Aunt Yetta. She wore her shiny ash-blond hair in a blunt cut that framed her oval face; she dressed in tailored clothes that flattered her size-six shape. She had a standing weekly manicure appointment, rubbed shoulders with diplomats and newspaper editors, traveled to Europe every year, had subscription tickets to the theater, and spent treasured time with her nieces, nephews, and their children.

And yet in my early thirties, I feared Rachel. I believe I even avoided her, because on an unconscious level I thought "never-married" was a contagious disease. Remember, in my family, single was not an option. At that time I felt romance ruled, that my life lacked something essential when my life lacked a man. I felt sorry for Rachel.

Looking back now, I can laugh. I see Rachel through different eyes. She is a woman of passion, style, commitment, and energy. She is my role model. She taught me that I can carve whatever life I want.

Rachel, 86, meets me at her door wearing black-and-white walking shorts, Keds, and a black T-shirt. Her nails are a pale pink. From the back, she can pass for a woman half her age. We sit in her screened porch drinking lemonade and noshing on ripe Indian summer fruits. She talks about her career as a writer. Rachel still freelances for local newspapers.

Ever since I can remember, I've wanted to write. I didn't have to go looking for an interest. My mother used to go to my teachers and say, "Why is my child always failing arithmetic?" They said, "She doesn't have to know arithmetic, she can write."

Rachel's father, a prominent lawyer, stressed learning. She heard Poe's "The Raven" before she knew nursery rhymes and read Ibsen's *A Doll's House* by the time she was seven. There was no question that Rachel would go to college. She graduated from Goucher in 1933, during the heart of the Great Depression.

My family really supported me about my career goals. When I got out of college, I wanted to find a job as a copywriter, and I was lucky to have a mother who said, "OK, walk the streets till you get what you want." I would knock on doors and get turned down by the very best.

I would answer every ad, take courage in my hands and go to the ad manager of an agency or particular company. I took the streetcar. Either they would see me or not. I got one job at a big agency, Van Sant Dougdale, after answering an ad for a man with experience.

They said, "If we didn't have a job for you, we'd make a job for you." That was in 1933. In 1935 I got a job at Lansburgh's Department Store in Washington, D.C. It was the lowliest job, a basement copywriter.

My boss at Lansburgh's told me there was a public relations society in D.C. He wanted me to talk to them about how to get into advertising. I got down there thinking I was going to be talking to neophytes. The ad manager of Woodies [Woodward and Lothrop Department Store] and the manager of a radio station were in the audience. I was telling them how to get into advertising. I gave them the speech as I had memorized it.

I was always happy doing what I was doing, writing basement copy or institutional ads. In the late '30s, early '40s, I started writing feature stories for *The Baltimore Sun*. I wrote about various topics: the Peabody Library, a chimney sweep, and an antiques shop built by two seafaring brothers. I also wrote for *The Times Herald*.

My family, which includes nieces and nephews, and writing have been the two greatest passions in my life. I always got a thrill when I got a byline. Unfortunately I'm the kind of person you have to sit down and hit over the head to write. I made a name for myself in the public relations community, and I know others who made greater names for themselves. I did what I liked and always had jobs I liked— that's the important thing.

My mother liked me to meet people; she never put pressure on me to get married. My life was my life and she just encouraged it. Marriage was never an issue; it was never discussed.

The one or two guys I wanted to marry didn't want to marry me, and I just wasn't going to settle. A friend of mine said, "It's important to have 'Mrs.' on your tombstone." I don't think so. There are so many things in life to enjoy. I've always had enough friends to do them with.

I've never been really lonely. There are some days when you get a little pang. I had a guy to take me to the theater, and I did have dates. For many years, there was always some guy around.

It's funny, I never felt there was a stigma to being single. I lived my life. I'm probably more confident now than I was when I was younger. You have to feel good about what you do, how you look. Maybe that's being vain, but maybe we need some vanity. There's no point in crying over what you can't have. It's a lot about attitude. I decided early on, "I'm not pretty, so I'll be smart looking; I will go to the hairdresser and work on me." At least I got satisfaction, if no one else did.

I'm the kind of person, with the good and the bad, who always thinks what she has is the best. I'm very happy with it. I never felt that anybody had anything better than I did. I had a beautiful home, and enough money to do what I wanted to do. I was very comfortable, middle-class. I would have liked to be real pretty and real popular, but I wasn't. I found interests—things I always wanted to do. I took up golf and horseback riding.

You know, being single isn't at all a bad thing. I earned enough money. I have a very loving family. I live with my sister, so I'm not living alone. I have nieces and nephews who are like my own children. My nephew just got married, and he calls me every Friday night. I don't feel like I missed out by not having a child. I have such wonderful memories of my nieces and nephews.

Rachel suggests that single people find something they are interested in and learn as much as they can about it. A strong supporter of education, she encourages people to go to a good liberal arts college—at any age.

If you already have a degree, start another one. Try a career change. Stick to it, stick to your guns, don't compromise. Find a job you love. If you want to do something badly enough, you can do it. You have to be content with your own abilities and limitations. That's what the key is. Accept what you've got, make the most of it, and stop being envious. You don't know what's in that other person's life. Look at Princess Di. She had a hell of a marriage and a tragic death. I believe that most people should be able to find contentment whether they're single or married.

I want my nieces and nephews to remember me as being an important part of their lives. I want people to remember that I had some kind of talent and I didn't waste a life. The only regret I have is that I should have made myself do more writing. I have a wonderful story I'm sitting on. I want to write a feature story about my cousin's experiences as a POW in World War II, based on his memoirs. He has a marvelous sense of humor.

I guess that a love of life and sense of humor run in Rachel's family.

Jill, 40, is a television station manager in a small Maryland town. I met her on a job interview a few years ago and admired her positive attitude, accomplishments, and independence. Well, I didn't get the producer job (they promoted from within), but I left with a great interview for *Celebrating Single*.

Voted "most-liberated" by her all-girls high school class of 1978, it's no surprise that Jill enjoys her freedom and the lifestyle of a never-married baby boomer. A spirited woman, Jill exudes radiance and a knack for celebrating life. I suspect she gets her passion for adventure, the arts, people, and the outdoors from her Native American and Irish forebears. Jill says that while exploring her Native American roots, she has experienced a spiritual awakening and feels a strong affinity for nature-based religions.

I have some Indian blood—my grandmother, whom I never met, was half Native American. She died when my father was very young. I'm very interested in finding my Indian roots. I've gone hiking in Arizona and throughout the Southwest. Some traveling I've done by myself. I'm not afraid to do things by myself; I do things I want to do.

While tracing my roots, I've enjoyed getting back to nature. When I was a kid I hated camping. Now I love to do things outdoors like bird-watching and hiking. I joined a hiking club through the recreation and parks department. We take day trips with 30 people. It's not a singles' group. The group is half single and half couples. In November our group is going to Berkeley Springs, West Virginia, on a spa vacation. We're renting a five-bedroom place.

I have always dreamed of going to Ireland. I'm part Irish and I'm very interested in pagan and Celtic culture and lore. Next year, I'm traveling by myself through Ireland on a hiking tour. We will hike about 10 miles a day and then we'll take a bus to bed-and-breakfasts, where they'll serve gourmet lunches and dinners. We'll get to see the countryside and taste the essence of what Ireland is like. I want to feel the earth. It's a spiritual thing, too.

I just turned 40 this year and I feel healthier and better than I did when I was 30. I've filled my life with friends, daily yoga practice, and a healthy diet to balance a somewhat stressful job. I've also changed my dating practices. I was in a very unhealthy relationship with a man and stayed with him for five years. Only one year was good. He was very into sports. I like sports, but I'm also interested in cultural things. I went to sporting events with him so we could be together. He refused to go to the opera, museums, or the theater. I thought, "If he won't share any of my interests, there must be something wrong." The problem was, he was friends with all my friends and I couldn't get rid of him. When I broke up with him it led me to a spiritual journey. I wanted to discover my self, nature, the world.

Now I have a group of friends, who are couples, single, engaged. We all have a good time. Nobody in the group makes me feel uncomfortable because I'm single. When they complain about their problems in relationships and marriages, I find it hard to sympathize with them. I'm very happy single; for me, now, single is better than being married. My friends who are married say they are envious of me.

When I get together with my girlfriends, one of my married friends goes off on a tangent about her husband and all his flaws; then she complains about her mother-in-law. She's a pain in the neck. I don't want to hear about these problems every single week. Her husband is pouty. I never liked her choice of husbands. He thinks I manipulate her. He doesn't like my influence on her. So many of my friend's husbands are controlling and don't give their wives freedom.

I just haven't found the right person yet. I'm not a man-hater. I'm not actively looking—if it happens, it happens. I'm not going to put ads in the paper. I want to be friends and really want to get to know someone; I want a meeting of the minds, to find a soul mate, before there is intimacy. I have ideals.

I don't want to spend all my free time searching for the perfect mate when there's so much more in this world to explore. We all meet people along the way. I don't want to spend time on meaningless dates. It's like going on a job interview. You try to learn as much about this person as you can in one night. People need time to get to know each other. Dating is like a formula: on the first date you do this; second date do this; if by the third date there's no sex, then it's over, ended. It has to do with our media culture—television and movies. People think it's normal to get intimate quickly.

I believe "It"—meeting someone—will happen through common interests. I go hiking, do yoga, work out every day. I belong to a health club. It's not a meat market. My friends from the health club do Happy Hour the first Friday of the month at a pub or at one of our houses. It's a group of 20 people; it's very social and fun.

I know so many women who are afraid to be alone. It's all in their minds. I don't know where they get it from. I guess it's pressure from their parents and our culture. I've had pressure from my mother to get married and have children. Many people feel they will be looked down upon by society if they're not part of a couple. It's like it's a goal, something to strive for. I find that attitude in my generation of women. I also see it in the younger generation. Young girls are obsessed with the way they look. They crave the attention of guys.

Maybe I've always had the sense of being liberated, being free and doing my own thing. I'm not afraid to go against societal norms, peer pressure, and family pressure. There were times in my life I could have gotten married. My mother said, "You marry him, don't let him get away." I won't be miserable just to be married.

If the right man came along, he would be a lot like me. College-educated, professional, financially secure, same interests, open-minded, supportive of my goals, interesting enough that I could learn from him and experience things. He would be independent, not needy. "I'll do my thing sometimes, you do yours." And until that special man comes along, I'm living my life, I'm not waiting for it to happen.

The Heart of Her Life

Imagine you are single, 47, living in Berkeley, California, and struggling financially. You've spent your entire life savings trying to conceive by in vitro fertilization, without success. You work two jobs, one as a travel agent, to make enough money to support yourself and to attain your dream—adopting a child. You locate a baby girl in an orphanage in Nepal and want to bring her home more than anything in the world. But you need to raise $7,000 in three months to make it happen.

Four years have passed since I interviewed this determined woman. Her name is Buffy and this is her story. At times, Buffy's life and accomplishments read like a Hollywood screenplay in which the heroine overcomes overwhelming financial and political obstacles. Like Buffy the Vampire Slayer, the tenacious Buffy Murphy fights back and wins.

The adoption of my daughter, Roma, was meant to be. It has been the best thing I have ever done in my life. The desire to be a mother has been one of those deeply personal growth experiences that has had a powerful and life-affirming affect on me. Adopting Roma was a leap of faith in myself and my ability to be a single mother; my experiences during her adoption influenced my personal journey to such a degree that it refocused my life.

Prior to Roma's adoption I had done volunteer work for abused children programs, Native American communities, and my martial arts school's program for children. My focus has always been children, because I believe they are the heart of what matters in my life.

Roma brought a new joy into my life, one that I felt was important to share with other women and couples unable to conceive. My personal experiences adopting Roma and my sister's previous research expanded my knowledge of Nepalese adoptions and led to the creation of an adoption support group and two new Nepal adoption programs for international adoption agencies in the United States, Bay Area Adoptions and Maine Adoption International.

In 1997, just prior to Roma's adoption, I lost my job working for a trekking company handling treks to Asia. It was devastating. I thought it was going to be my final dream job in the travel business. I had tried to work for this company for ten years, but when I finally started working for them I found out it looked great on the surface, but the soul of the company was in turmoil.

Because I was great at my job, a skilled negotiator, and they needed my expertise to train the new person, I was able to parlay a deal upon my departure. No one could know I was unemployed, because I risked losing my adoption. My negotiated deal with the company allowed me to not work for three months so I could devote my time to raising the funds necessary to complete the adoption. Aside from the adoption costs, I needed tickets for flights to Nepal for me, my sister, her daughter, adopted the year before, and a place for us to live in Nepal while I was finalizing the adoption.

I needed to raise a minimum of $7,000 in three months. Remaining hopeful and determined, I wrote a letter to all my friends and family asking for their support in my adoption garage sale and raffle. Donations of goods came pouring in, and some friends and families chose to donate money—checks ranged from $25 to $200, for a total of $700. The first garage sale raised $2,800; the second sale raised another $1,200. One friend helped by donating a beautiful wedding quilt to raffle off, and we sold off all of the raffle tickets. That brought in another $1,000. I painted the interior of someone's house and made another $1,500. It was miracle; with the assistance of family and friends, I'd managed to raise $7,000 in three months!

My commitment and spirit were tested a lot during the year leading up to the adoption. Adoption tests you on a wide range of emotional issues, bringing up so many questions—from motherhood to financial resposibility. Adoption is a complicated process of trusting your heart. I also trusted my support system of family and friends to guide me through the challenges. It wasn't until I returned from Nepal with my three-month-old daughter, Roma Rai, that it dawned on me. I was meant to lose my job so that I could raise the funds necessary for my adoption in Nepal. When I look at all the obstacles and how I managed with my family and friends to overcome them, in my heart I know Roma and I have a soul connection. We were meant to be mother and daughter.

It was also a miracle that Roma survived the conditions to which she was born. In many Third World countries, hundreds of babies die every day, along with their birth mothers. Roma was two months premature and only 1.65 kilograms at birth. That's just three pounds! In Nepal, women have virtually no prenatal care, and there is no preemie infant care hospital that I know of.

The orphanage is a very old palace, sorely in need of repair. It's quite shocking for Americans at first sight; we're not used to these conditions of poverty. The orphanage has no electricity after 5 P.M.—the children, as young as four, drip wax on their palm and put a lit candle in it. It's their only source of light in this very dark, cold place at night.

Despite these conditions, I'm in awe of the magnitude of joy, hope and love the children share with one another. They always welcome strangers who are hoping to become their mommy and daddy. When I felt their little hands snuggle into mine and saw the happiness on their faces, all fear melted away.

Buffy's experiences visiting and working in Nepal changed her career goal. She decided to help other families adopt babies from Nepal and improve conditions in orphanages there.

Some people adopt and go on with life the way it was before. For me, there was a soul connection. That was the turning point in my life. I knew I had to return home and focus my life on working toward helping some of these children in the orphanages.

Upon returning from Nepal in 1997 with my daughter, I organized and facilitated a support group for single women and couples interested in adopting from Nepal. Maine Adoption Placement Services International (MAPS) contacted me and asked if I would live in Nepal for five months and work as a liaison with Nepal Children's Organization. They knew I loved Nepal, was familiar with both the customs of the country and the procedures for adoption, and had spent a great deal of time building personal relationships and contacts in the country. I returned to Nepal as the in-country director of the Nepal Adoption Program for MAPS, along with my daughter.

Prior to living in Nepal, I had looked into jobs working for international children's organizations like UNESCO and CARE, where I thought, with my experience, I could really make a difference. But I didn't meet the basic requirement, a bachelor's degree. I had always dreamed of completing my degree. In order to begin the process of change, before I left to live in Nepal and facilitate the program for MAPS, I immediately registered for college.

I'm attending the College of Marin, a junior college, where I'm completing my undergraduate studies so I can major in cultural anthropology and Third World studies. I'm focusing on women's health issues, discrimination issues such as gender inequity in childbirth, and nutrition for Third World women and children.

Although she is currently struggling financially, Buffy knows getting a college degree, a lifelong dream, will ultimately improve her chances of achieving her career goals and building a more financially stable life for Roma and herself. She has recently been accepted to Smith College's Ada Comstock Scholars Program for the fall 2001 term.

Smith College is a top women's college with special scholars programs for women who are resuming their education. I feel very grateful to have been accepted, and I can't wait to move and begin this new phase in Roma's and my life.

When I complete my education, I would like to return to Nepal for a year or two to advocate for the improvement of the lives of women and children. I would also like to live there because I feel it's important for Roma to experience her birth culture firsthand.

There have been other sacrifices in Buffy's amazing life journey. She explains that there hasn't been any romance in her life because she has had to be completely focused on her dream of being a mother.

> I wasn't able to spend the time working on a relationship with a man who might not want to be a part of my dream of being a mother. And when I thought I could still have a child, I wasn't willing to work out all the issues and problems so many of my women friends faced when they had a child with a man; the parenting part was working for them, but the relationship-with-the-father part wasn't.

> I haven't given up yet. Someday I hope I will meet a man interested in developing a loving partnership, one in which we each support the other's spirit.

Buffy believes that any woman who wants to be a mother should not wait and let motherhood pass her by. "Do it now," she suggests, "because life goes on regardless and meeting the 'right' man can take years." For Buffy, "life has been about being a mother, not about being a wife."

> Adopting a child as a single mother was the best thing I've ever done in my life. All the adoptive parents I've met since I adopted my daughter have agreed with this feeling, and their children are happy and healthy.

In spite of her hectic schedule—going to school full-time and helping clients adopt children from Nepal—Buffy finds time to celebrate life with Roma every day.

> While living in Nepal with Roma, I chose to celebrate motherhood by going on a week-long trek in the gorgeous mountains of Nepal with my beautiful daughter and friends. I am celebrating life daily by going back to college and completing my degree, even though it means living on very little income and struggling by on scholarships and loans. I celebrate life by working, mostly on a volunteer basis, to unite children with families. In addition to handling my own adoption, I facilitated four other adoptions in the past three years. I cele-

brate daily the importance of maintaining a loving relationship with my family and friends. Mostly I celebrate life and my spiritual connection to it by being an active participant in whatever challenges life throws at me and by trying to stay centered and positive.

I learned early on that in order to take care of my daughter, Roma, I need to take care of me. One of the ways in which I celebrate life myself is by studying martial arts. I'm about to attempt my black belt, and I just turned fifty. If I can do it, other women can do it too.

One of my key words is resilience. If one path doesn't work, you find another path and eventually the Universe will support you if you've found the right one.

Joan: The Gift of Love and Giving Back

Have you ever met a truly radiant woman? She walks into a dimly lit room and brings the sun in with her. Karen Panasevich radiates warmth, vitality, and optimism. She is beautiful inside and out; and naturally attracts people.

I met Karen in August 1999 at the Berkshire Craft Show, where I was helping my friend Janice Cline sell her glorious batik paintings. Karen entered Janice's booth, looked around wide-eyed and said, "Wow, are you the artist?"

"No," I said. "That's why I can brag about her work."

I sold Karen a painting and we talked about decorating, her family, and her 25-year career as a social worker helping teens with severe behavioral problems in Boston's inner city. She said she was 45, never-married, and loved her life.

When I caught up with Karen a year later, we talked about society's expectations for single women and how she broke the mold by carving out a lifestyle that suits her current needs.

Society tells us you must have a husband and kids, a house with a garage, and do lawn work on Saturdays. A few years ago I thought, "Gee, I'm supposed to be doing all of that." Then I realized I'm happy just the way I am. I really like my lifestyle.

Now I'm 46 and I've decided I'm not going to have kids. I always have the option of adopting. I adore my job. The kids I work with need that parenting so much. The love and attention I would give to my own kids, I give to my clients at school. I just have the benefit of sending them home after school. It's a very intense, fulfilling job. I do things I wouldn't normally do if I had kids because I have more time. I had some kids from school come out to my house. I rent a house on a lake. These inner-city kids were frolicking in the country.

Society has great expectations of us. I expect myself to be a decent human being; to live life in a truthful, honest, kind manner; to forgive people when they do less than perfect things; and to forgive myself when I mess up. I don't expect much more than that.

A professional singer and painter, Karen comes from an artistically accomplished family. Her father played in the Boston Symphony Orchestra for 46 years and her mother still teaches French horn and piano full-time. Yet Karen inherited her greatest gifts from her mother—the gifts of forgiveness, generosity, and love.

Because I was raised by the most loving mom that could ever exist, I have a lot of love to give, and I can give it to the children and my relationships. I have a need to give love because it fulfills me. My mother taught me that it's our duty and responsibility as human beings to give back to the world. There's healing in service to others. In the Bible it says, "Be not overcome of evil, but overcome evil with good."

Sadly, it's such a take-take society. I think we missed the boat. No matter how much we acquire and how many material possessions we surround ourselves with, we'll come up feeling empty because those things are just things. All my life, since I was a little girl, I have felt called to give back to the world, or to try to heal that which needs to be healed in the world. My mom is my inspiration for this.

From the time I was a toddler, I remember my mother bringing me to "help" at muscular dystrophy drives. I started doing volunteer work when I was eight, working with a Down Syndrome girl. I knew when I was eight I was supposed to do this, that I wanted to be involved in healing the world and working with children. At 14 I started volunteering at a group home for disturbed children; I also volunteered for Head Start.

Karen says her mother has been very influential in shaping her life. She taught her to look at the loving part of a person, believe the best of people, and not harbor any animosity.

My mother's philosophy of life is, no matter what you see on the outside of a person, you must look for that loving part inside. People present themselves in different ways because of their own struggle and fear. There's goodness inside; you just have to transcend that initial barrier. You may have to get through a lot of walls to reach that [goodness]. If you believe it's there, it changes the way you live. My mother has a tremendous capacity to forgive. She's been the living, breathing force behind my understanding the importance of forgiveness in my life. For example, even after a painful divorce, she's been able to maintain a wonderfully close friendship with my father and stepmother. We have family gatherings together. The night Dad had a stroke, from which he'll have a full recovery, my stepmother had invited my mother over for dinner. When they went to the hospital, my mother gave the first 25 years of his medical history, and my stepmother gave the second half.

I saw my father recently, right after his stroke, and the first thing he said to me was, "Thank you for all you've done for me, and I know your birthday is this week." He was worried about recovering, but he remembered my birthday.

Karen says her relationship with her father hadn't always been as healthy as it is now.

My dad was difficult for lots of years. We just had a lot of miscommunication, and differences in style. I had a lot of anger toward him for years; I never felt I could live up to his expectations. We used to go head to head with this arguing.

When my father was 69, he said to my brother and me, "I've not been a perfect parent, I've made a lot of mistakes. I don't necessarily deserve a second chance, but would you give me one?" We said, "Of course." I found out I had always lived up to his expectations, I just didn't know it. He said, "I always loved you, always bragged about you to everyone else." Who gets that opportunity, that recognition, that chance to say, "Now let's try to work together?"

For the last 10 years we've had an amazing relationship. Working on that relationship has helped me understand more about myself and be better in my field. I learned that holding onto anger and trying to get back at someone when they've hurt you doesn't work. It's good to experience your feelings and stand up for yourself, and also to realize that 90 percent of the time people are not doing something to hurt you intentionally. We mess up—that's what we do.

My spiritual philosophy has shaped my entire life. It's a spiritual outlook that's just right for me. If you believe this is it, that there's no God force or life force, you miss the fact that there's meaning in everything, even the struggle. When I'm in the midst of the muck, I say, "This really stinks but it will balance out." I've had several difficult family crises over the past years. Now I'm happy things are so good, I'm feeling grateful—all the time—to have a career I adore, family I love, and people that add so much to the fabric of my life.

Although Karen has always maintained this spiritual belief, she sought professional help in her early twenties to sort out some painful childhood issues and to overcome a low self-esteem. Karen had been sexually abused by a neighbor when she was eight, and therapy helped her understand what had happened to her emotionally.

Some people go to therapy and talk about the same thing over and over again. At some point you have to take a spiritual leap and put it behind you. You have to say "OK, whatever happened happened, and I'm going to have to live this life," rather than "What are people doing for me?" or "I don't have a good life."

The answer for me is to give back. Everyone has pain. There has to be a point where you say, "These were the cards I was dealt, this was my situation, this is what I could learn from it, this is how I can transcend it." Then I looked at my patterns of choice and patterns of action to see, "Where is my responsibility? Where now can I make a difference?" You can hold onto resentment and become embittered. But not me, I'm not having it. I look for the goodness that comes out of pain. I look at any problems I had in childhood, and they make me more sensitive and attuned to people's needs. I don't have to understand from a book, I know. I look at how my past struggle with my father created a strength, [helping me] in what I wanted to do in life. I could persevere undaunted. I gained strength from that.

The whole seven years in therapy I worked on childhood stuff and losses, like sadness and how you resolve issues and family matters when you feel conflicted. A few years later, I went back to therapy for one more year. We worked on reasons why I kept picking men who weren't good for me. At that point I decided I didn't need therapy because I understood things. It was a matter of loving myself enough. That was the bottom line. At one point I said, "I deserve to be happy. I stopped worrying about it and then it came to me.

Karen's years in therapy paid off; she learned what she needed to get from a relationship in order for her to be happy. That's when she met the love of her life, her current boyfriend, Richard.

Before Richard, I had been in a relationship that had been better than my other relationships. I left the relationship because I knew it wouldn't be emotionally supportive for me. He wasn't forgiving and would harbor animosity. I realized I couldn't live with this. If a person is like this at 40, what would he be like at 60? I knew I couldn't fix this.

I asked myself, "Am I going to love who I am with this person, get my needs met, live in a decent way, and still be happy?" I knew it wouldn't work and if I let it go, it would be OK. You have to trust whatever the Universe has to offer and be open to it.

I have an ongoing conversation with God, and there was a point I just said "God, it would be nice if a relationship with a wonderful man happened, and if it doesn't happen, let me be content with it." All of a sudden, Richard popped up. In my relationship with Richard, I don't have to fix him. He is who he is.

Richard and I met when I was on the hiring committee at my school and he interviewed with us for a teaching position. Fortunately, he got the job. He teaches, and my background is social work, so I do the clinical part. He admitted to me later, "As soon as I saw that smile line, I knew I had to kiss it." Imagine, he's attracted to my wrinkles!

I always thought that if you're single you have to push this social life to meet someone. Now I have a long-term relationship. Richard and I have been seeing each other for four years. We're both independent; we maintain separate homes. We accept each other's differences. For example, I'm more of a "people person" than he is. At one time I thought we have to be alike, have the same needs and interests. That's garbage. You don't need to.

I don't have answers about marriage. We get along famously. Do I love him enough to marry him? Sure. Is there a need for it? I don't know. I have a lot of friends who are married, and I don't want their lives or their husbands. They struggle constantly. I wouldn't want to live with some of their husbands. Some married too young, some married quickly and found they weren't compatible intellectually. I also know some very happily married couples.

Richard is my rock; he is the voice of reason. I'll be all worried about something and he'll say, "You can worry about that in September when you have to." He's constant. He's devoted. He's strong. I can always depend on him. He puts everything in perspective. He doesn't let the little things destroy the joy in life.

Richard is not perfect, although he would say he is. He's competent. We both hate to argue. We disagree. That's OK. He's secure enough in himself that, if he gets mad, he'll tell me and then he'll get over it. He doesn't have to prove a point. And he's forgiving.

We started out as friends. Now it keeps getting better, because I'm not scared anymore. I used to be scared of just being vulnerable, being left. I trust this man, so I'm not afraid. We're in a relationship in which I can say he's my equal, like when you meet your match.

Karen says she celebrates life by living in the moment, being close to nature, and giving love wherever she can. A sense of humor is another ingredient in Karen's recipe for enjoying life. This multitalented lady also saves time for her many artistic passions.

I paint abstracts and scenes in acrylics and watercolors; I sold or gave away most of my paintings. I go through phases when I paint a lot. I sing with the Catholic Church on Saturdays and with the Unitarian Church on Sundays; I sing at small functions, too. I celebrate life by writing poetry, cooking, climbing mountains, and cross-country skiing. I'm always looking for a new activity. This year I went scuba diving in Aruba. I'm planning trips to Hawaii next summer and Morocco next year.

I have a lot of fun celebrating single. I don't feel grown-up. I have a childlike fascination with the world, and I have fun—more than I did when I was a kid. I work hard at my job, and afterwards I want to play. I go to the gym every day after work. Sometimes I'll take a canoe out on the lake and barbeque for myself on the deck overlooking the lake.

My work has taught me what a crisis is and what it isn't. Unless you have a gun to your head or someone is jumping out of a window, it's probably not a crisis. I was driving up to my family's country house and got caught in the middle of a traffic jam. It took four hours instead of two to get there, so I wrote letters, did my nails, put on the blues, and read clinical summaries.

I know I'm grown and 46, but I feel that childlike wonder. I'm grateful for the happiness and experience and I believe that it will all work out. Life is good. I have a job, family, man, and things I do that I love. And I love me, too.

A Passion to Survive

When Sara, a successful, single, 46-year-old advertising executive, learned she had a rare and virulent form of breast cancer, she had many choices to make. One she never considered was giving up.

> When I told people I had cancer, I wanted to tell them it wasn't so bad, "Don't worry about it." I didn't give myself a choice; I've got to be OK. Since this had been my worst fear, the worst thing that I could imagine for myself, facing it finally made it less scary. Both my mother and one of her sisters died of breast cancer, so I was always just waiting for that shoe to drop. It dropped, and it didn't devastate me. If I could handle that, I could handle anything.
>
> My doctor made me angry by telling me that I should bring my sister with me when I got the results of the test. He didn't want me to be by myself. When he gave me the news that I had cancer, he said, "I know how devastating this is." I couldn't relate to the word devastating. The idea that somebody could think I could be devastated by anything, the idea I would need someone to help me home or support me, burned me up, too. I cried for a couple of hours. That was the last time I cried. It was almost like I had something to prove: They're not going to get a weepy, inconsolable, and devastated woman, if that's what they're expecting.

Sara was prepared for the bad news because she had watched helplessly as cancer wiped out most of her mother's family: two brothers and her mother's father had also died of cancer.

> I assumed that when it happened to me, I wouldn't want to go through surgery. That was unimaginable. But I didn't have regular breast cancer, I had inflammatory breast cancer. My breast became

huge and swollen, and it ached like a toothache; nothing could have hurt more. I said, "Cut it off."

With inflammatory breast cancer, it's diffuse, not a lump. When it's not a lump, you don't find it with self-examination, a doctor's exam, or a mammogram. What normally happens at some point with this disease is some of the dead tissue of the cancer clogs up the mammary glands, which causes infection, and then a doctor can find it.

They started me on very strong oral antibiotics, and if that didn't work, they would put me in the hospital. In the meantime they figured it wasn't an infection, and they were pretty sure it was cancerous. They had to do a biopsy and it came back positive.

Next was chemotherapy—eight courses, one every three weeks. I scheduled them on Fridays so I wouldn't lose time from work. The first time I got sick, but never again.

At the time of my diagnosis, I was an executive at an advertising agency, where I managed the account services and media departments. I managed $10 million and worked at least 65 to 70 hours a week. Throughout my entire chemotherapy, I didn't lose one day of work. I take it back—I lost one day. I could have gone in that day; I was waiting to feel bad. But I didn't feel that bad. My boss asked me if he could do anything to help. I said, "Yeah, get me a laptop so I can work while I'm getting treatments." After eight months it never happened. I never got the laptop.

Then I went in for the mastectomy. The doctors gave me a month to recover from that. After that I started the stem cell transplant. After that was radiation. I went through one year of treatment.

Sara took fate into her own hands. She quit her job the day before she went into the hospital for the stem cell transplant. Even though the agency said they would pay her for her three-month recovery time, she refused to stay on their employee role because she knew she would not be returning.

At that point I had faced the big bugaboo: If I was going to live one day, one year, or 100 years, I was going to live the way I wanted to. I wasn't going to live one more day doing something that wasn't right for me, especially if it meant taking money from someone I didn't want to work for anymore. It wasn't what I wanted, what would make me happy. I would have felt indebted to them.

By the time I resigned I had decided I would start my own business. I knew I had one account and I wondered if that was enough for me to live on, to pay my mortgage. The worst-case scenario was, I would work that account from home and figure how to get more business. Then I survived the stem cell transplant without feeling ill. Everything my doctor said would happen, didn't; I didn't feel weak as a kitten.

I did things to try to take good care of myself. I walked all the time, everything I could do to keep my strength up. They had told me it would be a horrendous experience, and it wasn't as bad as I thought. That made me feel very strong. I felt I could do anything. If I could do anything, I could start my own business.

Not having someone to lean on made me feel stronger. When you have to depend on yourself, you realize you are stronger than you know. Sometimes when you have the opportunity to depend on someone else you take advantage of it. I never felt I had anybody who was going to do things for me; as long as I kept going I could do almost everything. Whether I felt tired or not, I had to make meals, go to the store, let the dogs out. I had to find the will and energy to do everything I normally did. I never got the opportunity to lie down and feel sick.

Facing death changed Sara's life in many positive ways. Instead of feeling sorry for herself, she learned to cherish the moment and not take life for granted. Her illness changed the way she would work and play.

I think almost dying made me braver about living. It does make everything seem different. Things you took for granted you appreciate more, like how the air smells.

Having survived cancer made me more spiritual, more interested in thinking about whether I was doing the right thing in terms of life and my work. There were days I was so focused on what I was doing for work that I would not have noticed if it was the most beautiful day in the world.

Now, how I do things—how I get to where I'm going—is just as important as getting there. It's more important for me to know that everything I do is the best that I can do.

Now I work with people I like working with, co-workers and clients. I'm not interested in just finding clients that spend the most, but ones that have similar philosophies about work ethics. Since I started my business two years ago, we're billing $2 million.

Business is good. It can always be better. It's a constant challenge. I feel very responsible for everyone who's gotten in this with me. I'm constantly having to figure out how to get my business to the next level. Running a business is much harder than I ever realized. It's more responsibility than ever occurred to me. Yet I can't imagine going back to work for anybody else now.

Sara has found balance in her life. Her work brings her enormous satisfaction and her home is her oasis.

I'm working on making my home more of a place that gives me joy. That wasn't a word I ever thought about before I got sick. I thought it was something you hear about at Christmas; it wasn't a word that applied to my life. Now I think of it as something more important to me, than working toward financial goals.

I want my home to have colors that make me feel good. I'd like to have art. Art makes me feel good every time I look at it. Clothes you get tired of. I want to have sculpture around, some art with dimension. I want books, lots of books around, and things that appeal to all the different senses: smells that smell good, colors that look good, fabrics that feel good to the touch, like the texture of suede. I want to be surrounded by golden yellow and periwinkle blue.

Sara cherishes her time alone and her time with friends. She has chosen a life as a single woman and has no regrets about her unmarried lifestyle.

Not everyone who is single can truly say they are happy about being single. I wouldn't want not to be single. I would not want someone living in the house with me. I am happy single. It's not the same as someone who wishes it were another way. I don't want to be married. This is the life I would choose for myself.

Things I would change have nothing to do with having a husband or significant other. I would like to have more time to read, be a size 10, have more money. It wouldn't be having a guy.

I think celebrating life and celebrating single are the same thing. I can't ever think: "I'll do that or I'll go there when I meet somebody." You can't delay any of the things that are important to you in life and make them contingent on having someone to share them with, like vacations, going to dinner, getting tickets to the theater. There are lots of things you may think you need someone else to do them with, but you don't. For example, going to a wedding: Taking a friend is great, but some people won't ask if they can take a friend.

I find friends who want to do things with me, or I do them by myself. I'm much happier doing things by myself than most people. I think the hardest thing for people to do is be by themselves. People sometimes settle for a mate because being alone was horrible for them. If you can't get through being alone, and get used to it, and like being with yourself, then you will only get into situations that aren't right for you. People get into bad situations because being by themselves scares them.

If you can get through that fear and do end up being in a relationship, it will probably end up being a good one for you. The alternative doesn't scare you anymore. You know you can walk away and survive. It means you're not dependent upon being in that situation.

I share my life with three dogs and three cats. I enjoy taking them to the park. One night I was in bed with six animals and said to them, "I always thought I wanted to be part of a big family." It was so cozy.

I also enjoy getting friends together to go out to dinner. I go to the movies and read. I find I never have enough time to do everything, and I've reduced my work week to 50 hours from 80.

I think that I have come to appreciate and enjoy everything about life. I don't want to steal time from one part to give it to another. In order to keep up with work, I used to rob myself of downtime, time to relax. Now I know that's important if I'm going to be creative and vital and do the best I can. I've got to feel good, and a big part of feeling good is being happy.

Sara is a cancer survivor. A business owner. A woman making a difference. She is strong and healthy. She is proud of her accomplishments—and her appearance.

I have learned that I am tough as nails and losing one part of me isn't that important. You're not the measure of one quality or attribute. What is essential to the core of who you are is something that surgery and physical stuff can't touch. The fact that you're not young anymore, not as thin as you like, have wrinkles—all of the things we think are so important about who we are—they're really not that important. Sometimes it takes something that's real, something that's truly awful, to make you realize that stuff isn't that big a deal. Who you are isn't reflected by how many boobs you have. If someone is basing their opinion of you on the number of boobs you have, then they think you're only half as good as someone who has two. I know that has nothing to do with it.

I feel as good about myself as I ever did before. Whatever I lost in body parts, I gained in so many ways, that I wouldn't undo it if I could.

Marc: Planting Healthy Roots

I think that growing older without growing wiser is a sin against Nature and yourself.

Unfortunately, society doesn't seem to place the same importance on learning as it does on making it big. I can't imagine having as my major goals in life a giant house and an elegant car. So why would I place more importance on having a partner for the sake of having a partner than on being able to grow intellectually and spiritually?

Am I indifferent to women? Well, you can tell from the stories of my experiences scattered throughout this book, I'm obviously not indifferent. But I have learned enough about relationships and my own foibles to know when to avoid getting into stultifying or vexatious relationships.

I'd rather take a drive through the Shenandoah Valley than drag myself through another day in a relationship that is sapping my energy. Loneliness between relationships? Sure, that's a problem sometimes. But now I think of loneliness as being caused by a lack of creativity in how I use my spare time. There is so much to do in this world. I'm just glad I was able to learn, and internalize that knowledge.

Contemplating the years from my divorce to the writing of these last words of the book is like looking at the miracle of my rebirth. And I witnessed the miracles of the births of both of my sons, so I don't use that analogy lightly.

This appreciation for birth and growth is nowhere more obvious than in my apartment. I've lived in four apartments in four cities over the past decade. And for much of that time I didn't have the initiative to hang pictures or even place potted plants in the windows.

Today I live in an apartment that has a living room looking out onto a highway. That side of the living room is all windows—big windows. But I can hardly see cars when I look out of them because of the plants growing amok there. I've even stretched twine from wall to wall across the inside of the windows to encourage the stems to push along those vines, adding to the rampant greenery.

My walls sport pictures of water scenes and other pieces of art and calligraphy I've bought at outlets and boutiques over the last few years. I'm especially proud of the plants, though. I water them, give them Miracle-Gro, and play them mellow jazz on the stereo.

The roots of those plants are sinking deeply into the soil. They consume sunlight, water and funny-sounding chemicals. They learn to turn their stems toward the sun and offer up the flat parts of their leaves to the light. And they grow. It took me years to figure out how to do the same thing in my life. But at least I'm not sinning against myself and Nature. I'm learning. I hope you are, too.

14

Just Friends

When our egos overstep
eggshell boundaries,
you mend my cracks
with kindness.

We are not lovers.
When we hug
you pat my back
with fatherly hands.

Yet if fiery walls
fell around us—
I would seek your arms
to embrace my soul.

—JOAN

JOAN: I'll pose the same question that Harry asked Sally. Can men and women be "just friends?"

MARC: It depends on whether they're having sex.

JOAN: If they're having sex then they're not "just friends."

MARC: Just kidding. Just friends? The word "just" in front of "friends" seems to diminish the relationship. It's like saying there has to be sex to make the relationship worthwhile.

JOAN: You and I don't have sex with each other and our relationship ranks up there with chocolate. Based on the benefits of our friendship, why would you encourage other single men and women to be friends?

MARC: You mean besides having a professional shopper to help me pick out new business suits? Well, I learned more about women from you in a couple of years than I did in several decades of pre-Joan life. Especially about PMS. And I also learned from you how to engage in honest disagreements with women instead of stewing.

JOAN: I never really had a positive male role model in my life, a man I could trust not to come on to me sexually. (Even relatives my father's age have hit on me.) As I got to know you, I knew that I could trust you not to hurt me. Having a healthy friendship with you opened up a whole new way of seeing men. It gave me an opportunity to break the love addiction cycle. Without the sex, I didn't feel that emotional trauma or frenzy of rushing to the relationship finish line.

MARC: Our friendship has helped us put relationships in perspective; since we have each other in our lives, it's helped us to celebrate single.

JOAN: It has. And we've had some stumbling blocks in creating our friendship. When we first met, I was trying to control you by nagging you, like my mother tried to control me. I had a good teacher. But then I realized I can't control anybody or really anything. It was a big lesson. I also learned how to talk openly and honestly with you without the fear of abandonment. These are building blocks that will help me establish a healthy relationship with a lifelong partner.

MARC: Our friendship has helped me reorient my view of women as completely unreliable in relationships. The notion that women are unreliable came from my romantic misadventures. I was about to write off women in general in relationships. Our friendship helped me to see women in a new light and to learn how to avoid those women who are not prepared to enter a healthy relationship. So our friendship worked in tandem with discussions I had with my psychiatrist. Now I either avoid going out with women who are in the midst of divorce proceedings, or if I start up with them, I'm not shocked if things don't work out. I'm much more realistic about such relationships. I found a lot of joy in being single through my joy in having our friendship.

Joan: Sundays in the Park with Marc

It's tricky having a man for a best friend. He's not interested in playing in my closet when I buy a new outfit or in helping me pick out accessories or the hair tint of the month.

Recently when he was in town and stopped by for potluck dinner, I came to the door with my hair full of gooey red dye arranged in outer-space spikes. He wasn't sure what to say or how to hug me hello. Being a diplomat and a gentleman, he pretended I looked normal, and we ate dinner until the timer rang and I jumped up to wash the color out.

I'm sure I have my limitations as a friend for him, too. I'd rather fight rush hour traffic in searing heat than go to a football or basketball game; at least I can listen to books on tape. Marc bonds with males for these testosterone-filled events.

But hair color and ball games aren't important issues, especially when either of us is in trouble. We would do anything for the other. Once, when I locked my keys inside my car, Marc drove 45 minutes to open my car door with a spare set of keys. No questions asked, no sarcastic comments. Just, "I'll be right there." After he opened my door, he turned around and drove home. Didn't even stay for lunch.

During our friendship, Marc and I have nursed one another through the flu as well as broken hearts. Having a friend of the opposite sex to talk to after a breakup is "a good thing" as Martha Stewart says. We offer one another hugs, which help diffuse our anger at the other sex for hurting us, and precious insights into the male and female psyches.

I felt Marc needed more than a hug after his last breakup. His girlfriend of a couple of months felt she needed more time with him to make their relationship work. Knowing both parties and the circumstances, I could see her point.

I sat Marc down and handed him a cup of mustache-curling Starbuck's coffee. I made it a bit stronger to emphasize the importance of the advice percolating in my mind—advice I've wanted to share with him for a long time. But how to be gentle?

"Tell me again how it happened, what she said exactly." (I felt like a detective in a murder mystery.)

"She knew I went to see my boys every Sunday morning so I could spend the day with them. Because of this, she felt concerned that I would never want to go away with her on weekends."

"What did you say?"

"The reason I don't get away on romantic weekends is my relationships never last that long."

"And that's when she said she needs more intimacy and closer contact in a relationship?"

"Yeah. She didn't like it that I wasn't spending enough time with her. She didn't like it when after work, after I'd take her out to dinner, we'd go back to her place, have sex, and then she'd drop me off at the subway. She wanted me to stay over on weekdays and weekends. The first and only time I stayed over was on a Saturday night, and I left early the next day to see my kids, who, you know, live 90 minutes away. I promised them I'd take them out to breakfast. I'm trying to be a nice, thoughtful boyfriend and a good father."

I knew in this situation I would have felt just like the girlfriend. Although it's been a while, I still get emotionally involved after getting sexually entangled. Men frequently interpret this as clingy. So much for the Sexual Liberation Movement.

"My life is spread out over a large area; work, kids, girlfriend. So I left that Sunday morning to see the kids. It was all downhill from there. What did I do wrong?"

"Let me tell you an unwritten law about women and Sunday mornings, Marc. It's a primal instinct, probably dating back to cavewomen. It's about abandonment. After a romantic and intimate Saturday night that lasts into Sunday morning, a woman creates a fantasy about what Sunday will look like with her lover. She probably starts this fairy tale even when she's between relationships: 'I'll slip on my new Victoria Secret lace gown, he'll find me irresistible, we'll make love again. Then we'll go to that adorable outdoor cafe for continental breakfast and we'll read *The New York Times*. We'll linger over cafe mochas and finish the crossword puzzle in ink. We'll browse in the book store, go for a bike ride. . . . '"

"I had no idea."

"I know," I said with more sympathy. "So when you got up and got dressed that Sunday, no matter how much you had warned her that you'd be leaving first thing in the morning to see the boys, she felt rejected. If a man bursts this bubble, a woman may feel disenchanted, confused, angry—take your pick. The good news is, I know there's a compromise so you can have a relationship and also visit your children on Sundays."

"Yes, I could spend Friday night with her, all day Saturday, and Saturday night. Doesn't that count?"

He means well, but he still doesn't get it. I will be gentle, but I want to smack him.

"Not really. You can spend Friday and Saturday night, and Sunday till about 1:00. That will probably take care of it."

"I could see the boys later in the day and take them to dinner instead of breakfast!" he says with enthusiasm.

"That will work."

Marc tells me I was put on earth to torment him. Ditto.

Marc: Friends First

I think that, generally, men don't intuitively understand that women can be full-fledged, three-dimensional human beings and friends. Men have to grow into this knowledge.

At least that's so, I think, for most men—and certainly for me. It's a problem men have to overcome in order to enjoy the benefits of being good friends with women. Such friendships are a treasure in their own right, a gift and a valuable emotional sounding board. And such friendships offer the benefits of a sure date with someone you care about, an enjoyable dinner or movie companion, someone to share a home-cooked meal with while you talk about the mysteries of the opposite sex.

I think the difficulty many men have in forging a solid friendship with a woman—especially one they're romantically interested in—has its roots early in life.

For example, I'm the middle of seven children and grew up fighting with my older sisters. Not all the time, but sometimes. Mostly because I thought they were members of an alien species trying to take over my world. Now, of course, I realize they were actually human beings disguised as aliens.

When I was in third grade, I started to get a new perspective on girls. I attribute this emotional growth to a pretty blonde girl named Barbara, who appeared sporadically in the neighborhood. I remember her teasingly walking away from me on the sidewalk, denying me her company, and then flirtatiously, stopping, bending over, and flipping up her dress at me. This gesture carved a psychic rut deep in my memory and crushed any budding notion that she and I could be "just friends."

A few years after Barbara flashed me, I entered full-fledged puberty. During that transition from flaccid response to silly girls to rigid attention at the sight of anything living that bore the remotest resemblance to a female, I realized I'd been very wrong about something. I realized women weren't aliens. Rather, I was the alien—or at least I started to feel like one. I spent much of the next four decades of my life learning the benefits of becoming fully human around women. But even now I have no illusions that I'll ever get rid of all my alien feelings toward them.

One of the major hurdles to my developing the ability to form lasting, close, and fulfilling relationships with women is the way I got socialized about the opposite sex. Which was pretty much the way most boys I knew got socialized. Sometime during junior high school, Nature decreed that boys should start pursuing girls for sexual enjoyment rather than just for friendship. Over the next few years, girls started to wear makeup and serious bras—not the training variety. Some sprouted prematurely. Rock 'n' roll songs offered images of 16-year-old goddesses. There was flirting in class, Saturday night cruising, stolen glances, an occasional dirty magazine and lots and lots of erections.

Growing into adulthood, I think I had stuck in the back of my head the thought that being "just friends" with a girl was a state of affairs tinged with failure—failure to make the relationship go anywhere near sex. And how can the subconscious image of failure nurture a friendship with a woman? So here was an entire half of the population that represented potentially valuable friendships at risk of going to waste. I certainly did have friendships with women in high school, college, graduate school, and beyond. But sometimes those friendships formed because there was no alternative to being just friends. I was already dating someone, married, or the woman was involved with someone. The key to having a fulfilling platonic friendship with a woman is to feel that the friendship exists because it gives each of you something important, nurturing, and downright special. Not because there's no alternative.

Even more challenging was remaining friends after breaking up with a woman. Sometimes it can be done, but that depends on the attitudes of the people involved—and probably a lot of other variables as well. It seldom works for me. Joan is an exception to this rule, and any explanation of why this is so would probably make a worthy subject for a graduate thesis in psychology.

Then there's the issue of couples becoming "friends first," before they become lovers. I understand the sexual drive that impels many men to push the envelope on sex. And I appreciate that many women want to establish a friendship first. But old habits die hard. If I'm sexually attracted to a woman, the notion of friendship isn't necessarily what automatically pops up first in my head.

That's where my friendships with women have been valuable to me. I've learned how to talk honestly with a woman. I'm becoming better at letting a woman know what makes or breaks a relationship for me. I'm also more comfortable being honest about my feelings toward her, whether or not I think that honesty might lead to conflict. Being diplomatic, I've learned, doesn't guarantee a good relationship. In fact, diplomacy can let problems fester.

So all in all, I'm better off being able to develop good friendships with women. It gives me solace and emotional nourishment and intellectual stimulation. It has taught me much about how to have a successful romantic relationship with a woman. And it also helps me walk planet Earth without fearing that men are living among aliens.

Epilogue

CELEBRATING SINGLE

Do not seek your mate.
Feel life's passion from within,
and love will find you.

—JOAN

JOAN: Marc and I met on a blind date on his birthday, seven years ago. Our mutual friend, Ellen Beth Levitt, and her husband, Jack Whitt, introduced us at a lovely brunch at their home. When the subject of dessert came up, I said I had been told I made the world's best brownies. Marc said he made pretty good brownies himself and challenged me to a brownie bake-off. The winner would be taken to the restaurant of his or her choice. "Very creative of this man," I thought. "This way he knows I'll go out with him again."

"You're on," I said.

The next day we set up the rules. We would each prepare our brownie recipe. Marc would pick my brownies up on his way to work. He did media relations at Johns Hopkins Hospital at the time. The people in his office would do a blind taste test and vote. Marc called me the day of the contest with the news. "You won," he said.

MARC: It wasn't a blind taste test. They had already had my brownies before. And they still voted for yours.

JOAN: But then you asked me out again because I had to collect on my prize, the dinner.

Actually, our friendship turned out to be the prize. That's an unexpected gift from a blind date, one for which I'm grateful. And in the spirit of blind dates and as a tribute to our friendship, Marc and I are sharing our brownie recipes.

Marc's Brownies

I just created this recipe out of my sick mind. I needed something to make chocolate-addicted women grateful to me. On a good night it serves just one woman. If you have to share it, eight to ten people can partake.

1 double chocolate brownie mix
Enough butter to grease pan
1 egg
1 bag miniature peanut butter cups
Grand Marnier or Amaretto

Follow directions on box, using whatever amount of butter, eggs, and cooking oil the recipe calls for. Don't substitute anything healthy. Mix batter till smooth. Then fold in gently by hand, using a large spoon, the unwrapped miniature peanut butter cups. Spread batter into a well-buttered 8" by 8" pan.

Put in pre-heated oven and bake for the amount of time and temperature noted on the box, plus five minutes. Remove from oven. Cover with foil and put in refrigerator overnight. This is to ensure the brownies become firm. Next day, cut into squares and cover liberally with Grand Marnier or Amaretto.

Testimonial of a Fan of Marc's Brownies:
"They are fabulous. You are like the devil sitting on my shoulder—eat, eat."

—KAREN, 34

When I told Marc the following story about my brownies, he insisted that I include it with the recipe. He said it's wonderfully weird in a John Waters way.

I was dating a man who's friend had lost his father. To support my boyfriend and his friend, I made a plate of brownies for the Shiva house (a Jewish wake). The grieving mother sampled a brownie, covered them with foil, and left the room with my coat and the brownies. As we were leaving, when I picked up my coat on her bed, I noticed the plate of brownies peeking from under her pillow, far away from the guests.

Joan's Sinsational Brownies

Makes 36 small squares.
Preheat oven to 350 degrees.

I prefer a rectangular glass baking dish (13 ½" by 8 ¾" by 1 ¾").

2 sticks of salted butter
4 eggs
1 cup pre-sifted flour
2 cups sugar
1 teaspoon vanilla extract
pinch of salt
4 ounces of unsweetened chocolate
one 12-ounce bag of double-chocolate or semi-sweet morsels

Melt 4-ounce block of unsweetened chocolate in a glass bowl in the microwave. When it's almost completely melted, add butter and microwave till butter is very soft, about 45 seconds (depending on your microwave). Combine all ingredients except chocolate morsels in a food processor till mixture is smooth, about 10 to 15 seconds. Add half the bag of morsels and process for one or two pulses. Pour batter into buttered baking dish. (Vegetable oil cooking spray is fine.) Cook for 20 minutes. Take out of oven. Add remaining morsels to top of hot brownies. Allow them to melt and spread evenly with knife. Cool, cut, and watch them disappear. If there are any leftovers, freeze them in an airtight container.

Testimonials for Joan's Brownies:
"You are not a cook, you are a sorceress."

—STEVEN, 47

"I feel like I have committed a mortal sin."

—GERTIE, 83

Marc and I hope you've enjoyed *Celebrating Single*, and we look forward to hearing your comments and questions. Contact us at our Web site for more interviews, recipes, stories, and information about my matchmaking business, Happy Endings. If your business or organization would like to schedule Marc and me for a reading or lecture, you can reach us at www.celebratingsingle.com.

Notes and Acknowledgments

Kind acknowledgment is made for permission to excerpt the following:

Hillman, James. *The Soul's Code: In Search of Character and Calling.* p. 8. New York: Random House, 1996.

Leonard, Linda Schierse. *The Wounded Woman: Healing the Father–Daughter Relationship.* p. 11. Athens, Ohio: Ohio University Press/Swallow Press, 1982.

Mellody, Pia. *Facing Love Addiction: Giving Yourself the Power to Change the Way You Love.* p. 12. San Francisco: HarperSanFrancisco/A Division of HarpersCollins Publishing, 1992.

OSHO © Osho International Foundation, www.osho.com. (Poem by Osho)

Phillips, Jan. *Marry Your Muse—Making a Lasting Commitment to Your Creativity.* pp. 85, 224. Wheaton, Ill.: Quest Books, 1997.

Quinn, Janet F. *I Am a Woman Finding My Voice.* p. 3. New York: Eagle Brook/Morrow, 1999. Reprinted by permission of HarperCollins Publishers, Inc./William Morrow.

Sanford, John A. *The Invisible Partners: How the Male and Female in Each of Us Affects Our Relationships.* pp. 13–15, 19–20. New York: Paulist Press, 1980.

Toffler, Alvin. *Future Shock.* pp. 250–251. New York: A Bantam Book/with Random House, Inc., 1970.

Wilson, K.J., Ed.D. *When Violence Begins at Home: A Comprehensive Guide To Understanding and Ending Domestic Abuse.* pp. 10–13. Alameda, Ca: Hunter House, Inc., 1997.

Yogananda, Paramhansa. *Moments of Truth, Excerpts From The Rubaiyat of Omar Khayyam Explained.* p. 11. © J. Donald Walters. Nevada City, Ca: Crystal Clarity Publishers, 1995.

Notes

Bureau of the Census, U.S. Department of Commerce, "Current Population Reports," 1998, 1980, 1970. (Statistics in Prologue)

The actual quote by Eckhart is "The seed of God is in us. Given an intelligent farmer and a diligent fieldhand, it will thrive and grow up to God whose seed it is and, accordingly, its fruit will be God-nature. Pear seeds grow into pear trees; nut seeds into nut trees, and God-seed into God." Blakney, Raymond B. (trans.) *Meister Eckhart: A Modern Translation.* p. 75. New York: Harper and Brothers, 1941.

Suggested Reading by Topics

Dating, Love, and Relationships

Blinder, Martin, M.D. *Choosing Lovers*. Macomb, Ill: Glenbridge Publishing, Ltd., 1989.

Gordon, Sol, Ph.D. *Why Love Is Not Enough*. Holbrook, Mass: Bob Adams, Inc., 1990.

Hendrix, Harville. *Getting the Love You Want: A Guide for Couples*. New York: Harper Perennial, 1988.

Kaplan, Basha, Psy.D. and Prince, Gail, M.Ed. *Soul Dating to Soul Mating*. New York: The Berkley Publishing Group, 1999.

Kasl, Charlotte, Ph.D. *If the Buddha Dated*. New York: Penguin/Arkana, 1999.

Rabin, Susan, M.A. *101 Ways to Flirt*. New York: Penguin, 1997.

Wallace, Marlene. *Playing Chess With the Heart: Beatrice Wood at 100*. San Francisco: Chronicle Books, 1994.

Whitfield, Charles L. *Boundaries and Relationships*. Deerfield Beach, Fl.: Health Communications, Inc., 1993.

Meditation, Spirituality, and Finding Your Purpose

Anderson, Greg. *Living Life On Purpose: A Guide to Creating a Life of Success and Significance*. San Francisco: HarperSanFrancisco, 1997. An Imprint of HarperCollins Publishers.

Bonheim, Jalaja. *Aphrodite's Daughters: Women's Sexual Stories and the Journey of the Soul.* New York: Fireside, 1997.

Boorstein, Sylvia. *It's Easier Than You Think: The Buddist Way to Happiness.* San Francisco: HarperSanFrancisco, 1995. An Imprint of HarperCollins Publishers.

Breighner, Fr. Joseph. *Stops Along the Country Road.* Baltimore: Cathedral Foundation Press, 1996.

Jeffers, Susan. *Feel the Fear and Do It Anyway.* New York: Fawcett Columbine, 1987.

Kabat-Zinn, Jon. *Full Catastrophe Living: Using the Wisdom of Your Body and Mind to Face Stress, Pain and Illness.* New York: Dell Publishing, 1991.

———. *Wherever You Go You Are There.* New York: Hyperion, 1994.

Moyers, Bill: *Healing and the Mind.* New York: Doubleday, 1993.

Williamson, Marianne. *A Return to Love.* New York: HarperCollins Publishers. 1992.

Psychology and Family of Origin

Ball, Carolyn M., M.A. *Claiming Your Self-Esteem.* Berkeley: Celestial Arts Publishing, 1990.

DePaulo, J. Raymond, Jr., M.D. and Ablow, Keith Russell, M.D. *How to Cope With Depression: A Complete Guide For You and Your Family.* New York: Fawcett Columbine, 1989.

Herst, Charney, Ph.D., *Mothers of Difficult Daughters: How to Enrich and Repair the Bond in Adulthood.* New York: Villard Books, a division of Random House, Inc., 1998.

Johnson, Robert, A. *We: Understanding the Psychology of Romantic Love.* San Francisco: Harper, 1983. A Division of HarperCollins Publishers.

Peck, M. Scott, M.D. *The Road Less Traveled.* New York: Simon & Schuster, 1978.

Steinem, Gloria. *Revolution From Within: A Book of Self-Esteem.* Boston: Little, Brown and Company, 1992.

Whitfield, Charles L. *Healing the Child Within.* Deerfield Beach, Fl.: Health Communications, Inc., 1989.

———. *A Gift to Myself.* Deerfield Beach, Fl.: Health Communications, Inc., 1990.

Sex and Love Addiction

Carnes, Patrick. *Don't Call It Love: Recovery from Sexual Addiction.* New York: Bantam Books, 1991.

Schaef, Anne Wilson. *Escape from Intimacy: Untangling the "Love" Addictions: Sex, Romance, Relationship.* San Francisco: Harper San Francisco, 1989. A Division of HarperCollins Publishers.

Resources for Adoption

(There are so many more. This list will jumpstart your research.)

Magazines and Books

Adoptive Families Magazine (800) 372-3300, P.O. Box 5159, Brentwood, TN 37024

Alperson, Myra. *Dim Sum, Bagels and Grits: A Sourcebook for Multi Cultural Families.* New York: Farrar, Straus & Giroux, 2001.

Evans, Karin and Min, Anchee. *The Lost Daughters of China: Abandoned Girls, Their Journey to America, and the Search for a Missing Past.* New York: J. P. Tarcher, 2000.

Veron, Lee. *Adopting on Your Own: The Complete Guide to Adoption for Single Parents.* New York: Farrar, Straus & Giroux, 2000.

Other Contacts for Adoption

Buffy Murphy's e-mail address: memurphy@ricochet.net (information about Nepal Adoption and Sponsorship Program). Buffy is also associated with Bay Area Adoptions at 465 Fairchild Drive, Suite 215, Mountain View, CA 94043, and Maine Adoption Placement Services at 277 Congress Street, Portland, ME 04101.

Patsy Schneider's e-mail address: Patkarl1@hotmail.com. She is happy to help anybody who wants to know how to get started with international adoption.

The Ametz Single Adoptive Parent Network of Jewish Child Care Association: (212) 558-9949, 120 Wall Street, N.Y., N.Y. 10005

Index

7/02

Lucy Robbins Welles Library
95 Cedar Street
Newington, CT 06111-2645